Intellectual Traditions in Islam

Intellectual Traditions in Islam

Dr Suhail Saheed

MD PUBLICATIONS PVT LTD
NEW DELHI
www.mdppl.com

"Views represented in the book are personal views of the authors and have no association with the organisations with which the authors are working."

Published by :

MD Publications Pvt Ltd
"MD House", 11, Darya Ganj,
New Delhi - 110 002
Phone : +91-11-41563325 (Customer Service)
+91-11-41562846 (Editorial)
E-mail (orders): order@mdppl.com
Website: www.mdppl.com

ISBN: 978-81-7533-234-8

Published and Printed by Mr. Pranav Gupta on behalf of **MD Publications Pvt Ltd** at Times Press, New Delhi.

Preface

The transformation of Islam into one of the great civilisations of the world has been the subject of many studies in recent decades. As Islam spread beyond the Arabian Peninsula into the neighbouring regions of Syria, Iraq, Iran, Egypt and beyond to North Africa and Central Asia, it became enriched by the intellectual contributions of a multitude of individuals, communities and cultures in regions that eventually comprised the Muslim world. Indeed, within three centuries, the Islamic world had already become one of the dominant civilisations of the world, characterised by a diversity of literary and intellectual traditions in various fields of learning, while Islam as a religion became elaborated in a plurality of expressions and interpretations.

The present intellectual crisis in Islam does not help in countering extremist interpretations. A closer look at Islam's rich intellectual traditions from the past, however, might offer chances for fostering a climate of dialogue, mutual respect and understanding. In this regard, the potential contribution of Shi'ism has often been overlooked.

There is no denying that the intellectual contributions of Sunni Islam had been manifold. Yet, it is Twelver Shi'ism – the majority denomination in Iran and Iraq revolving around the Twelve Imams – that is usually associated with a certain pioneering spirit in terms of philosophy and thought. Shi'ism is commonly though somewhat rashly associated with political assertiveness of a militant character.

However, what is lesser known is that this rather recent, post-1979 phenomenon is mainly related to the events in Iran. Thus, a more sober, fact-oriented and less sensational attitude might be helpful in understanding contemporary Shi'ite Islam.

A great deal of controversy, confusion and disunity among Muslims is caused by a careless use of the argument that such and such a thing did not exist in the days of the Prophet and the rightly guided caliphs or was not allowed by them and therefore it is un-Islamic. Often this argument is used with a measure of hypocrisy and intellectual dishonesty, in the sense that an *'alim* (Muslim jurist, scholar) or a group objects to one thing on the ground that it has no precedence in the days of the Prophet and the *sahabah* (companions of the Prophet) and at the same time accepts something else which also does not have any precedence in early Islam.

The fact that Islamic tradition grows continuously does not mean that revelation did not come to an end with the Prophet Muhammad or that it was not perfected by his work. For the entire growing Islamic tradition is the Prophet's work. It is like a planter who plants a tree and the tree that continues to grow even after the planter departs from this world.

I am very grateful to Mr. Pranav Gupta, Director of MD Publications Pvt Ltd, New Delhi for his kind cooperation and support for this book.

Dr Suhail Saheed

CONTENTS

1

Intellectual Traditions in Islam

An Introduction

Islam and Science present an articulate and concise historical introduction to intellectual developments that have shaped Islamic civilization, both religious and scientific. The work attempts to 'construct a coherent account of the larger religious and cultural background' in which the Islamic scientific tradition came into existence and to explore the 'vexingly complex' issue of its decline. The main thesis is that scientific traditions 'arose from the bosom of a tradition of learning that had been grounded in the very heart of the primary sources of Islam: the Qur'an and Hadith.' The latter are reports of the deeds and statements of the Prophet that became the sunna, or tradition of the Prophet. The first chapter covers the emergence of an Islamic scientific tradition during the first two centuries of Islamic civilization: both the emergence of new religious sciences, with the study of Qur'an and hadiths, and the presence of scientific traditions (atomism of the theologians, astronomy, medicine, alchemy).

A closer examination of the work may explain why this might be so. A first methodological difficulty the work encounters is rooted in a conceptual confusion over what constitutes the 'Islamic scientific tradition,' since it includes: Islamic 'religious sciences,' esoteric traditions influenced by various Greek hermetic and alchemic traditions, medieval theological cosmologies, medieval philosophical speculations (theological, metaphysical, ontological, cosmological), various theological discussions about time, causality, motion, and creation and their attempts at harmonizing theology and metaphysics, an Islamic aesthetic experiential component (architecture), and specifically scientific disciplines (astronomy, medicine, mathematics, physics). An all-encompassing notion of Islamic scientific tradition can then provide support for the main thesis, encapsulated in such statements as 'the Qur'an is the foundation upon which everything Islamic is built . . . the primary source, the essential textbook' of all knowledge, both religious and secular, that emerged from the Islamic civilization. Such claims become the basis for what is then taken as demonstrations of the existence of an inherent 'nexus' between Qur'an/religion and all sciences, both religious sciences and the specifically scientific (secular) disciplines.

Holding that certain Qur'anic beliefs were at the heart of scientific explanations and that methodologies developed by the religious Qur'anic sciences provided some elements of the methodology used by natural sciences is quite problematic. The work fails to properly explain why most scientific works did not refer to the Qur'an. Stating that what infused their works was the metaphysics of the Qur'an, which implicitly assumes the existence of a relationship between metaphysical knowledge and the scientific traditions, is not a historical or a scientific explanation. The premises of such arguments can only lead to the more serious problem of drawing erroneous conclusions that ascribe to the Qur'an and its central message the role of establishing a 'nexus between the physical cosmos and the metaphysical realm' as objects of a scientific investigation. If one argues that the Hebrew Bible is similar in this regard, how would one account for the lack of scientific impact in the Jewish tradition.

The work assumes that there was no distinction between Islamic metaphysical principles and the scientific tradition. In the classical period, Islam infused all aspect of the intellectual activities of Muslims as well as the scientific tradition, by providing the latter with its core Islamic metaphysical principles from which it was not divorced. The history of such sciences as mathematics, biology, astronomy (or the new sciences of molecular microbiology, genetics, astrophysics, etc.) in the Islamic world cannot be reduced to or explained by appealing to Islamic metaphysical principles. The work illustrates the difficulties that a non rigorous use of what constitutes a 'scientific' tradition can generate. This brings us to a second methodological problem that is rooted in the presentation of evidence. The work's account of the development of sciences in Islam provides fodder for the main thesis. Examples provided to illustrate the process of appropriation, translation and naturalization of new knowledge abound, e.g., for the religious sciences and for theology, but the work falls short of convincingly illustrating and demonstrating that this was the case in the realm of natural or theoretical sciences to the extent that only what was Islamic was retained and naturalized.

This was certainly not the case with al-Khwarazmi or Ibn Hayyan whose works were certainly more influenced by ideas that were non Islamic, e.g., Greek, Egyptian, Indian, Persian, Babylonian. Equally problematic are unsubstantiated claims that the sciences of early Islam developed a Qur'an methodology that was used by the scientific tradition. The work also adduces examples of theologians (mutakallimun) who worked on ideas that embraced logic, epistemology and cosmology, failing to note that the latter were all at the service of their theological metaphysics, e.g., their atomism to account for an Islamic understanding of the world and of God's actions. The work notes that the Islamic scientific tradition was only one part of the larger context of the Islamic tradition, or what it calls the 'cultural matrix' that gave it birth, but maintains a reductionist assumption that every scientific development in the Islamic world was shaped by Islam and its worldview and glosses over much of the more complex issues that lie at the heart of the historical development of scientific traditions in the Muslim world.

The source of these methodological problems lies perhaps with the work's holistic approach that places the Qur'an (revelation) and the sunna of the Prophet at the heart of the religion/science nexus, in order to argue that an 'intrinsic nexus between various levels of existence transforms the multiplicity of appearances into a unity. The ultimate foundation of their interrelatedness at the level of cosmic existence is their ontological dependence on God.' This ontological unitive principle, derived from the Islamic notion of unity (tawhid), is projected onto all facets of human experience (ethics, moral, metaphysics, sociology, politics) that extend to the 'numerous internal links between all branches of knowledge in Islam as well as the process through which an integrated and holistic theory of knowledge had emerged from the twin sources of revelation and the tradition of the Prophet of Islam.'

This particular holistic approach accounts for a number of problematic claims that the Islamic scientific tradition was 'intimately connected with the worldview created by Islam and so thoroughly rooted in the Qur'an's and that the same Islamic metaphysical truths that produced Islamic medieval metaphysical discourses (theology, cosmology, philosophy) were – and are still – capable of producing Islamic sciences. Such claims are controversial from historical, sociological and epistemological perspectives, but this does not prevent the author to affirm that 'for a creative exploration of the relationship between Islam and modern science, one needs to examine modern science from the perspective of the Islamic concept of nature taken as a whole and within its own matrix which is based on the revealed text, the Qur'an, and supplemented by the Sunna of the Prophet of Islam.'

Less ideological is the forthcoming Bennacer El Bouazzati's 'The Formation of the Scientific Tradition within Islamic Culture'. In his *Islam and Science: A false Statement of the Problem* published in Islam & Science: Journal of Islamic Perspectives on Science, Gutas has, perhaps, best illustrated the problem that this type of approach encounters in its attempt to ascribe some sort of historical 'agency' to religious beliefs, i.e., to Islam and its metaphysical worldview, over scientific activities. Islam and Science holds that a society dominated by Islamic values, nourished by the teachings of the Qur'an and the hadiths, provided the impetus for the development of the rich Islamic scientific tradition and thus incorrectly suggests that religious beliefs/worldviews, i.e., Islam, can be the main driving forces behind the development of a scientific tradition.

This was certainly not the case in the West where the rise of the scientific tradition occurred without the metaphysical principles of the Qur'an and the sunna. The work notes the impact of foreign (Greek) knowledge, but argues that the advent and decline of the Islamic scientific tradition owes everything to the presence or absence of the Islamic/religious worldview. On the contrary, theological and metaphysical worldviews that religious traditions produce and postulate neither produce science, nor scientific explanations. Theological and metaphysical explanations are by definition 'scientifically' non demonstrable and, therefore, not part of a scientific method or explanation. The work's theological and metaphysical explanations fail to take into account any sociological, economical, or political factors in its explanation of the development (rise and decline) of a thriving scientific tradition, with research projects, funding, institutions, and patronage. Efforts to demonstrate the existence of an inherent 'nexus' between Islam and science constitute part of the 'ideological' underpinning of the work.

Arguments for the role of this nexus to explain the vitality and the decline of the scientific traditions in the Islamic world are used to suggest that a revival of this original medieval religion/science symbiosis provides the conditions for the establishment of the needed 'new nexus.' The ideological underpinning of the work constitutes the hallmark of a familiar holistic revivalist (fundamentalist) discourse. At the heart of all revivalist projects is an 'idealized' version of Islam that the 'vanguard' (term used in the work and made famous by Sayyid Qutb, one of the leaders of the holistic revivalist project of the Muslim Brotherhood) attempts to re-actualize and implement via the establishment of an Islamic Society/State. In this work, Islam's idealized role is projected onto the development of scientific traditions.

This is made evident with the implicit prescriptive solutions for the revival of a truly Islamic scientific tradition: (i) the revival of the umma (political entity), (ii) a return to Arabic as lingua franca of the Islamic world, (iii) the reintroduction of the traditional (religious) system of education, and (iv) a return to an Islamic political system and its (traditional) institutions. Islamic sciences will once again thrive when scientists will be educated and trained in an 'organic' and living Islamic tradition (read: a re-Islamized society). Islamic beliefs and worldviews will become producers of an Islamic scientific tradition once the Qur'an and the sunna reintroduce this 'matrix', productive of knew Islamic knowledge.

Once more, the problem of agency attributed to Islam in the medieval period resurfaces as the conditions for the naturalization of new knowledge become the re-Islamization of Muslim societies, through education. The work rests on the (false) assumption that Islam, or any religious tradition, was and, more problematic, can be the driving engine that produces a scientific tradition. The work provides a useful historical overview of the development of different intellectual traditions and debates in Islam, but it does not provide philosophical discussions on contemporary issues or on their philosophical implications (e.g., theory of evolution, theory of relativity, quantum mechanics, chaos theory, stem cell research). Such contemporary debates are deemed a mere 'historical anomaly' in Islam. Islam is unique. These religion/ science debates are foreign to Islam and only occur today because of a lost of the original religion/science 'nexus.' Once reestablished via the 'new nexus,' this anomaly will disappear.

For similar reasons, Islam cannot be classified in any of the traditional typologies (e.g., Ian Barbour) that try to explain the religion/science relationship. Again, Islam is unique. The work is a Muslim's 'urgent and creative response' to the 'triumphant force of modern science that seeks to replace all worldviews other than its own,' i.e., the Islamic worldview. On the whole, the work does not quite succeed to overcome the intellectual paucity of contemporary studies on the religion and science debate in Islam. The work, however, provides a useful review of existing scholarship on various scientific (religious, philosophical, theological, natural sciences, etc.) traditions that took place in the Islamic world and of some of their historical developments. A work that explores the philosophical problems that arise with the contemporary Islam and science discourse has yet to be written.

Of all those who have stood against the currents of modernism, Alasdair MacIntyre stands out as the philosopher who has offered the most profound critique. His *After Virtue,* which was first published in 1981, sent shock waves through the Western intellectual world. He committed what for many was an unforgivable sin when he claimed that the project of the Enlightenment period of European thought was a failure. This rejection of modernist thinking was focused upon moral philosophy, but it attracted the attention of a readership much wider than what could be expected for a book in ethics. There were even articles in the popular press about the revival of Aristotelian thought initiated by MacIntyre's work, and in the article on the history of twentieth century Anglo American Ethics in the *Encyclopedia of Ethics,* Alan Donagan predicts that MacIntyre's attention to Thomistic thought will influence the philosophical work to be done in the twenty fast century.

MacIntyre's work has also sparked controversy among political theorists and social critics, as well as professional philosophers. Conferences have been convened to discuss his ideas, critical studies of his work have been compiled, and several of his books and articles have been translated into foreign languages. In the field of ethics, MacIntyre has spawned a revival of interest in Aristotelian ethics with such force that it is now generally recognized as a serious rival to the two major strands of moral philosophy that have been dominant in the West since the Enlightenment: untilitarianism and Kantianism. Numerous books and articles have been written since the publication of *After Virtue* proclaiming the advantages of an Aristotelian virtue ethics over utilitarian consequentialism and Kantian deontology.

In political theory, there has been a steady stream of writings in which liberalism is defended against MacIntyres criticisms, or those criticisms are elaborated, often in the form of a communitarian theory which MacIntyre himself has repudiated. In religious thought, MacIntyre's work has prompted a renewed interest in Neo Thomism, especially as it is related to ethics and social political thought. MacIntyre's emphasis on the importance of history has also led to heated discussions in which he has often been accused of being a relativist. It was largely in respopse to this sort of misunderstanding which followed the publication of *After Virtue* that MacIntyre was motivated to write the sequel, *Whose Justice? Which Rationality?* MacIntyre's rejections of historicism and relativism in this latter work have also contributed to the depth of the discussions of these issues.

So, one reason for reading MacIntyre is because his work has been tremendously influential, even among those who disagree with his positions. Another reason would be interest in the topics he discusses: history, politics, ethics, religion, epistemology, philosophy in general and the relations among them. For Muslims, however, there are additional reasons to read MacIntyre. One of the most important issues in Islamic social and political thought since the nineteenth century has been the confrontation of traditional Muslim societies with European modernism, and one of the most important facets of modernism about which Muslim thinkers are concerned is that of political liberalism. Muslims who argue that liberal ideals and institutions are compatible with Islam are usually classified as modernists. At the other extreme are those who would claim that liberal and Islamic thought agree on nothing.

The vast majority of Muslim intellectuals and scholars, however, fall somewhere between these extremes. The interesting discussion in contemporary Muslim social thought is not over whether modernists or conservatives hold a more defensible position, but what aspects of liberal thought may be accommodated and what aspects must be rejected. MacIntyre's writings are interesting in this context because, like many Muslims, he is very strongly opposed to many aspects of modernism and liberalism for what turn out to be ultimately religious reasons. Furthermore, the philosophical perspective he seeks to defend, a form of Neo Thomism with a strong emphasis on Aristotle, is more similar to the philosophical perspective of traditional Islamic thought than are any of the other major tendencies to be found among contemporary Western philosophers.

Of course, there remain important differences between the attitudes of Muslims and those expressed by MacIntyre, to be discussed below, but regardless of our differences, the thought of the most profound critic of modernism and liberalism in the West should be of great interest to those who feel a need to resist the imposition of modernist and liberal thought on Muslim societies, such as those inspired by the warnings of the Grand Leader of the Islamic Revolution against the 'cultural invasion.' Muslim liberals who await a repetition of the European Enlightenment in Islamic culture would also be well advised to read MacIntyre, who has declared the Enlightenment project to be a failure and ultimately incoherent. Perhaps if Muslim modernists would read MacIntyre they would become more critical of the claims made on behalf of liberalism, and would come to recognize the need to examine the intellectual history of their own traditions, as well as those of the West, to find the way forward. Perhaps MacIntyre's books can serve as a kind of vaccination against the infatuation with Western culture which Persians call *gharbzadigi.*

After Virtue

The book which initially provoked the great storm of controversy was *After Virtue,* and in order to understand the true significance of *Whose Justice? Which Rationality?* one must understand something about the earlier work.

After Virtue begins with the disquieting suggestion that moral discourse in the West has lost its meaning, that it serves as a disguise for the expression of preferences, attempts to gain power, emotions and attitudes, but that it has ceased to have any relation to what is truly good or right. MacIntyre pins responsibility for the collapse of Western ethics on the Enlightenment. Much of the book goes on to criticize various aspect of Enlightenment thought in Hume, Kant, the Utilitarians, the emotivists, and in contemporary liberal political philosophy, especially as elaborated by John Rawls.

MacIntyre sees only two ways to pass beyond the errors of modernism and liberalism: either we must accept a Nietzschean nihilism or we must return to an Aristotelian ethics. However, the Aristotelian alternative is not a simple return to Greek or medieval systems of thought. For the Enlightenment criticisms of scholasticism to be successfully answered, the return must be to a reformed Aristotelianism consonant with modern science. This means that the *telos* or end of man is not to be understood as determined by biology, rather it is to be fathomed by reflection on history, and the human practices and traditions that have evolved over the course of history. The second half of *After Virtue* consists in MacIntyre's elaboration of this historically grounded Aristotelianism and its development as a theory of the virtues.

Like the Nietzschean critics of the arrogance of the Enlightenment, MacIntyre accepts that there is no absolute standpoint from which we can arrive at absolute moral truths. Each of us must view the world from his own position in history and society. It is this admission that led many critics of *After Virtue* to accuse him of relativism or historicism, and it is largely in response to this criticism that *Whose Justice? Which Rationality?* was written. Unlike the Nietzscheans, or *genealogists* as MacIntyre refers to those often called post *modernists,* MacIntyre does not accept the claim that because we are bound to our finite perspectives conditioned by history and social position, we are barred from certainty or absolute truth. Rather, he holds that man has the ability to understand rival perspectives even when one cannot be translated into the idiom of the other. On the basis of this understanding, rational evaluation and judgment can be made with regard to the strengths and weaknesses of the rival world views and ideologies.

MacIntyre extends this discussion in *Whose Justice? Which Rationality?* beyond ethics, which was the focus of his attention in *After Virtue,* to the very principles of rationality, thus bringing the insights of his ethical thought to bear on epistemology. There are two major themes developed in *Whose Justice? Which Rationality?:* first, there is a continuation of the critique of liberalism found in *After Virtue* coupled with an affirmation of a religious perspective; and second, there is a rejection of relativism coupled with an insistence on the significance of historical considerations for the adjudication of disputes across traditions. When two traditions of thought are so different that what is considered self evident or obvious in one tradition is considered dubious or incomprehensible in the other, the very principles of reason come under question. In contemporary Western thought, what are often considered to be principles of reason are those which have proven indispensable to the natural sciences and mathematics.

If one wants to judge whether this view of rationality is correct or that, for example, found in the works of Muslim philosophers, one must be very careful to avoid begging the question by using the very principles in one's evaluation that are under dispute. Relativists have considered such controversies to be irresolvable. They claim that we are stuck inside our own world views, unable to make judgments on any of them. MacIntyre distinguishes two forms of relativism, which he terms relativist and perspectivalist. The relativist claims that there can be no rationality as such, but only rationality relative to the standards of some particular tradition. The perspectivalist claims that the central beliefs of a tradition are not to be considered as true or false, but as providing different, complementary perspectives for envisaging the realities about which they speak to us. MacIntyre argues that both the relativist and the perspectivalist are wrong. They are wrong because they fail to admit the absolute timeless character of the truth, and would replace truth by what is often called warranted assertibility. Instead of truth, they hold that the best we can attain is the right or warrant to assert various statements in various circumstances.

MacIntyre's solution to the problem of how to reach absolute truth from a historically limited position is that attention to history itself may reveal the superiority of one tradition over another with respect to a given topic. To have passed through an epistemological crisis successfully enables the adherents of a tradition of enquiry to rewrite its history in a more insightful way And such a history of a particular tradition provides not only a way of identifying the continuities in virtue of which that tradition of enquiry has survived and flourished as one and the same tradition, but also of identifying more accurately that structure of justification which underpins whatever claims to truth are made within it, claims which are more and other than claims to warranted assertibility. The concept of warranted assertibility always has application only at some particular time and place in respect of standards then prevailing at some particular stage in the development of a tradition of enquiry, and a claim that such and such is warrantedly assertible always, therefore, has to make implicit or explicit references to such times and places. The concept of truth, however, is timeless.

MacIntyre argues that since a tradition can fail to pull through an epistemological crisis on its own standards, the relativist is wrong if he thinks that each tradition must always vindicate itself. MacIntyre further argues that there are cases of cultural encounter in which one must come to admit the superiority of an alien culture in some regard, because it explains why the crisis occurred and does not suffer from the same defects present in one's own culture. It is in this way that the people of Rome could come to accept Christianity, and the people of Iran, Islam. Each people saw that their own traditions had reached a point of crisis, a point at which further progress could only be made by the adoption of a new religion. The relativist claims that there is no way in which a tradition can enter into rational debate with another, "But if this were so, then there could be no good reason to give one's allegiance to the standpoint of any one tradition rather to that of any other.

To the contrary, MacIntyre claims that the question of which tradition to which one is to give one's allegiance is far from arbitrary, and the intellectual struggle of all those who have changed their minds about the correctness of an intellectual or spirit" tradition is more than ample evidence that the question, "Which side are you on?" is one which requires rational evaluation, however much other factors may come into play. Perhaps MacIntyre is reflecting here on his own brief membership in the Communist Party and subsequent rejection of Marxism and conversion to Catholicism. One who adopts an intellectual position must always ask himself if it can adequately respond to criticism,

criticism which can mount to produce what may be termed an epistemological crisis. "It is in respect of their adequacy or inadequacy in their responses to epistemological crises that traditions are vindicated or fail to be vindicated."

MacIntyre also argues that the position of the relativist is self defeating. The relativist pretends to issue his challenge from a neutral ground where different traditions may be compared and truth may be proclaimed relative to each of them. But this is as much a claim to absolute truth as any other. This argument and others similar to it which are to be found in *Whose Justice? Which Rationality?* have provoked penetrating criticism. John Haldane has argued that one need not assume that there is some neutral ground from which to issue the relativist claim. Within an intellectual tradition, one may observe that there are other incommensurable traditions and decide that relativism best explains this. MacIntyre accepts Haldane's point, admitting that the case against relativism in *Whose Justice? Which Rationality?* needs to be amended. At the same time, 'he points out that within every major intellectual tradition, various claims are presented about morals and rationality as absolutely true.

The problem is then raised as to how this anti relativistic commitment to truth can coexist with the recognition of rival intellectual traditions with their different standards of rationality and morality. MacIntyre's solution is that common standards are to be sought, even where none exist, by dialectical interchange between the rival viewpoints. One tradition of inquiry will be in a position to uphold the truth of its claims against rivals in which those claims are not recognized when it develops the intellectual apparatus to explain the rival viewpoint, and why the disagreement has arisen, and why the rival is incorrect. In other words, through intellectual conflict between traditions, a tradition can vindicate itself only when it can enrich its own conceptual resources sufficiently to explain the errors of its rivals. This kind of conflict and progress is only possible when there is a commitment to finding the truth.

With relativism there can be no intellectual advancement, because there is no attempt made to adjudicate among different theoretical viewpoints, and without the attempt to reach a more comprehensive position in which truth and falsity can be distinguished, traditions cannot evolve rationally, nor can they maintain their previous truth claims. MacIntyre sees relativism as tempting those who despair of intellectual advancement, and for the sake of intellectual advancement, he sees it as a temptation that must be avoided. MacIntyre dismisses the perspectivist position with the rebuff, "theirs is not so much a conclusion about truth as an exclusion from it and thereby from rational debate." The perspectivalist, like the reductive religious pluralist, states that rival traditions provide different views of the same reality, and none can be considered absolutely true or false. MacIntyre objects that the traditions really do conflict with one another, and the fact that they are rivals itself bears testimony to their substantive disagreements over what is true and false.

The claim that there is no ultimate truth of the matter is really just a way of avoiding the work that needs to be done in order to determine exactly where and in what respects in each of the rival traditions the truth lies, and when the differences in the rivals is so deep that the very principles of rationality are called into question, the rivalry produces an epistemological crisis, but even here, the need and duty to provide a rational evaluation of the rivals remains. MacIntyre contends that epistemological crisis occurs when different traditions with different languages confront one another. Those who learn to think in both languages come to the understanding that there are things in one language for which the other does not have the expressive resources, and thereby they discover a flaw in the deficient tradition.

In this way he shows how rational evaluation of different traditions is possible, although this evaluation itself must begin from within a specific tradition. His emphasis on the fact that the starting point of our inquiry is tradition bound is comparable to a common theme among writers in the hermeneutic tradition, such as Gadamer. The fantasy of universal standards of reason to which all rational beings must submit by virtue of being rational has been abandoned. This separates MacIntyre from traditional writers, as Thomas McCarthy has observed:

> Even arguments like Alasdair MacIntyre's for the superiority of premodern traditions are not themselves traditional arguments but the traditionalistic arguments of hyperreflexive modems.

What distinguishes MacIntyre from others who share his sensitivity to context dependency is his robust sense of the truth. The incommensurability of competing traditions, according to MacIntyre, is not as absolute as some have imagined. Logic retains authority, even if its principles are disputed, and what is sought is truth, and although he rejects correspondence theories of truth that would pair judgments to facts (because he considers the concept of fact to be an invention of seventeenth century European thought), the theory of truth to which he gives his allegiance is still a correspondence theory. In response to a sympathetic comparison between his position and views current among certain philosophers of science, MacIntyre objects:

> I had hoped that what I had said about truth in enquiry in Chapter 18 of *Whose Justice? Which Rationality?* would have made it adequately clear that I regard any attempt to eliminate the notion of truth from that of enquiry as bound to fail. It is in part for this reason that I regard the Nietzschean tradition as always in danger of lapsing into fatal incoherence.

MacIntyre's solution to the problem of relativism is especially important for Muslims because it offers a way to break the deadlock between Muslim intellectuals who, over impressed with the intellectual traditions of the West, deny that Islam asserts any absolute truths that man is capable of grasping, and those 'Mama' who insist on the self evidence of the fundamental troths of their own traditions without seeing that such claims are ineffective against rival systems of thought in which there are profound differences about what, if anything, is to be considered self evident. The solution MacIntyre offers is one in which there is hope that the absolute truths of Islam can be rationally defended against opponents as certain, but only by developing the Islamic intellectual traditions to the point that they are able to explain the successes as well as the failures of their rivals.

MacIntyre's disappointment with liberalism is more extensive and more profound than that of other Western critics: more extensive because it applies to the political theories of both the left and the right, more profound because it traces the failings of liberalism to its origins in the Enlightenment, and traces the injustice of the modern nation state to its very essence. As Ronald Beiner observes:

> What makes MacIntyre unique is that for him the problem is not merely individualism or liberalism but modernity as such. Therefore he includes even Marxism within the scope of his critique.

In some ways, MacIntyre's rejection of liberalism is similar to his rejection of relativism. Just as the relativist contradicts himself if he would proclaim the absolute truth of the proposition that there are no absolute truths, the liberal contradicts himself by proclaiming neutrality between all ideologies, when, in fact, liberalism itself is an ideology. Liberalism is an intellectual tradition as ideological as any other, and it allows for scholarly inquiry only after initiation into accepted modes of appraisal which deny the worth of serious challenges to liberalism itself.

Just as Haldane argued that the relativist need not claim that relativism is absolutely true, independent of any tradition, defenders of liberalism have responded to MacIntyre's criticism of liberalism by admitting that liberalism is an ideology, that it is not absolutely neutral. *Whose Justice? Which Rationality?* MacIntyre responds that liberalism is a defective and ultimately incoherent ideology. His insight into the defects of liberalism is one which was first expressed in his first book, *Marxism: An Interpretation,* which was written when he was only twenty three years old. In the revised edition of this work MacIntyre emphasizes the need for an ideology on the scale of Christianity or Marxism that can offer an interpretation of human existence by means of which people can situate themselves in the world and direct their actions to ends that transcend their own immediate situations. He argues that liberalism is an ideology that cannot function effectively as such. The axis about which the failure of liberalism turns is its assertion of the fact/value gap.

Liberalism fails as an ideology because it does not permit one to discover one's own identity and appropriate ends by gaining knowledge of nature and society, or by under-standing human existence in relation to al Haqq, the Exalted. In liberalism, all values are personal except the value of respecting personal values, and this is simply not sufficient to orient one's life. Modernism inhibits orientation because from the point of view of modern liberalism, religious traditions seem irrational. The standards of rationality to which the religious traditions of enquiry appeal are so different from those which dominate the natural and social sciences in the West today that traditional and modernist ways of thinking have become nearly mutually. incomprehensible. Nevertheless, a tradition may come to be rationally accepted by those who live within the horizons of Western liberal culture once they come to recognize themselves as imprisoned by a set of beliefs which lack justification in precisely the same way and to the same extent as do the positions which they reject but also to understand themselves as hitherto deprived of what tradition affords, as persons in part constituted as what they are up to this point by an absence, by what is from the standpoint of traditions an impoverishment.

The impoverishment of which MacIntyre speaks here is one which Islam excels at eradicating. What the individual posited by liberal thebry lacks is an effective ideology to provide understanding and purpose on the basis of which communities can be established. Modern liberal thinkers imagine themselves to be independent, but MacIntyre charges that from an Aristotelian point of view they have refused to learn or have been unable to learn that "one cannot think for oneself if one thinks entirely by oneself," and that it is only by participation in rational practice based community that one becomes truly rational.

MacIntyre admits that this kind of recognition amounts to a sort of conversion. Individuals at the point of conversion will invite a tradition of enquiry to furnish them with a kind of self knowledge which they have not as yet possessed by first providing them with an awareness of the specific character of their own incoherence and then accounting for the particular character of this incoherence by its metaphysical, moral, and political scheme of classification and explanation. The catalogs of virtues and vices, the norms of conformity and deviance, the accounts of educational success and failure, the narratives of possible types of human life which each tradition has elaborated in its own terms, all the invite the individual educated into self knowledge of his or her own incoherence to acknowledge in which of these rival modes of moral understanding he or she finds him or herself most adequately explained and accounted for.

Not only does MacIntvre explain how someone in a liberal society may evolve to the point of being able to convert to a religious tradition, his astute observations regarding the logic of liberal thought also helps to illuminate the West's failure to understand the current Islamic movement and its hostility towards it. The liberal's moral analysis is one which begins by abstracting the claims to be debated from their contexts in tradition, and then proceeds with an evaluation of rational justifiability which is supposed to convince any rational person. The liberal fantasy of universal progress implies that the most rational standards are those which dominate the most recent trends of its own thought. To the extent that Muslims are unwilling to adopt the standards of modernism, they are thought to be irrational. Islamic intellectual traditions are taken to be more or less the same as what the West progressed beyond when it abandoned medieval scholasticism.

The caricature of Islam drawn by the liberal West requires neglect of the particularities of character, history, and circumstance. This makes it impossible to engage in the kind of rational dialogue which could move through argumentative evaluation to the rational acceptance or rejection of a tradition. Thus, the kind of debate which is enforced in the public forums of enquiry in modern liberal culture for the most part effectively preclude the voices of tradition outside liberalism from being heard. Materialistic consumerism is a direct result of the liberal's pretense of neutrality. Since all the citizens of the liberal state are supposed to be free to pursue their own happiness, and since despite their differences about what ultimate happiness is, the vast majority seem to be in agreement on the idea that its pursuit is aided by ever increasing acquisition and consumption, which goes by the euphemism of economic development, it becomes nearly self evident that it is in the national interests of the liberal state to pursue economic development.

MacIntyre explains that those who adhere to the standpoint dominant in peculiarly modern societies recognize that acquisitiveness is a character trait indispensable to continuous and limitless economic growth, and one of their central beliefs is that continuous and limitless economic growth is a fundamental good. That a systematically lower standard of living ought to be preferred to a systematically higher standard of living is a thought incompatible with either the economics or the politics of peculiarly modem societies...But a community which was guided by Aristotelian norms would not only have to view acquisitiveness as a vice but would have to set strict limits to growth insofar as that is necessary to preserve or enhance a distribution of goods according to desert. From the Aristotelian point of view advocated by MacIntyre, the problem with the modern liberal state goes way beyond its worldliness. There is no way, MacIntyre insists, for those who rule in a modern state to avoid doing injustice.

Modern nation states which masquerade as embodiments of community are always to be resisted. The modem nation state, in whatever guise, is a dangerous and unmanageable institution, presenting itself on the one hand as a bureaucratic supplier of goods and services, which is always about to, but never actually does, give its clients value for money, and on the other as a repository of sacred values, which from time to time invites one to lay down one's life on its behalf; it is like being asked to die for the telephone company ... [T]o empower even the liberal state as a bearer of values always imperils those values. His criticism of the liberal state is so harsh that it could be mistaken for a form of anarchism were it not for the fact that he explicitly advises his readers to cooperate with the state by paying their taxes. What sort of politics does MacIntyre advocate? MacIntyre suggests that the focus of the political life of an Aristotelian of the sort he lauds should be "the family, the neighborhood, the workplace, the parish, the school, or clinic, communities within which the needs of the hungry and the homeless can be met."

Are we then to leave the state to "the barbarians" mentioned at the close of *After Virtue?* And what are we to do about the hungey and homeless who live outside our parish? Is it not incumbent upon a religious society to take the reins of state power out of the hands of those who are driving it to ruin, even if the nation state of its own momentum will not readily change course? A more realistic political Aristotelianism than the one advocated by MacIntyre would not shun the need to shoulder the burden of the modern state in full recognition of its deficiencies and in the hope that it could be transformed into something better. MacIntyre does not see this as a live option because he seems to be thinking of Europe and the U.S., whereas the prospects for anything better than liberal government are unpromising, because the major alternative there to liberalism is nationalism, and nationalism easily degrades into fascist rage we have witnessed in the attempt to exterminate the Muslims of Bosnia. Within Muslim societies, however, there is an alternative to both nationalism and liberalism which is not taken seriously by Western theorists?

MacIntyre's retreat to the local takes the punch out of his critique of liberalism. Liberals do not oppose local associations with substantive ideologies, values and purposes. Liberal political theory is a theory of *government,* not of local voluntary associations. If MacIntyre had announced at the start of his book that his quarrel with liberalism was over how local associations are to be organized, and not about government, it would not have attracted the attention it has. Indeed, if one were to read *Whose Justice? Which Rationality?* from the start with the assumption that the critique of liberalism was not to extend to liberal theories of government, much,of what MacIntyre says would not make any sense. Consider the passage quoted above in which limits to economic growth are advocated.

What is at issue here is how whole societies conduct their economic affairs, and no matter how large and thriving the private sector of any society is, the role of governments in directing the economic affairs of the societies they rule is undeniable. So, what MacIntyre is objecting to is the flaws of liberal governments and of liberal theories of how governments should conduct their affairs. Here again, MacIntyre's work should be helpful for those engaged in the development of Islamic political theory. If we accept MacIntyre's critique of the modern form of nation state, the creation of Islamic republics cannot be the ultimate goal of Islamic political activity, but only an .intermediary stage in a development leading to more perfectly Islamic forms of governance, culminating in the governance of the *Wali al 'Asr,* may his emergence be hastened.

2

Tradition and Globalization and Present Day Islam

The various geopolitical configurations of the world each produce a dominant discourse. During the period of ideological rivalry between the two superpowers, the choice was between westernization or, alternatively, sovietization, with a reluctant Third World in between. Since the implosion of the Soviet empire and China's entry in the international market, the "assertive" cultures and religions are the ones who find themselves in trouble. The pressure of global standardization exercised by the sole superpower and the prevailing view of neoliberal globalization has produced identity countercurrents. In the large cultural areas of the world - China, India, Africa and Islamic lands - ground swells surge to oppose the standardizing pressure, in favour of the right to authenticity and difference. The most striking example is China, a colossus of 1.3 billion inhabitants, which achieved the highest rate of growth in the world during the last twenty years through a strategy of openness, modernization and internationalization which is quite different from the western model.

The so-called socialist government, while controlling the project, combines an authoritarian one-party state and a network of multinationals that bring hefty investments and technology. With its low-cost exports and the enormous surplus of its commercial and financial deficit with the United States, China has already become a driving force of the world economy. In India, the strategy centred on the creation of niches of sophisticated technology is more autonomous. And its modernization is more democratic than that of China, in accordance with its multicultural genius for synthesis. In Malaysia, a new unified wave of Islam supports a remarkable economic dynamic. During the 1990s, multiple trajectories of non-western modernization emerged, even in Latin America where the postmodernist current is proudly called modernidad periférica.

Thematic areas and texts about the various possible angles on this subject are increasingly debated in conferences throughout the world. In the Muslim world, since the end of the 1990s, seminars and conferences in Beirut, Cairo, Damas, Rabat, Lahore and Kuala Lumpur on globalization's issues and global governance have taken place. Multiple Internet networks have spurred transnational contacts; they act as opening catalysts in circles that had until recently been closed or had existed in an ethnic, cultural and religious cleavage. From the point of view of western neoconservative or fundamentalist commentators who are influential theorists of the prevailing discourse, these multiple ways of asserting identities will inevitably lead to a clash of civilizations. From a hegemonic perspective, Western publicists judge the policies and practices of other civilizations on the basis of principles and ideals prevailing in the western world.

According to this method, the non Western cultures are judged according to criteria which are not theirs. We would like to reverse this trend so that we may listen to Muslim intellectuals and understand, especially on the challenges that globalization represents for them. In spite of well-known differences between fundamentalist, liberal and innovative thinkers, they are commonly critical of our practices in the field of global governance. They consider that our principles are not universal and moreover not convincing. Indeed, some of the ideals we present as the most important appear to them as trampled and disavowed by our neo-colonialist behaviour. To open this intercultural dialogue, it will be necessary to critically assess not only the thoughts and the prejudices of the others but ours as well, accepting the test of contradiction wherever it may come from. Dialogue implies that everyone can present his argument while listening to the Other.

Trajectory of Islam

From the eighth to the fifteenth century, Islam was at the core of the dominant cultures and peoples which prevailed in the Mediterranean area: Arabs, Persians and invaders coming from Asia such as the Turks and Mongols. During this period, Islamic culture deployed its splendour and was hegemonic in the Mediterranean basin, reaching as far as Spain. Its scholars picked up where the Western world left off: Greek philosophy, mathematics, the beginnings of medical science, and numerous technologies for irrigation, agriculture and architecture. These transfers accelerated our take-off in the 11th and 12th century. Then came the decline. One of the great Maghreb masters, Ibn Khaldoun (1332-1406) theorized the causes of the decline in his historical work Muqadimmah. Later, stagnation in the material sense and in the intellectual sphere brought political colonization as well as grudgingly adopted modernization. The movement of reform (nahda) at the end of 19th century did not hold its promises because it was not supported by the masses that remained anchored in tradition.

Decolonization brought to the Islamic world its share of more or less authoritative governments. Currently, there are some 1.3 billion Muslims dispersed in about fifty nationstates around the world. OPEC's oil crisis marked the first divide. And the Ayatollahs' Iranian revolution started a trend in which religion and culture override imported secularization and models. In the wake of this spiritual and political revolution, the Muslim world was vivified by a movement of cultural and religious revival: Al sahwa Al islamiyya. In the large, diverse Islamic world (Arab, Asian, African, and the diaspora with its numerous Muslim intellectuals and university professors), it is impossible to give due place to the complex dynamics which animate these cultural areas with their different schools of fiqh and theology. The leaders of a cultural Islam (Al Islam hadari) have become more influential than the protagonists of the Islamic state. In spite of an enormous financial support for Saudi Wahhabite fundamentalism, liberals and innovators gain ground in most areas.

However, fundamentalists received a gift from heaven when the American army, supported by some Western forces, invaded and occupied oil-rich Eurasia. Muslims who were sympathetic to the Western culture were not rewarded. Even sympathizers disapprove of democracy when it is imposed by foreign military force like a suppository. Imposed westernization hurts nationalism and national pride and consequently works like a contraceptive. Debates on globalization build on those of modernization, however they are more about geopolitics and strategies for economic development.

Culturalist and Religious Debate

A great number of Muslims see globalization (Al aulama) as an elegant neologism which hides reality; they see globalisation as a powerful lever for westernization (Al taghrib) whereas pro-Westerners favour it and see as a highway to modernity. Fundamentalists demonize globalization as an invasion and even as cultural rape. They argue that Western mass-industry (pop art, cinema, television and other media, consumerism, Mc World, etc) brings perversion through seduction. Secularization presented by Westerners as liberating in fact destroys the canonical hierarchy of values where religious morals control the social, economic and political processes. Secularization is perceived as a lever to push religion out of the public sphere. Its purely instrumental rationality deprives life of its fundamental dimension. In the Western world, demystification or desacrilization led to dechristianization.

Churches are empty. Structuring principles no longer guide fundamental values. Culture becomes merchandise and values (including economic morals) dissolve. While reading fundamentalist texts, the learned reader has sometimes the impression they are hearing the great master of Western rationalization, Max Weber, discussing the other side of modernity: disenchantment of the world, loss of direction as a result of secularization. On the other hand, liberals and innovators underline the obsession of the fundamentalists for models of the past. Admittedly, cultural heritage is a value but it should not function as an obstacle to the present.

All cultures have a dynamic which takes in external elements and contributions. Islam cannot paralyse itself through excessive glorification of past values. Each culture like each religion has appeared in the world at a historical moment and in a particular cultural context. Thus, innovators say, our culture like our religion must evolve in order to serve as an existential anchor for the faithful who wish to progress in their historical trek. According to these new scholars, Islam must be situated in history, just like Western culture that proclaims itself universal. The evolution of the Western world, its secularization and particularly its economism (priority given to material development) must be understood within the framework of its particular historical course.

Viewed as a product of history, the Western world has moved away from models that are more grounded in the human tradition of the long term. Thus it became the exception and cannot aspire to universality. Our post-modernists have also deconstructed the myth of universalism, of the isms of modernity through the recognition of difference, specificity and endogeneity. The Muslim revival thus tends to outfit imported models with its own intellectual productions,, especially in the social sciences. Great intellectual centres are reformulating economy, sociology and political science in new terms on the basis of the Islamic system. However transition to Western modernity rests on the critique of traditional knowledge and the evacuation of religious morals.

This model of secularization implies autonomy in the spheres of knowledge and life in accordance with their own validation and operational processes. Through this evolution, politics, society and economy free themselves from the religious morals by which they were governed. Without structural regulation, conflict between these spheres of values is unsolvable, say even the innovative Muslims. But a group of new scholars of international reputation plead for a religion that is not subdued to jurisprudence (fiqh). They contend it should open the way to hermeneutic debates (ijtihad) in order to reconcile the spiritual foundations of religion, its existential value, and its contribution to the future of umma. A religion that mingles constantly with turmoil and the variations of day-to-day political options becomes an ideology and loses its transcendental substance. Intense and profound thematic topics reflect the cultural creativity and theological renewal that has arisen through the debate on globalization.

The Muslim world very strongly resents the militarization of international relations which touched on aspects of its historical splendour. For them, the globalization process seems to be pushed less by an earnest care for democracy and development than guided by material interest. A Muslim is deeply stung when he feels he is being "bedouïnized" by an arrogant Westerner.

Economic Analysis of Geopolitics

In the view of publicists writing from an economic perspective, the geopolitics of security is a project imagined and directed by the Western world to ensure its vital raw materials supply (such as oil) and to retain its capacity to attract world savings towards Western financial markets. Wall Street is the epicentre of the recycled savings of the whole world which serve to finance deficits in the US trade balance and American public sector deficits. In order to control the rate of the dollar and thus world trade, it is vital to control oil reserves on which competitors (Japanese, Chinese, Europeans) are even more dependent. Global governance produces a view and a strategy of development that suits Western needs as a whole, including also Europe.

These strategies of development are passed down to staff and think tanks associated with the institutions with economic capacity such as the World Bank and the International Monetary Fund. In order to allow them to impose their discipline (by punishing the uncooperative through the Malthusianism of loans and privilege for those that yield to structural adjustment), their financial means and their capacity of intervention have become considerable. While researching on the Chinese course of action, read similar critical analyses. In China, the questioning of global governance is formulated by the intellectuals of the New Left and the militants of cultural nationalism (cf analysis of Wang Hui, Liu Kang and Zheng Yongnian). But criticism of consumerism is absent from Chinese discourse, while it is very present in Muslim publications that recommend a reserved attitude towards consumption.

From a planetary perspective, the Western consumerist model is a false utopia, because it is impossible for the Western model of consumption to apply to the 6.5 billion inhabitants of the world without bringing about an ecological explosion. For innovators, development is a project of civilization. Their writings laden with principles of social ethics support the harmonious development thesis. In this way, they come close to some Western reformers, such as Indian Amartya SEN and also the inspirers of the Kyoto school, notably Yasusuke Murakami.

A comparison of Asian and Islamic courses of action is

all the more interesting because modern Malaysian Islam has played an important role in the economic success of this country. This is partly due to Mohamed Mahathir who was during 12 years (1981-1993) its bold Prime Minister. As an enthusiastic Muslim, he associated Islamic masters to the doctrinal framing of his development.strategy. Some innovators of the Arab world, like Hassan Hanafi, see the modernized Islam of Malaysia as a model.

In spite of the constraints exerted by global governance, a counter-current exemplifying courses of non-Western modernization is shamelessly emerging. In order to understand correctly these trends and perspectives from inside, a recommended method is to read and to analyse their intellectuals' writings and publicists' writings. If one is uninformed of ongoing controversies and trends as they are viewed from inside, one cannot understand the real situation. Western analysts are often blamed for reading only western scholars and for ignoring or neglecting indigenous sources even on issues such as globalization. If this debate is to become really a dialogue with multiple voices on world issues and the future, it must not shun but rather include the views of Others.

Now you can learn about Islam from one of the world's top experts. The events of September 11 brought the Muslim world into direct confrontation with the West. 19 hijackers not only killed thousands of innocent people, but also created one of the greatest paradoxes of the 21st century: Islam, which sees itself as a religion of peace, is now associated with murder and mayhem. Islam is the world's fastest growing religion. About 1.4 billion Muslims live in 57 countries, including 25 million living in the West. Some of America's strongest allies and greatest enemies are Muslim. In this environment, understanding the World of Islam is not a luxury but an imperative.

In these audio lectures, renowned Islamic scholar Akbar Ahmed introduces you to the Islamic world, an exploration few Westerners have experienced. Islam, argues Professor

Ahmed, does not mean the subordination of women, contempt for other religions, opposition to modernity, or violence against non-believers. One can learn to appreciate the beauty, depth, and variety of Islamic tradition by turning to its sources and rich history. Through this unique lecture series, you'll explore the life of the Prophet of Islam, and the Quran's five pillars, which govern the beliefs and behavior of Muslims everywhere. Learn how the extraordinary legacies of the great Ottoman, Safavid and Mughal empires influence the present day Arab world, Iran, and South Asia, and explore Islam in other parts of the world.

The current Muslim struggle to preserve traditions in an age of globalization and ethnic and religious strife are examined in detail. Professor Ahmed explores all these issues with insight and sympathy, penetrating beyond stereotypes to the realities of Islamic life. Professor Ahmed offers a message of hope and reconciliation between the West and Islam by leveraging the power of dialogue to build bridges across ethnic, religious, and cultural divides. With dialogue comes knowledge and understanding. This lecture series is essential for anyone hoping to learn more about the Islamic world and its people and to understand the world in which we live.

Globalization and Counter Terrorism

The Quran states that Islam is the universal religion and is a mercy to all creatures. Islam is a religion of peace. As a universal faith that has been subject to diverse interpretations Islam offers a living demonstration of qualities to which all human beings can relate: compassion, mercy, tolerance, and love. Bearing the label "Muslim" is no guarantee of living by its teaching since Muslims are not a single, homogeneous entity. Grave risks arise from thinking that they are. Islam is more than a system of theology, it's a complete civilization. The classical history of Islam proved the Islamic universality: Islam rejects discrimination, racism, and teaches men and women to disperse within the land and seek the bounty of God. More clearly the tradition of the Prophet

Muhammad instructs his followers to seek knowledge, even to China. Indeed, this hadith calls for globalization at doctrinal and practical levels. Islam became the global power when the peoples of Arabia, Africa, Europe and Asia admired and followed the Islamic civilization and culture.

The presence of Islam has contributed to the welfare and the prosperity of the peoples. The civilized peoples closely related to the basics of Islamic doctrine, ethics, values, morals, law, and their customs. Islam and its history have taught globalization at the most general level, that refers to a process of change which affects all regions of the world in a variety of sectors including the economy, science and technology and to some extent – politics, the media, culture and the environment. The characterization of globalization may be thought of initially as the widening, deepening and speeding up of worldwide interconnectedness in all aspects of social life, from the cultural to the criminal, the financial to the spiritual.

The 12th Century was "The Golden Age of Islamic Globalization". The majority of Muslims are not located in the motherland of Islam, but Indonesia, India and Pakistan. The faces of Islam in these geopolitical locations are more moderate than what has developed in the Middle East. However, the global interaction among the people of Muslim countries does not only introduce moderate Islam, but also militant ideas and practices as the resistance to the common enemy, namely the West. With this in mind, this chapter attempts to explain the nature of Islam, its interaction with the West and its responses to the Western global economy and military as part of the triggering factors of how global resistance towards the West is expressed in the most inhumane form, such as terrorism. This is not to say that terrorism is acceptable in Islam and to Muslims. Terrorism is not Islamic at all and will never become part of the Islamic teaching.

Unity in Diversity

Although Muslims maintain that there is one divinely revealed and mandated Islam, there are many Muslim interpretations of Islam. There are two major branches of opinion about political and religious leadership after the death of Muhammad: Sunnis (85 percent of the World's Muslims) and Shi'is (15%). There are diverse school of theology, law and mystical tradition that includes many Sufi orders or brotherhoods. Islam represents a basic unity of beliefs within rich cultural diversity. Islam practices itself in different ways within a vast array of cultures that extend from North Africa to Southeast Asia, as well as Europe and America. As a world religion, Islam is practiced in diverse cultures in Africa, the Middle East, Asia, Europe, and America. Differences in religious and cultural practices are therefore wide-raging. Like all faiths, Islam has developed divisions, sects, and school of thought over various issues. Islamic law provides one of the clearest and most important examples of diversities of opinion.

While many law schools existed, only a few endured and were recognized as authoritative. While all Muslims share certain beliefs and practices, such as a belief in God, the Quran, Muhammad, and the Five Pillars of Islam, divisions have arisen over questions of political and religious leadership, theology, interpretations of Islamic law, and responses to modernity and the West. Perhaps nowhere are differences in Islam more visible than in responses to modernity. Since the nineteenth century, Muslims have struggled with the relationship of their religious tradition developed in premodern time to the new demands of the modern world (viz. religious, political, economic, and social demands).

The issues are not only about Islam's accommodation to change but also about the relationship of Islam to the West, since much of modern change is associated with Western ideas, institutions, and values. Muslim responses to the issues of reform and modernization have spanned the spectrum from secularists. The other groups are more "Islamically" oriented but have different opinions as to the role Islam should play in public life.

Islam and the West

The highest tide of Islamic culture, 800-1100A.D., was coincident with the lowest ebb of European culture. While the Muslims enjoyed general standards of living equal to, if not surpassing those of the proceeding Graeco-Roman civilization, the Europeans were living in the semi-barbarous squalor and restricted regime of feudalism – a pattern unalleviated by comforts and luxuries. One of the strangest dramas of history is that at the very moment when Europe, prodded by contacts with the Islamic culture in Sicily and Spain and by the Crusades, began to recover from its prolonged descent towards darkness, Islam entered a decline that was to carry it down into the very fog of obscurantism from which it had helped to rescue Europe philosophy of capitalism in economy and secularism in the politics. Both capitalism and secularism supported by sciences, technology and the military had created the Superpower State, especially after the Cold War.

The Islamic civilization has a significant contribution to drive the Enlightenment in the West and the modern world. The immenseness of the Arab-Islam contribution can best realized by recapitulating the most significant of her activities, considering at the same time their impact to a Europe struggling upward through the barbarism of the Dark Ages. The Arabic-Islamic science and technology, reaching Europe via Sicily and Spain, awoke her from the Dark Ages in which she was slumbering. The detailed elaboration of the actual routes by which this transference took place have only recently been outlined by historians. A hundred years ago a statement of the full influence of the Arabic culture on Europe would have been incredible. But modern research has firmly established its incontestability. The principles of Western political systems typically are democracy and the rule of law. Together democracy and the rule of law save people from arbitrary whims of dictators and tyrants, and make all people politically equal. Democracy was pioneered by ancient Athens.

The rule of law is to a great degree a product of Islam. Democracy in the words of Abraham Lincoln is similar to the syura' in the Islamic concept derived from the Quran by Fuqaha. The West learned the scientific method from Islam and has used that method to develop, amongst many other things, technologies for communication that have shrunk the world. The global civilization may be regarded as the joint legacy of Islam and the West. The three most influential thinkers of the Western civilization represented the three Abrahamic faiths: Ibn Rusyd (Averroes) the Muslim, Maimonides the Jew, and Thomas Aquinas the Christian. Rationalism initiated the new modern world and ignited the secularism that only takes the Christian's ethic; meanwhile, ethics are a changeable point of view on what is good or bad.

Conceptually, Islam and the West were born within the tradition of monotheistic religion, - Jews and Christianity - referred to the Abrahamic faith. In the spheres of politics and economics Islam and the West are often in conflict, where as in knowledge and ideas they are often in harmony. When there is a rivalry between Islam and the West (Christianity) or between capitalism and Islam, one of the solutions is military power and war. Therefore, there is a significant relationship between the economy and politics on one side and belief and religion on the other. The only superpower State nowadays is the United States (U.S.) that has become the "World Cop" who always monitors and unashamedly forces the other State or States to be under its control. This condition is globalization or hegemony. The Western world as a whole previously clashed with other civilizations long before the Cold War of Ideology. Firstly, there was genocide against the native ancient civilization of the Americans. Secondly, there was later enslavement of millions of Africans for use in the so-called New World.

Thirdly, there was the phase of European imperialism and colonialization of most of the world. Is the fourth phase the United States as an imperial superpower? America has now become a new form of empire, controlling millions of people through a variety of inducements and intimidations. In addition, the global development that began after the Cold War left a vacuum from the influence of the two Super Powers or West and East Block represented by the USSR and the U.S. This area is well-known as the Middle East. The victory of the West pioneered by the USA, soon followed by founding the Israel State in the middle of the Middle East countries. The State, in the eyes of the world, inflicts injustice on the Palestinians. Muslims around the world consider the invasion of the Palestinian land as the core problem that creates the rebellion of the oppressed people (Palestinians) by the powerful and unjust state institution and government (Israel). Such rebellion is called "terrorism".

War on Terrorism

The lack of information and deeper misunderstanding of Islam may lead some to think that the war on terrorism is a war on Islam. That's why most Americans and Europeans think of Muslims as strange, foreign, and frightening, inevitably linked to headlines of terrorist events. This is not true since the war on terrorism is not a war on Islam. Islam and Islamic law have consistently condemned terrorism (the killing of non-combatants). Like the members of all religious faiths, Muslims have had to deal with religious extremism and terrorism from their earliest days. The responses of the mainstream majority to groups like the Kharijites and the Assassins and more contemporary groups like Islamic Jihad in Egypt or al-Qaeda have been to condemn, combat, and marginalize them. From the origins, the Islamic community faced rebellion and civil wars, violence and terrorism, epitomized by groups like the Kharijites and Assassins. The Kharijites were a pious but puritanical and militant extremist group that broke with the Calip Ali and later assassinated him. The Assassins lived apart in secret communities from which they were guided by a series of Grand Masters, who ruled from the mountain fortress of Alamut in northern Persia.

The Assassins' jihad against the Seljuk Dynasty terrorized the princes, generals, and ulama (scholars), whom they murdered in the name of the Hidden Imam. They struck such terror in the hearts of their Muslim and Crusader enemies that their exploits in Persia and Syria earned them a name and memory in history long after they were overrun and the Mongols executed their last Grand Master in 1256. The response of Sunni Islam and Islamic law was to marginalize extremist and develop a political theory that emphasized stability over chaos and anarchy. This, of course, did not dissuade all from the extremist path. In more recent decades, alongside mainstream Islamic political opposition, terrorist groups have risen up to challenge the regime and terrorize their populations and attack foreign interests. Often they portray themselves as the "true believers" struggling against repressive regimes and in the midst of a "pagan" society of unbelief.

They attempt to impose their ideological brand of Islam and "hijack" Islamic doctrines such as jihad, claiming to be defending true Islam, to legitimate their illegitimate use of violence and acts of terrorism. In Egypt, groups like Egypt's Islamic Jihad and other extremist groups assassinated President Anwar Sadat and government officials, slaughtered tourists in Luxor, burned churches, and killed Christians. In Algeria, the Armed Islamic Group has engaged in a campaign of terror against the Algerian government. Osama bin Laden and al-Qaeda undertook a global war of terror against Muslim governments and America, distorting Islam and countering Islamic law in issuing their own fatwas (legal opinions) in an attempt to legitimate their war and call for an attack on civilians (non-combatants). The Suicide Bombing in Jakarta, Bali and Poso by Indonesians terrorists under their commander of Malaysian citizenship "the late Dr. Azahari" and his close companion and successor Nordin Top. They have distorted the true Islam and seemed to endorse the mistaken view so common in the West that

Islam is essentially a fanatical and violent faith. Terrorism has multiple faces and may be hiding under the name of a religion, philosophy, politics, or any other name. Terrorism is a way of life.

It may be a part of the history of human civilization and culture. Defining terrorism is most important in order not to be changeable between "terrorism" and "the warrior of freedom". The scholars have their own definition of terrorism based on their point of view and field, or they define it as the ruler's outlook. Anyway, how divers those definitions, but the might is the rulers' definition who enforce their definition to be accepted by the people either using military, political, economic, technology or cultural power. Terrorism may be derived from religious doctrine or motivated by any other beliefs. Terrorism may be come to the true when the terrorists regard themselves as the victim of a repressive and hypocritical regime that never takes care of them, for instance: the IRA, EPTA, and some groups of terrorists in Latin America, and the intifada movement of the Palestinians. The beginning of the terrorist's movement seems to be Hassan Bin Sabbah (1057 AD), the leader of the impressive movement in the Middle East, Hashashiyyin or Assassins as mentioned above.

Meanwhile, Maximilien Robespierre of France was the father of modern terrorism, as claimed by the scholars. Vladimir Lenin (b.1870-1924) is the modern terrorist. His ideas and theories of terrorism are followed by his successor as Vladimir Lenin (Vladimir Ulyanov) said. Joseph Stalin (d. 1953) is the master executive of terror. Furthermore, the greatest terrorist of the East was Mao Tse-Tung. Mao led a world class of terror. Mao believed that the government needed to be a dictatorship to remain in control; using terrorism as a means to oppress the people to obey all the governments will. Mao modernized terrorism and made it more effective, more powerful and more horrific than before. America has been described as "conceived and born in violence". Noam Chomsky has stated that the USA is a rich and powerful country that practices international terrorism on smaller States. Noam Chomsky stated that Osama bin Laden has caused the USA to bomb poor countries, such as Afghanistan. Osama bin Laden is the creation of the U.S. For Kuwait, the U.S. is the savoir and the defender against Saddam' aggression.

For Egypt, the U.S. is the donor of millions of dollars in order to take Egypt out of alignment with countries against Israel. For Saddam Hussein, the U.S. is the big enemy who removed him from his crown. For many countries of the world, the U.S. is a never ending Superpower State. There is no state in history that has made more progress in economics, the military, science, technology and politics, than the U.S. In both good and bad, the U.S. is an incomparable State. Globalization or hegemony is a new phase of the U.S. as an iperium having global power, including economic power and power over, information such as the internet. After the Cold War, the U.S. was the winner. Recently this State successfully brought freedom and democracy for peace. The U.S. seems to pull the rest of the world to follow its system. Unfortunately, the U.S. is trapped in imperializing other States. It represented the Jew-Christian ethic that created the capitalist system in economics and secularism system in politics. Anti-Americanism (along with anti-Europeanism) is a broad based phenomenon that cuts across Arab and Muslim societies. It is driven not only by blind hatred of religious zealotry of extremists but also by frustration and anger with U.S. foreign policy among the mainstream in the Muslim world.

The West's espousal of self-determination, democratization and human rights is often seen as a hypocritical "double standard" when compared to its policies, what is actually does – for instance, imposing sanctions upon Pakistan for its development of nuclear weapons while failing to press Israel and India on their nuclear development. The moral is so evident in America's helping

Kosovo is seen by many Muslims totally absent in the U.S. policy of permissive neglect in the Chechnyan and Kashmiri conflicts. The impact of sanctions on more than a half million Iraqi children does not seem to have been considered when they were imposed. Another inflammatory issue involves the significant presence of U.S. military and arms in the Gulf, which critics perceive as a neo-colonialist military influence. The American presence is equated with support for unpopular authoritarian regimes and pressure of Arab governments to comply with U.S. foreign policy objectives, especially with respect to Israel and Palestine. This long litany of grievances stretching over many years feed the anger of many mainstream Arabs and Muslims, as well as extremists. Globalization of communications has created a situation in which Arabs (Muslims and Christians) and Muslims around the world often see more than before.

Unlike the past, today international Arab and Muslim media are no longer solely dependent on Western reporters and channels. While America's overseas media presence (reporters and overseas posts) and coverage have waned over the past decade, television stations like al-Jazeera and others provide daily coverage of the violence in many Muslim countries. They show, for example, the violence and acts of terror committed by both sides as well as the disproportionate firepower used against Palestinians by Israelis armed with American-supplied weapons, F-16s, and Apache helicopters. America's record of overwhelming support of Israel-witnessed in its levels of aid to Israel, the U.S. voting record in the United Nations, and official statements by the administration and State Department - has proved to be a powerful lightning rod for Muslim anger over injustice.

Terrorism and Misconception of Jihad

Osama Bin Laden is the only terrorist leader to have formally declared a jihad- holy war – against the United States. This declaration of holy war is not an empty gesture. Laden's objective was the establishment of a "true" Islamic

State under the Sharia. The realization of his objective would require confrontation with the United States because Saudi Arabia had been turned into "an American colony". Asked if he was declaring war on the West, he replied, "It is not a declaration of war – its a real description of the situation. This doesn't mean declaring war against the West and Western people – but against the American regime which is against every Muslim". He hates the United States passionately and considers it his principle enemy. He accuses the U.S. – the locus of Westernization and modernity – of being the source of all crises and trouble afflicting the Muslim world. Bin Laden is convinced that U.S. presence in the Muslim world, particularly in his home country of Saudi Arabia, prevents the establishment of real Islamic governments and the realization of the Islamic revivalism to which he and other Islamists aspire. Since a frontal assault is out of the question, the U.S. must be terrorized into withdrawing from the Muslim world.

While the atrocities and acts of terrorism committed by violent extremists have connected Islam with terrorism, the Islamic tradition places limits on the use of violence and rejects terrorism, hijacking, and hostage taking. As with other faiths, mainstream and normative doctrines and laws are ignored, distorted, or hijacked by a radical fringe. Islamic law, drawing on the Quran, sets out clear guidelines for the conduct of war and rejects acts of terrorism. Islam, like all world religions, neither supports nor requires illegitimate violence. The Quran does not advocate or condone terrorism. However, Quranic verses also underscore that peace and warfare are the norm. Permission to fight the enemy is balanced by a strong mandate for making peace. The root of terrorism within the Muslim community refers to the misconception and misinterpretation of the jihad as the Quran's command. Jihad (to strive or struggle) is sometimes referred to as the Sixth Pillar of Islam.

The Quranic teaching of jihad have been of essential significance of Muslim self-understanding, piety, mobilization, expansion, and defence. Jihad as struggle pertains to the difficulty and complexity of living a good life; struggling against the evil in oneself-to be virtuous and moral, making a serious effort to do good works and to help to reform society. Depending on the circumstances which one lives, it also can mean fighting injustice and oppression, spreading and defending Islam, and creating a just society through preaching, teaching, and if necessary, armed struggle or holy war. The two broad meanings of jihad, non-violent and violent, are contrasted in a well-known Prophetic tradition. It's said that when Muhammad returned from battle he told his followers: "We return from the lesser jihad (warfare) to the greater jihad". The greater jihad is the more difficult and more important struggle against one's ego, selfness, greed, and evil. Jihad is a concept with multiple meanings, used and abused throughout Islamic history. Although jihad has always been an important part of the Islamic tradition, in recent years some have maintained that it is a universal religious obligation for all true Muslims to join the jihad to promote Islamic reform or revolution.

Some look around them and see a world dominated by corrupt authoritarian regimes and a wealthy elite minority concerned solely with its own economic prosperity and awash in Western culture and values. Western governments are perceived as propping up oppressive regimes and exploiting the region's human and natural resources, robbing Muslims of their culture and their option to be governed according to their own choice and to live in a more just society. Better understanding and a comprehensive study of Islamic teaching in respect of relations between Islam and the West, both by Muslims and the others (Westerners) will eliminate the misconception of a jihad in one side; and misconception of Islam and the Muslims in the other one. Understanding Islam and Muslim peoples will be one of eliminating terrorism. But the most importance is how Muslims all over the world have a good understanding of how the Prophet explained what really jihad is. Jihad is not "holy war", but "struggle" and "effort". This is a very important religious principle. The term jihad reminds all Muslims that Islam as a religion (al-din) is never something achieved or finished. The revelation is given, but those who follow it have to make an effort, day by day, year after year, to put it into practice in a flawed and tragic world.

Islam Post 9/11

Within hours of the planes hurtling into the World Trade Center of New York and Pentagon on 911, Americans were crying out in anguish: "Why do they hate us"? The question was echoed throughout Europe, since no doubt the attack was directed not just at America, but at the whole of Western civilization. However, the tragic events of 911 and the fear and paranoia they have generated have set Muslims back. America before 911 was on the verge of accepting Islam as one of it own, but after the attack of 911 it has paused to once again reassess Islam and Muslims. What happened on 911 and afterward has had significant and mostly negative consequences for the Muslim communities in Europe, and has set back the process of mutual accommodation between Muslims and European populations and the integration of both Islam and Muslims into Europe's social, cultural and political landscape. In the aftermath of 911, people of goodwill on both sides of the divide between the Judeo-Christian and Muslim worlds were filled with deep anxieties. For Westerners, it seemed that a dreadful clash of civilizations had become imminent and unavoidable. For Muslims, it was clear that serious injury had been done to the most powerful nation on earth – a wound that could only call for terrible retaliation. Many Jews and Christians seized on the belief that something feral and evil in the faith of Muhammad had made 911 inevitable.

Many Muslims feared that a new "crusade" against Islam would ensue, expressing deeply ingrained impulses in the West. Indonesia has the biggest Muslim population in the world. Some Western educated or Western civilized leaders (Prime Ministers or Presidents) regarded Indonesia as a heaven and paradise for terrorists. They saw Baasyir as an example of the Indonesian terrorist and that this was proven by some of the Islamic doctrines taught at Pondok Pesantren Ngruki where Baasyir typically teaches his students. The popular words of wisdom among the Santri that says "be alive honourable or die as a martyr" are regarded by Westerners as the doctrine of Islamic extremism and terro-rism. Meanwhile, the well-known words of wisdom among Indonesian Muslims are just a motivation of achievement and teach the students how to live in dignity.

This prejudice was supported by the fact that some actors involved in suicide bombings were the alumni of Pesantren or Islamic institutions. Suicide bombing was introduced as a new type of warfare in the Palestinian-Israeli conflict as a response to the brutal aggression by the Israelis. On February 25, 1994, Dr. Baruch Goldstein, a Jewish settler who emigrated to Israel from the United States, walked into the Mosque of the Patriach in Hebron and opened fire, killing twenty-nine Muslim worshipers during their Friday congregational prayer. In response, Hamas (Islamic Resistance Movement) introduced suicide bombing promising swift revenge for the Hebron massacre. The Hamas militia, the Qassem Brigade, undertook operations within Israel itself, in Galilee, Jerusalem, and Tel Aviv. In Israel-Palestine, the use of suicide bombing increased exponentially during the second (al-Aqsha) intifada (uprising), which began in September 2000? The most horrific example of suicide bombings or attacks was seen in the attacks of 911.

Traditionally, Muslims are unconditionally forbidden to commit suicide, because only God has the right to take the life he has granted. There is only one verse that appears relevant to suicide in the Holy Quran, Q, 4:29. Could we have the globalized world with no discrimination and aggression? Such view of globalization requires all citizens of the world to have mutual understanding of their similarity with other humans and their need for safety. As humans of different races, religions and civilizations, it is important that we continue to learn from one another our glorious past as well as our pain. In the process of this mutual dialogue, all religious leaders and policy makers should attempt to carry on responsibility for the creation of a peaceful world.

Muslims certainly carry the heaviest load since Islam has been consistently described as the epitome of radicalism, terrorism and evil religion. Such a hijacked portrayal of Islam does not accord with Islamic teaching that promulgates tolerance and understanding of other religious beliefs, languages and civilizations. In the process, it is important for Muslims to reinterpret Islamic teaching so that Muslims combat the misuse of the Quran and Hadith in the name of religion as has been done by the global terrorists. Along with this attempt, the changes in the foreign policy and public opinion of the rest of the world would decrease the prejudices against Islam and Muslims.

3

Epistemology in Islamic Jurisprudence

Islamic sacred law, the Shari'a, has been regarded by Muslims as a perfect, divinely ordained religious-ethical-legal system. The Shari'a relates Muslims to God's purposes by providing comprehensive directives in the two spheres of human activity: those actions that relate humanity to God, and those that relate humans to fellow humans. The former actions are categorized as 'ibadat (literally, "acts of honoring God", technically, God-human relationships) and the latter are known as mu'amalat (literally, "transactions", technically, interhuman relationships). Whereas the God-human relations have remained more or less immutable in the Shari'a, the area of interhuman relationships has demanded rethinking and reinterpretation of the normative sources like the Qur'an and the Sunna (Tradition) to deduce new directives under changed social conditions. There are, however, epistemological problems connected with the way normative sources are retrieved and interpreted by Muslim jurists which have hampered the necessary progress towards one particular area in the interhuman relationships, namely, the personal status of Muslim women.

The juridical deliberations in the exclusively maleoriented traditional centers of Islamic learning, the madrasa, have disregarded female voices in the emerging discourse connected with women's issues and human rights. The redefinition of the status of a Muslim woman in modern society is one of the major issues that confronts Muslim jurists' claims to be authority on legal-ethical sources of Islam. But such a redefinition is dependent upon Muslim women's participation in the legal- ethical deliberations concerning matters whose situational aspects can be determined only by women themselves. Without their participation in legal-ethical deliberations, women's rights will always depend on a "representational discourse" conducted by male jurists who, in spite of their good intentions, treats the subject as "absent" and hence, lacking the necessary qualification to determine her rights in a patriarchal society.

Male Jurists and Female Related Rulings

It was in the late 1960s when I began my studies in Islamic jurisprudence at the madrasa (seminary) of the Ayatollah Milani in Mashhad, Iran. Studies in the madrasa were structured around texts, both initial expositions and commentaries on them. In general, classical Islamic juridical texts were organized to undertake "first things first." Hence, in the Shi`ite jurisprudence, with which I commenced my studies in Islamic law, immediately following theoretical discussion about the necessity of following one of the living mujtahids (theologian-cum-jurist), the teacher began with the rulings connected with ritual purification (kitab al-tahara = The Book of Purification). I always sensed some uneasiness in the teacher as well as all male fellow students when the rulings on tahara reached intimate matters connected with female purification.

At that point, as if sensing a need to justify the embarrassment, my teacher often told the story about the discomfort and inadequacy felt by the late Ayatollah Burujardi (d. 1961) when he had to lecture on the taharat al-niswan (women's ritual purification) to his largely male audience made up of senior members of the religious establishment of the Qumm madrasa. Such sessions were part of the advanced lectures given by Burujardi on juristic principles applied to deduce these rulings.

Since the traditional centers of Islamic learning neither allowed female participation nor public discussion on matters concerning women's specific physical condition, the lectures on taharat al-niswan dealt only with closing judicial decisions, leaving the detailed explications of the method and reasoning behind them for individual perusal. However, that does not seem to be the case in the early days of Islam. The Prophet himself was at various times asked questions regarding the rules of purification for women. Significantly, on many such occasions the women of the Prophet's household were the interlocutors and even the interpreters of the religious guidance that affected women's ritual purity. A'isha, according to the Muslim traditionist, al-Bukhari, was present when a woman in Medina came to ask the Prophet about the rules of cleanliness after finishing menses.

He replied: "Take a piece of cloth perfumed with musk and clean the private parts with it thrice." The Prophet felt shy and turned his face. So I (A'isha) pulled her to me and explained to her what the Prophet meant. In the same section another tradition reports that when the Prophet replied that she should purify herself with a piece of cloth scented with musk, the woman asked: "How shall I purify myself with it?" He said: "Glory be to God, purify yourself!" At that point A'isha came to the rescue of the Prophet and pulled her to herself and taught her the method of cleansing herself.

The traditions clearly show that in the early days of Islam in issues dealing with women's ritual purification leading Muslim women provided with the necessary instruction. The Prophet could not and did not exclude women in dealing with their own particular situation in the performance of their religious duties. Moreover, as one can sense in some of these traditions, the Prophet himself sensed discomfort in going beyond expressing simply the rulings dealing with women's ritual purification. This feeling of inadequacy in dealing with peculiarly female concerns in Islamic rituals continues in the way later jurists treated juridical decisions affecting women. Certainly, the difference was that while the Prophet's wives and daughters were full participants in the legal deliberations affecting Muslim women, we have no record to suggest that the womenfolk of the jurist had similar opportunity to intervene in female ritual concerns.

Anecdotes about the male legal scholar dealing with intimate female issues and the problems he faces in conveying innermost contents of female ritual purification constitute legitimate entertainment among the "puritanical" members of the Muslim religious class. The subtle language of the Muslim "seminarians" speaking about the "unspeakable" deserves a separate study. But the contents of these anecdotes that lead modern researchers to the contextualization of the rulings about menses and sexual intercourse also point to the way in which powerfully gender-oriented Muslim culture treats matters connected with the "other gender:" excluding it in the interpretive process.

In the male-dominated religious discourse of the madrasa, information about women's experience is mediated through the "intertext" of the oral transmission of the anecdotes about women. The previous anecdote about the senior male legal scholar embarrassed by female ritual purification provides a symbolic link in contextualizing the experience of something absent - the elicitation of the condition of being a woman by a man in a legal investigation. While intelligible reenactment of the subjective experience of the "other" through the formation of figurally represented relations is not entirely impossible, its cognitive content is not free of suspicion. For instance, in the context of a legal ruling pertaining to a woman's situation in a society, the legal language constitutes the meaning of utterance about the female "other" mediated through male representations of interpersonal relations, the mu`amalat.

The legal utterance, in such circumstances, without taking full account of the concerns and conditions peculiar to female life, is promulgated and interpreted by a male jurist to apply to all women in a society. Hence, what we have in the text is figural rather than the actual representation of woman's situational and objective condition. To overcome this cognitive impediment one needs to undertake the analysis of the symbolic network of Islamic legal discourse. In other words, contextualization of rulings about sexual segregation, for instance, that still stand unvitiated among the religious-minded Muslims today, cannot be provided by merely referring to the textual and cultural validation of the practice in Muslim societies.

One needs to understand the intertextual network of symbols expressed by means of the narratives developed through interlocutory devices in which women are represented as actors, as questioners, even occasionally as disputants. To be sure, these narratives extend beyond the legal rulings about the male-female segregation. They in fact contribute to the formation of a symbolic configuration of Islamic cultural values. Further elaboration on this particular issue of segregation is in place. In general, rulings about female segregation are based on the concept of 'awra, meaning "indecent to expose." On the basis of this concept, jurists regard a woman's body, including her face, as 'awra. However, there are controversial texts ascribed to the Prophet and some of his companions that regard even her voice as 'awra and hence, "proper for veiling or covering" at all times.

Through such an extension of the 'awra to include the voice, Islamic law seems to advocate the position in which a woman is legally silenced, morally separated, and religiously veiled. Going beyond the text and the context of these rulings, as I want to demonstrate in this essay, could lead us to such an analysis of the intertextual dimension of the cases that form an entire genre in Islamic juridical texts. It could, furthermore, direct us to pose a fundamental question in the Muslim juridical studies: Can the male dominated religious epistemology provide an authentic voice in the interpretive process connected with the female "other"? How can male jurists undertake to map the subjective experience of the silent "other" of a Muslim society? At this juncture I need to point out my reservations about lending whole-hearted support to feminist jurisprudence that regards male dominated legal decisions as being conditioned by ideological interpretation of law, and the male bias being the source of violation of women's human rights.

Even in the male dominated Islamic culture, at the level of figural representation, male jurists have been able to transmit female existence and experience, however imperfect, by eliciting that segment of their ideological utterances that consider both genders to be part of humanity. Without such an acknowledgement of essential humanness of men and women, it would have been impossible for them to transmit those values in the culture that saw woman and man in relational terms as parents, sister and brother, daughter and father, mother and son, and husband and wife. Islamic legal discourse has not always conceived of male-female relations in terms of gender power struggle. The argument to be developed in this chapter is that the major part of the present epistemological crisis in Muslim jurisprudence over women's issues is due to the blatant absence of female voice in Islamic legal discourse.

It is remarkable that even when women transmitters of adth were admitted in the 'ilm al-rijal ("science dealing with the scrutiny of the reporters") dealing with source criticism to authenticate adth-reports in the Sunna, and even when their narratives were recognized as valid documentation for deducing various rulings, they were not participants in the intellectual process that produced the prejudicial rulings encroaching upon the personal status of women. More importantly, the revelational text, regardless of its being extracted from the Qur'an or the Sunna, was casuistically extrapolated in order to disprove a woman's intellectual and emotional capacities to formulate independent decisions that would have been more sensitive and more accurate in estimating her radically different life experience.

The demand today for new and expanded methodology of usul al-fiqh among the Muslim fundamentalist leaders, clearly shows the crisis that faces male-dominated epistemology in coming to terms with the demands about the recognition of the women's personal status and the substantive-cognitive role of their reason in reversing prejudicial decisions that deny her dignity as a full person. In order to demosntrate the seriousness of this crisis in Muslim legal studies, let me begin by setting forth some preliminary observations about Muslim religious epistemology. There are four basic components that constitute legal studies:

1. *The usul:* Fundamental sources that provide paradigm cases and the general principles that are behind them;
2. *The furu'*: Present instances for which legal decisions are being sought in the light of paradigm cases provided in the fundamental sources;
3. *The mawdu'at*: "Objects" or "situations" that determine the status of present instances and the ordinances that could be based on them to decide whether it is an obligatory act, a recommended act, or an act permitted at discretion, and so on.
4. *The ahkam*: Ordinances that specify the religious practice.

Whereas Muslim scholars are in agreement that acquisition of knowledge regarding the usul (fundamental sources) is incumbent individually on the community members who should undertake investigation of these sources themselves, in matters of ahkam (religious ordinances) they must follow the judicial rulings of a qualified jurisprudent, mujtahid. However, the practice of the community throughout the history has been to follow the juridical authority in acquiring knowledge regarding both fundamental sources and the rulings derived from them.

This method of acquisition of religious knowledge on the authority of a learned member of the community is identified as taqlid (following the authority of a leading legist), which is theoretically permissible only in the matters related to religious practice. What is the status of mawdu'at (objects in a case)? Is taqlid permissible in acquiring knowledge about "objects" and "situations"?

Mawdu' (singular of mawdu'at) signifies the actual state of a thing before a ruling can be deduced. For instance, before a jurist issues a ruling regarding the shortening of the daily worship for those who travel between two neighboring cities, such as Berkeley and Palo Alto, he needs to define the legal extent of a large city. Such an explanation of the size of a city for legal purposes is known as mawdu', that is, substantive information about factors that characterize a city. Or, in order to rule about ritual impurity of the blood that stains a shirt, a jurist needs to ascertain that it is definitely human and not insect blood, because the status of human blood is different in determining ritual impurity of the shirt.

Muslim scholars acknowledge that in investigating the mawdu'at one need not be an expert. In fact, an ordinary believer is in some instances even more proficient than a scholar in determining the factual state of an object or a situation. What matters is the practical knowledge about an issue under investigation. As such, one need not follow another person's knowledge in mawdu' if he or she is certain about its actual state. Moreover, juridical principle states that knowledge about mawdu' does not fall under the category of taqlid, that is, one need not follow the juridical authority in order to determine objects and situations of a case; rather, one should undertake its investigation individually. The presumption is that determination of the state or contextual situation of the case is a rational process open to all who possess sound reasoning.

One should not let someone else determine the object on which a judicial decision would be based. However, there is a stipulation in Islamic law that in the case of a legally incompetent person or a minor, determining the mawdu' could be assumed by a legal guardian (wali), including a jurist. To recapitulate, of the four fundamental components of Islamic legal system it is only ahkam -ordinances- that require following a jurist's research and conclusions based on the main sources of Islamic legal formulations. The other three parts are open to individual research and their ultimate acknowledgment or rejection. More importantly, it is in the area of mawdu'at, as they affect the religious practice, that there exists the space in which interpersonal negotiations between different groups and individuals are possible. The usul that should be based on firm rational inquiry have their place in the hearts and minds of the believers.

Unlike the mawdu'at, the usul (the paradigm cases in the Qur'an and the Sunna) have only an indirect influence on the final outcome of a juridical ruling. This male dominated religious epistemology has given rise to several fundamental questions related to the determination of the situational aspects of cases in connection with women. First of all, are women any different from men in understanding the process of identifying objects and their contexts as required prior to issuing the legal decision? How about their role in ascertaining the particular substantive state of woman's situation related to sexuality and reproduction, marriage and divorce? Is there any principle in the juridical theory that would suggest a form of thinking that distinguishes between the concerns of men and the concerns of women?

If one follows the prerequisite individual rational inquiry in the mawdu'at it would be correct to conclude that the Islamic belief system dictates that women need to represent their own concerns in all matters of family and maternity care. Implicit in this proposition is the recognition of women's right to assess their particular social situations and determine the legal applications in accordance with their sense of priorities. Furthermore, since the Islamic belief system does not speak about justice in terms of equality of sexes and treats the underlying difference of sex as natural, not the creation of society, defining a particular mawdu' has to be undertaken by the party concerned. From the juridical literature examined in its historical context, it is evident that, relatively speaking, Muslim jurists succeeded in pursuing the Qur'anic impulse towards family relationships and asserting individual rights on the basis of God- centered equality. And, although man retained wide authority over the wife, laws were enacted to give woman unprecedented respect and protection in the patriarchal context.

In family law, the rights of women, children, and other dependents were protected against the male head of the family, who, on the average, was stronger than a woman and more independent, since he is free of pregnancy and immediate care of children. Islamic marital rules encouraged individual responsibility by strengthening the nuclear family. Islamic law protected male prerogative on the grounds that men were required to support the household; whereas women were protected primarily by their families. All legal schools gave a husband one-sided divorce privileges because for divorce initiated by a woman would mean unsettle her husband's economic investment. Under these rules a husband could divorce a wife almost at will; but a wife who wished to leave her husband had to show good reason. The main legal check upon the man in divorce was essentially financial and a matter of contract between equal parties that included a provision about bridal gift. Part of the gift (sidaq or mahr), which might be substantial, was paid at the time of marriage; if he divorced her without special reason, he had to pay her the rest.

The equality of women in the law carried with it an important financial independence. Muslim women could own property which could not be touched by any male relative, including her husband who was required to support her from his own funds. Moreover, women had a personal status which might allow them to begin their own business.

However, this potential female independence was curbed primarily by cultural means, keeping marriages within the extended family, so that family property would not leave the family through women marrying out. Hence, although wives and daughters were given a stronger position than they had in the pre-Islamic Arab culture, in one area the Qur'an left the status of women to become the mawdu' for laws that permitted, though mitigated, unequal status between men and women, reducing a woman to "half-the-man." Her distinctive contribution in determining her own social context was thoroughly excluded by eliminating her as the interpreter of her own objects and situations. Patriarchal structures of Arab culture, in the form of loosely camouflaged traditions ascribed to the Prophet, left her intellectually crippled, while the male jurists prepared the text of the laws for her insidious domination by male members of the society.

It is relevant that it is mainly in the sphere of interpersonal relationships, the mu'amalat section of the jurisprudence, that woman's input in clarification of her mawdu' - her substantive social context - was kept in check. In the sphere of God-human relationship, the 'ibadat section of law, her equality with man before God was never questioned. Nevertheless, the manner in which her input in the mu'amalat was circumscribed had implications for her performance of the 'ibadat, the requirements of God-human relationship. Thus, for instance, the prohibition of independent female travel, requiring the presence of a male relative, has directly affected her religious freedom to undertake the performance of the obligatory hajj (annual pilgrimage) in Mekka. This prohibition, it must be pointed out, was based on the juristic principle that "averting causes of corruption has precedence over bringing about that which has benefit" (dar'u al- mafasid muqaddam 'ala jalb al-masalih). Other similar juristic principles have also been regularly invoked to curb not only women's rights but also the rights of minorities to function as full citizens in some Muslim societies.

Paradigm Cases

The paradigm cases dealing with the status of women are derived directly from an investigation of the sources of law. The sources are treated hierarchally, reflecting the religious evaluation of the epistemes contained in the Qur'an and the Sunna. Thus in formulating judicial decisions (fatawa) a jurist goes first to the Qur'an, then to the exegetical works in conjunction with the Sunna, and finally, to the juridical corpus, in that order, to follow the process of extrapolating fresh decisions from paradigmatic cases. I follow this approach with the methodological concern that any study of this kind requires a normative interpretation of the religious underpinnings presented in the Qur'an.

It is foundational to my study to raise the question: Should "Islam," as a belief system, be defined and judged by its practitioners or should its practitioners be defined and judged by a normative standard provided by the revelational sources on which the religious belief system is constructed? I believe I need an interpretive standpoint from which I can judge that some affirmations regarding women are peripheral or incidental to the tradition and that others are central and essential, that some are privileged and can serve as a guide for the interpretation of others. With this in mind, I begin to respond to my question: "Woman, half-the-man?" by looking at the Qur'an and its exegesis as the source of religious affirmations that altered, in decisive ways, the objects and situations within which legal-moral judgements were made regarding women in Muslim society. The estimation of a woman's position in the jurisprudence, is contextualized in the following pertinent reference, where the Qur'an speaks about contracting a debt:

O believers, when you contract a debt one upon another for a stated term, write it down, and let a scribe write it down between you justly, and let not any scribe refuse to write it down, as God has taught him; so let him write, and let the debtor dictate, and let him fear God his Lord and not diminish anything of it.....And call in to witness two witnesses, men; or if the two be not men, then one man and two women, such witnesses as you approve of, that if one of the two errs the other will remind her; and let the witnesses not refuse, whenever they are summoned.....And fear God; God teaches you, and God has knowledge of everything. (emphasis added) (Q. 2:282)

The passage is regarded as the scriptural basis for the law of evidence (shahadat) in jurisprudence. Moreover, it has also been evoked to communicate the inferiority of a woman's evidence as compared to a man's. Exegetical literature discusses variations in the reading of the phrase: "....if one of the two errs ('an tadilla ihdahuma)," and consider whether the clause is conditional and if it connotes the superiority of male memory power. In fact, abars cites a specified opinion which he rejects and which maintained that the Qur'an made this provision of "reminding" in women's evidence because "forgetfulness overcomes women [inherently] more than it does men."

None of the commentaries in the classical age go beyond lexical and grammatical exposition of the statement to establish that women are in need of being reminded in order to render their evidence equal to that of a man who enjoys impeccable memory. To be sure, Baydawi maintains that the Shafi'ite jurists implemented the terms of this verse only in the case of business and financial transactions (amwal), whereas the anafites extended the requirement to criminology and law of retribution. Yet, the grammatical conclusion that the Qur'anic statement "if one of the two errs...." is a conditional clause had enormous implications in explicating the nature of divine commandment in jurisprudence. This grammatical specification had been acknowledged despite the fact that only one transmitter among the early transmitters of the Qur'anic text had insisted in reading the clause as conditional with 'in.

For the jurists looking at the denotation of the statement the question is: Is the conditional commandment given for the specific situation in the Medina society to be interpreted as an unconditional commandment, evincing the probable conclusion that regardless whether a woman errs or not, her evidence is to be reduced to half of a man's evidence? In fact, some later exegetes, like the Shi'ite Mulla Fath Allah Kashani, maintained that the statement is unconditional because woman is inherently weaker in her rational judgment than man who is intellectually stronger, and forgetfulness is far from his nature. Furthermore, he asserts that, according to Sufyan b. 'Uyayna, the verse's requirement of two women brings together the evidence of two women and raises it to be equivalent to that of one man. However, both the explicit denotation and the implied context of the verse in the exegetical literature strictly allowed a conditional commandment to be surmised.

It denied the unconditional purport with its implications for the inherent inferiority of a woman that was asserted in the legal decisions, including those maintained by the Shafi'ites in the limited area of financial transactions. In the legal texts, the object and the social situation of a Muslim woman, as extracted from the conditional commandment of the Qur'an, was defined in terms of her position in the regional culture. The cultural evaluation of a woman was transmitted in some of adth-reports that were used to overcome the conditional denotation of the Qur'anic law of evidence. These were used as evidentiary documentation to extrapolate unqualified stipulations that a woman's evidence equals half of that of a man's, regardless of the situational factors.

When we examine the hadith literature to determine how far Q. 2:282 had reinforced the cultural estimation of a woman's intelligence in providing evidence, we discover that al-Bukhari has preserved an interesting rubric in one of the odd places towards the end of his compilation dealing with the evidentiary nature of a "single" narrative (khabar al-wahid). Al-Bukhari's rubrics actually serve as his judicial decisions (fatawa) for which he produces hadith-reports that follow as documentation. Thus, under the rubric of Khabar al-mar'at al-wahida (narrative reported by a "single" woman), he cites the following tradition:

['Abd Allah] ibn 'Umar said: Some companions of the Prophet, including Sa'd, were going to eat meat. But one of the wives of the Prophet called them, saying: "It is the meat of a certain reptile (dabb)!" The people then stopped eating it. On that the Prophet said: "Carry on eating, for it is lawful." Or, he said: "There is no harm in eating it, but it is not from my meals."

An important dietary matter is the object of the narrative, on the basis of which a legal ruling permitting a particular kind of meat is being deduced. However, this permission is stated on the authority of the Prophet, who reportedly reverses an opinion prohibiting its consumption expressed by one of his wives. The implications of this hadith for the admissibility of a woman's evidence in specifying the object of a ruling cannot be sufficiently emphasized. The hadith indicates that a narrative related by a "single" woman, even if she happens to be one of the Prophet's wives, cannot be permitted as evidence for a prohibitive legal ruling. On the contrary, as reported in another tradition in the same section, a hadith reported by a "single" truthful male transmitter is admissible as documentation for all kinds of ordinances.

The purpose of al-Bukhari's compilation is not to provide additional documentation by citing the above verse as proof for his implied conclusion that regarding a "single" female narrator's credibility is vitiated by the absence of another female. However, the law of evidence in Q. 2:282 is the unmistakable context of this tradition. This and other similar traditions raise serious questions not only about the authenticity of these narratives that ignored the intertextuality of the daily details of the lives of women entrapped in male jurist's subjectivity and his skewed vision of her social role; it also puts in doubt the claim by the pious for the validity and applicability of these legal rulings in all age and at all times. Moreover, in the absence of reevaluation of the relevant authoritative texts within their historical and cultural contexts, Islamic jurisprudence has been impaired by irrelevant hairsplitting exercises, reflecting an acute formalistic rather than substantive approach to religious knowledge.

Hence, instead of squarely confronting the question of mawdu'at dealing with women's situation in Muslim society under variable historical circumstances, the jurists have vacillated between the prestige of the written tradition and nonessential conceptual and terminological devices developed in the Islamic legal theory to interpret it. Both the methods of inquiry and the forms of argument indicate the juridical tradition's inadequacies in furnishing solutions to the concrete problems faced by Muslim women. The nature of religious discourse employed in the madrasa setting makes it epistemically impossible to speak about specific objects and situations peculiar to Muslim woman's personal status, without referring to the revelational knowledge preserved in the prestigious texts. It is ultimately the written tradition - and not human reason that can negotiate the intertextuality of the judicial decisions made by a male jurist.

Application of human reasoning, in any of its forms, has been permanently crippled by the madrasa attitude, articulated in various works of Islamic thought, that human reason on its own is not capable of extracting practical knowledge regarding an ideal Islamic order. The legal rulings regarding the inferiority of woman's evidence were extrapolated mainly on the basis of the Qur'an 2:282, fortified by traditions that accepted the inherent inferiority of women in matters of religion and intelligence. These rulings reveal even more serious problems in defining the object and situational context (mawdu'at) particular to women's social and personal condition. Undoubtedly, it was in the area of evidence that it was inferred that al-Bukhari implied that a single woman's testimony is half that of a man's.

Yet the conditional commandment of the verse 2:282

could not be interpreted so explicitly in view of the contextual restriction imposed by the kind of transaction. To resolve this apparent contradiction between the restrictive and conditional terms of the verse, and the unqualified terms related in some traditions, jurists had to define the objects and situations in which female evidence and attending conditions could become operative. Investigation in the specific text and the context of the Qur'an and the hadith led jurists to recognize substantially different situations in Muslim interpersonal relations where women functioned as witnesses, providing objective testimony for ultimate judicial rulings. The Qur'anic law of evidence treated only one instance of the social situation in which her evidence in the matter of contract involving financial obligation was, for practical reasons, devalued. Muslim jurists were cognizant of other situations in which this conditional and situational enactment of the Qur'anic law could not be generalized.

Consequently, they promulgated three situations in the process of validating a woman's testimony on any interpersonal situation, including contractual agreements:

1. A non-permissible situation in which women's testimony is not admissible at all;
2. A permissible situation in which women testified with men; and, therefore, their testimony is admissible;
3. A permissible situation in which women's testimony is admissible, even if there were no men testifying with them.

It is worth noting that in none of these cases is a woman admitted as the only witness. In all instances she is mentioned in plural, not necessarily in the formula of two women equal to one man, as implied in the Q. 2:282. In most of the examples cited for each situation it is not difficult to find the underlying concern of the Muslim culture in which a woman's role was defined by the powerful male functioning as her manager. More pertinently, while her testimony was admitted in instances of marriage and debts or in areas of her expertise such as determining cases of rape and pregnancy, her evidence was excluded from cases of divorce and murder. When it came to cases of adultery, Islamic law admitted two women's testimony if accompanied by that of three men. However, if there was only one male witness and six or more female witnesses, their collective testimony could not be regarded as valid.

On the other hand, a single woman's claim that she is virgin when accused of adultery by four male witnesses, stands unvitiated provided a midwife establishes the validity of her claim. Rulings about woman's testimony have filled the sections of kitab al-qada' (administration of justice) where jurists have identified minutely where and when women can function as qualified witnesses. It is not difficult to discern underlying concern for justice when one takes into account stringent requirements to establish evidence for accusation against anyone in Muslim society. However, there is no doubt that the tone of the rulings is set by the powerful male jurist, who, in most cases, ignores the female evaluation of her own social situation, for instance in divorce, that furnishes the object of the ruling. There is almost an a fortiori argument derived from the Q. 2:282 to support the implied inherent inequality of sexes which then makes men take charge of a woman's affairs as determined by the competent legal authority.

The religious epistemology that was constructed on revelational knowledge in the juridical studies has served the Muslim jurists' endeavors in extracting unconditional commandments from the conditional and culturally conditioned references, both in the Qur'an and the Sunna dealing with the historical Muslim social universe. The treatment of women in Islamic legal tradition is a classic example of the "epistemological crisis" faced by madrasa-educated scholars of Islamic law. Honest and critical evaluation of this crisis is dependent upon the appraisal of the historical development of theoretical and conceptual structures of the Islamic religious sciences, including jurisprudence. In order to provide an authentic intertextuality to the text and the context of legal rulings that reduce women, in a mathematical fashion sometimes, to half a man, Muslim male jurists have to include women in communicating the mawdu`at about women.

Without such participation in the interpretive process of the text to communicate its context and intertext that has been the source of her cultural subjugation, Muslim women stand little chance to overcome being reduced to the legally silent, morally segregated and religiously veiled half-the-man. The issue of women in Islam is highly controversial. Any materials on this subject, whether in print or online, should be used with caution because of the lack of objectivity. While it is generally agreed that the rights granted to women in the Qur'an and by the prophet Muhammad were a vast improvement in comparison to the situation of women in Arabia prior to the advent of Islam, after the Prophet's death the condition of women in Islam began to decline and revert back to pre-Islamic norms. Yet just as the women's movement in the West began to pick up steam in the twentieth century, the same thing occured, although to a lesser extent, in the Muslim world at this time.

Feminists in the Muslim world in the twentieth century (until the 1980's) were generally upper class women whose feminism was modeled after feminists in the West. But just as modern socio-political models in the Muslim world after the colonial period began, in the 20th century, to shift from Western models of society and government to "Islamic" models, feminism in the Muslim world began to take on Islamic forms rather than aping the Western feminist form. This has been true not merely for Muslim women but for women throughout the entire third world. Having thrown off the schackles of colonial imperialism, women of the third world are increasingly growing resistant to the cultural imperialism marketed by the West, even in the form of feminism. Hence, third world women, like women of color in the West, are realizing that while they have certain things in common with the struggle of Euro-American feminists, what is best for Euro-American women is not necessarily going to be best for them.

Consequently Muslim women have been developing a distinctly "Islamic" feminism, just as women of color in the West have been developing "womanism" in contrast to feminism, which primarily was shaped by the concerns of upper-class Euro-American women. One example of the differences between Western feminism and Islamic feminism concerns the issue of "veiling." The *hijab* (often translated as "veil") is the form of scarf or hair covering commonly worn by Muslim women. It has always been seen by the Western feminist as oppressive and as a symbol of a Muslim woman's subservience to men. As a result, it often comes as a surprise to Western feminists that the veil has become increasingly common in the Muslim world and is often worn proudly by college girls as a symbol of an Islamic identity, freeing them symbolically from neo-colonial Western cultural imperialism and domination.

4

Reason and Mystical Experience in Sufism

The Sufis are not an ethnic or religious group, but a mystical movement that is found all over the Islamic world and that still has a deep influence on the varied populations of the Middle East. Sufism grew historically as a reaction against the rigid legalism of the orthodox religious leadership and as a counterweight to the growing worldliness of the expanding Muslim empire. One source of Sufism is to be found in the twofold presentation of God in the Qur'an: on the one hand he is described as the almighty creator, lord and judge, and on the other hand he is seen as abiding in the believer's heart and nearer to man than his own jugular vein. Sufism searches for a direct mystical knowledge of God and of his Love. Its goal was to progress beyond mere intellectual knowledge to a mystical (existential) experience that submerged limited man in the infinity of God. It used Jewish, Christian, Gnostic, Hellenistic, Zoroastrian and Hindu traditions that were brought into Islam by converts from the many conquered populations.

The name Sufi is derived from the Arabic word Suf which means wool. Early Sufis wore simple coarse woollen garments similar to those of Christian monks. Sufism believed that the Qur'an and Hadith have secret, esoteric, meaning and symbolism (Batin). In opposition to the literal method of interpretation (Tafsir), Sufism used an allegorical method (Ta'wil) which looked for the hidden meaning and symbols in the holy texts. Sufism had an important part in the formation of Muslim societies as it educated the masses and met their felt needs, giving spiritual meaning to their lives and channeling their emotions. Sufis were also great missionaries who converted new regions to Islam. Its cultural contribution was a rich poetry in Arabic, Persian, Turkish, Urdu, Sindi, Pashto and Punjabi, which spread its mystical ideas all over the Muslim world and enriched local literature and identity.

Several techniques were developed to achieve the goal of a blissful union with Ultimate Reality. They were known as Dhikr (remembrance, mention of God) and Sama' (hearing). In the Dhikr Sufis would recite the many names of God and sing hymns of praise. Special forms of breathing were supposed to aid concentration and help them attain to an ecstatic state in which they actually felt they had reached union with God. During the Sama', poetry, music and dance were used as an aid to reaching the ecstatic state. These informal groups later crystalized into Sufi brotherhoods gathered around famous leaders. In some countries even today most Muslims belong to one order or another. Around the Muslim world there are hundreds of orders and they are an important religious and political force.

Sufism is found amongst both Sunnis and Shi'a, being a movement within orthodox Islam. However it has many links with Isma'ilism and other extreme Shi'a sects (Ghulat) as it developed in similar times and circumstances. Sufism developed in the 8th and 9th centuries in three major centres: 1. The cities of Basra, Kufa and Baghdad in Iraq. 2. The city of Balkh in the Khorasan district of Persia. 3. Egypt. Muhammad is regarded as the first Sufi master who passed his esoteric teachings orally to his successors who also received his special grace (barakah). An unbroken chain of transmission of divine authority is supposed to exist from

Muhammad to his successor 'Ali and from him down to generations of Sufi masters (Sheikhs, Pirs). Each order has its own Silsilah (chain) that links it with Muhammad and 'Ali.

First Stage – Asceticism

Under the Umayads (661-749) there was a growing tendency to compare the wealth and luxury of the ruling class with the simple lifestyle of the first Caliphs. Devout believers were shocked by the worldliness and opulence of court life and they reacted with a growing concern for reality in their own personal relationship with God. Outward observance of the Shari'a laws could not satisfy their growing spiritual hunger, and they started to imitate Christian hermits who had discovered asceticism and poverty as a way to develop a close relationship with God. The first Sufis were ascetics who meditated on the Day of Judgement. They were called "those who always weep" and "those who see this world as a hut of sorrows." They kept the external rules of Shari'a, but at the same time developed their own mystical ideas and techniques. "Little food, little talk, little sleep," was a popular proverb amongst them. Mortification of the flesh, self denial, poverty and abstinence were seen as the means of drawing near to God, and this included fasting and long nights of prayer.

Some Early Sufis

Hasan of Basrah (d.728) was one of the first Sufi ascetics. He exhorted his followers against attachment to this evil world and encouraged them to reject it and to follow a path of poverty and abstinence. Ibrahim b. Adham (d. 777) of Balkh in Khorasan taught his disciples the importance of meditation and of silence in worship. Shaqiq of Balkh (d.810) taught that only a rigid system of selfdiscipline could lead to absolute trust in God (tawakkul) and to the mystical state (hal).

Al-Muhasibi (d.837 in Baghdad) taught that self-discipline and self-examination were the needed preparation for fellowship and union with God. Dhu an-Nun of Egypt (d.859) taught that Ma'rifah (inner knowledge, enlightenment, Gnosis) was necessary to attain real union with God.

Abu Yazid al-Bistami (d. 874) taught that union with God is achieved through the annihilation of self (Fana'). This is done by a total stripping away of a person's attributes and personality and by rigorous mortification of the flesh. He was the first "intoxicated" Sufi who in his ecstatic state felt that God had replaced his own ego and now dwelt in his soul. This caused him to exclaim: "Glory to me! How great is my majesty!"

Junaid of Baghdad (d.910), stressed the importance of wisdom and sobriety in achieving both fana' (dying to self, extinction of self) and baqa' (abiding in God). The first great Sufi martyr was Hallaj who was crucified in 922 in Baghdad for blasphemy. His offence was the statement "I am the Truth" which signified that he had attained union with God who now dwelt in his body instead of his own self. He saw Jesus as his great example of a holy man in whom God was incarnate.

Second Stage - Mysticism of Love

A woman from Basrah in Iraq, Rabi'a al-Adawiya (d.801) introduced the theme of Divine Love into Sufism. She yearned to love God only for Himself, not for hope of any reward (paradise) nor out of fear of judgement (hell). Following her death the love theme became a dominant feature of Sufism. It expressed the Sufi's yearning for the development of a love relationship with God that would lead to an intimate experience of God and finally to a total union with God. The love theme found its main expression in Sufi poetry in which the relations between God the Divine Lover and the man searching for his love were symbolically described. Early Sufi poems in Arabic express the soul's deep yearning for union with the beloved. Persian poetry often compared the soul's love relationship with God to that between a man and a beautiful youth.

In Indian poetry the loving wife yearning for her husband symbolised the soul's yearning for God. Later poets developed the long mystical poems called Mathnawis (Masnawis) which expressed in symbolical verse the manifold emotions of love to God and of unity with him. Persia had the greatest flourishing of Sufi poetry, and most of its classical poetry has a Sufi content. One example is the Mathnawi "Mantiq al-Tair" (speech of the birds) by Farid al-Din 'Attar, an allegory which portrays the mystic on his pilgrimage from asceticism through illumination to union with God. Jalal ad-Din Rumi (1207-1273), named "Mawlana" - our Lord or Teacher - was the greatest Persian mystical poet.

His famous Mathnawi of 26,000 rhythmic couplets is a real encyclopaedia of Sufi allegorical and mystical thought and experience. Persian Sufis regard it as next to the Qur'an in holiness. Rumi also founded the Mawlawi (Mevlevi) order of whirling dervishes. Sufi poetry uses the symbols of wine (God's intoxicating love), the wine cup (the Sufi's heart) and the cup bearer (the spiritual guide). The wine house is the religion of love and it is compared to the religion of law symbolised by the mosque. Learning the many Sufi symbols and their meaning is essential to an understanding of this kind of poetry.

Third Stage - Sufi Apologetics

Early Sufi masters gathered informal circles of disciples and transmitted their teachings orally. At first, the orthodox religious authorities were very suspicious of the Sufis and accused them of heresy and blasphemy. This led some Sufis in the 10th century to defend Sufism by writing handbooks of their teaching and practice in the hope of proving their orthodoxy. Al-A'rabi (d.952), Makki (d.996), Sarraj (d. 988), Kalabadhi (d.1000) and Hujviri (d.1057) were such masters who wrote in defence of Sufism. They also published histories and biographies of Sufism, trying to prove that it was based on the practice (Sunnah) of the Prophet and his companions. Al-Qushairi (d. 1072) defended Sufism against the accusations of antinomianism (lawlessness). In addition to writing biographies of Sufi saints he wrote "Risala", a book in which he defined Sufi doctrines and terms.

He defined the mystical stations (maqamat, a result of the Sufi's own labours), and states (ahwal, mystical states bestowed by God's grace). Abu Hamid al-Ghazali (d.1111), called Hujjat al-Islam - Proof Of Islam, was a great Muslim thinker who found no satisfaction in his extensive study of theology and law. Turning to Sufism he found in it the certainty of God he had yearned for and failed to find in his previous studies. In his book "The Revival of the Religious Sciences" (Ihya' 'Ulum ad-Din) he attempted to reconcile Sufism with orthodoxy. It was immensely popular and finally guaranteed Sufism an official place in orthodox Islam alongside Law and Theology.

Fourth Stage - Philosophical-Mystical Systems

Theosophy is any mystical system of religious philosophy that claims a direct intuitive insight into God's nature. Theosophical speculations on the nature of God and man were introduced into Sufism by Sahl al-Tustari (d.896) and at-Tirmidi (d 898). The greatest of all Sufi theosophical writers in Arabic was Ibn al-'Arabi (d.1240) who was born in Spain. He travelled to Tunis and Mecca and finally settled in Damascus. In his 500 books he teaches that all existence is but a manifestation of God, the one ultimate divine reality which is totally "other", an undifferentiated unity, but in whom the archtypes of all potential beings exist. This is the "unknown God" from whom emanates a hierarchy of divine beings (Names, Lords) the lowest of whom is the Lord of revelation and creation who is also called the First Intellect.

The emanations are the mediating link between the unknowable, transcendent God and the created world. This teaching was the basis of the Sufi concept of the Unity of Being (Wahdat al-Wujud). The First Intellect, an emanation of the God was also called the "idea of Muhammad". He is the archtype through whom man was made. This emanation is incarnated in a Perfect Man in every generation - the perfect

Sufi. This man most fully manifests the nature of God and he is the pole (Qutb, axis) around which the cosmos revolves. Ibn al-'Arabi saw himself as such a "pole" and he called himself the seal (the most perfect) of the saints. Another theosophical system, that of illumination, was developed by Shihab al-Din Suhrawardi (executed in Aleppo in 1191). He taught that all things exist as varying degrees of light, beginning with the Absolute Light, the Light of Lights who is God himself. Light then spreads out from God in ever weaker degrees (angels), each reflecting the light above it to those beneath it. The whole world of being is composed of innumerable angels of light spreading out in geometrical patterns.

Indian Sufis were influenced by Hindu mysticism and strayed far from Islamic orthodoxy in their speculations. The Naqshbandi order founded in the 13th century in Central Asia to preserve true Islam from the ravages of the Mongol invasions, succeeded in keeping them within orthodoxy. Ahmad Sirhindi (d.1624) taught that the Unity of Being was a subjective experience occurring only in the Sufi's mind - not the Hindu concept of total annihilation of the personal in the infinite.

Fifth Stage - The Rise of Sufi Orders

Sufi orders began to form in the 12th and 13th centuries centering around a master founder and stressing companionship (Suhbah, fellowship) as essential to the Sufi spiritual path. This was the time of the terrible Mongol invasions when the 'Abassid Caliphate in Bagdad was overthrown. Sufism was one of the forces that helped prevent the downfall of Islam. It helped convert the conquerors and had a stabilising influence on the community during those troubled times. This period was actually Sufism's golden age. In its first stages Sufism had been the prerogative of a limited spiritual elite. From the twelfth century onwards it succeeded in involving the Muslim masses on a large scale in its network of orders. Sufi hospices, (Zawiyas in Arabic, Khanagas in Iranian, Ribat in the Maghreb and Tekkes in Turkish) were founded all over the Muslim world from Morocco to Central Asia.

The Sheikh of each order, a successor of the original founder, presided over the hospice. In this centre he taught his disciples (Murids) and performed with them the Sufi rituals of Dhikr and Sama'. There was an elaborate initiation ritual for the disciple when he was admitted into full membership (usually after three years). In this ceremony he received from the Sheikh a special cloak (Khirqa) which symbolised poverty and devotion to God. Sufis had no rule of celibacy and most were married. The orders received endowments from sympathetic rulers and rich citizens and some eventually became fabulously wealthy. Sufi orders had an extensive missionary outreach into Africa and into Southeast Asia where they are still very influential.

Each order developed its own specific set of techniques for its Dhikr and Sama', used by its members to attain to the ecstatic state. These rituals also had a social function, helping to unify people from widely varying backgrounds into a spiritual brotherhood. The orders were thus a unifying force in society, drawing members from all social classes to their Dhikr and Sama' ceremonies as well as to their joyous celebrations of the anniversaries of the deaths of their founder ('Urs). They provided the masses with a spiritual and emotional dimension to religion which the hair splitting legalists could not supply. The orders also established trade and craft guilds and provided hospices for travellers and merchants which were located along the great trade routes (such as the famous silk road). Between the 13th and the 18th century most Muslims belonged to some Sufi Tariqah.

Some Famous Orders

There are more than two hundred known Sufi orders. Some are local, others universal. Some are rural and others are urban.

1. *The Qadiriyah*: It is the oldest and most widespread order. It has branches all over the world loosely tied to its centre at Baghdad. It was founded in Baghdad by 'Abd al-Qadir Jilani (d.1166), considered to be the

greatest saint in Islam. It later became established in Yemen, Egypt, Sudan, the Maghreb, Central Asia and India. The Qadiriya stresses piety, humility, moderation and philanthropy and appeals to all classes of society being strictly orthodox. It is governed by a descendant of al-Jilani who is also the keeper of his tomb in Baghdad which is a pilgrimage centre for his followers from all over the world.

2. *The Jilaliya: A* Qadiri branch in the Maghreb, worship al-Jilani as a supernatural being, combining Sufism with pre-Islamic ideas and practices.
3. *The Naqshbandiya*: It was founded in Central Asia in the thirteenth century in an attempt to defend Islam against the ravages of the Mongol invasions. It later spread to the Indian subcontinent. The Naqshbandis tried to control the political rulers so as to ensure that they implemented God's will. They were politically and culturally active, the great poet Mir Dad (d.1785) belonged to this order. They were also connected to trade and crafts guilds and held political power in the 15th century in Central Asia and in Moghul India. A Naqshbandi branch, the Khaltawiyah, had an important part in efforts to modernise the Ottoman Empire during the 18th and 19th centuries.

The Naqshbandiya developed mainly as an urban order with close links to the orthodox hierarchy. They recite their Dhikr silently, ban music and dance, and prefer contemplation to ecstasy. Their "middle way" between extreme asceticism and extreme antinomianism seemed acceptable to the orthodox hierarchy. They have been involved in underground movements against Soviet rule in Central Asia and supported the Afghan Mujahedin against the Russians. The Mawlawiyah - this order was founded by Jalal al-Din Rumi (d.1273, called Mawlana), the greatest Sufi poet who wrote in Persian. Their rituals are aesthetically sophisticated, and their Sama' is famous for its exquisite combination of music, poetry and whirling dance (in the West they are called "Whirling

Dervishes") which transports them into the trace like state.

4. *The Mawlawiya*: They were especially attractive to the educated elite of the Turkish Ottoman Empire and were widespread in Anatolia where they had close links with the authorities. The Bektashiya - a syncretistic order whose ritual and beliefs are a mixture of Shi'ism, Orthodox Christianity and gnostic cults. By the sixteenth century the Bektashis were the order of the famous Janissary corps, the elite military unit of the Ottoman Empire. Their magic-like rituals appealed to the illiterate masses of Anatolia. Their clergy were celibate, they practiced ritual confession and communion and had a trinitarian concept of God similar to that of the 'Alawis. The Tijaniya - founded by al-Tijani in 1781 in Fez, Morocco, extended the borders of Islam towards Senegal and Nigeria and founded great kingdoms in West Africa. They taught submission to the established government and their influence is still an important factor in these countries where it is associated with conservative businessmen.
5. *The Daraquiya*: It was founded in the early 19th century by Mulay 'Arabi Darqawi (d. 1823) in Fez in Morocco. It was the driving force behind the Jihad movement which achieved mass conversions to Islam in the mixed Berber-Arab-Negro lands of the Sahel. It is influential today in Mali, Niger and Chad and still widespread in Morocco.
6. *The Khalwatiya:* It was founded in northwest Persia in the 13th century and spread to the Caucasus and to Turkey. It was closely associated with the Ottoman Sultans and had its headquarters in Istanbul. It has also spread to Egypt and Indonesia.
7. *The Suhrawardiya:* It was started in Iraq by al-Suhrawardi (d.1234) who stressed serious training and teaching. They have many adherents in the Indian subcontinent. They were very involved politically in Iraq and Iran during

the Mongol threat, seeking to ensure the survival of Islam.

8. *The Rifa'ya:* It was founded in the marshlands of southern Iraq by al-Rifa'i (d.1187). They stress poverty, abstinence and mortification of the flesh, and are also known as the "Howling Dervishes" because of their loud recitation of the Dhikr. They focus on dramatic ritual and bizarre feats such as fire eating, piercing themselves with iron skewers and biting heads off live snakes.
9. *The Shadiliya:* It was started by al-Shadili (d.1258) in Tunis. It flourished especially in Egypt under ibn-'Ata Allah (d.1309) but also spread to North Africa, Arabia and Syria. It is the strongest order in the Maghreb where it was organised by al-Jazuli (d. 1465) and has suborders under other names. The Shadiliya stress the intellectual basis of Sufism and allow their members to remain involved in the secular world. They are not allowed to beg and are always neatly dressed. They appealed mainly to the middle class in Egypt and are still active there. It is said that the Shadiliya were the first to discover the value of coffee as a means of staying awake during nights of prayer!
10. *The Chishtiya*: It was founded by Mu'in al-Din Chishti in Ajmer, India. His teaching was simple and the order is known for its fervour and hospitality. They helped in the islamisation of the Indian subcontinent.
11. *The Sanusiya*: They are a military brotherhood started by al-Sanusi (d.1837) in Libya with political and military as well as religious aims. They fought against the colonising Italians and the former King of Libya was head of the order.
12. *The Nimatulahiya:* It was developed first in Persia and then in India as a specifically Isma'ili oriented Sufi order.
13. *The Ahmadiya:* The leading order in Egypt with its centre at Tanta. It was founded by Ahmad al-Badawi

(d. 1276). The orders helped spread Islam and their Sufi concepts in frontier lands such as India, Central and Southeast Asia, Sudan, Morocco and sub-Saharan Africa.

Sixth Stage - The Decline and Revival of Sufism

The Sufi orders grew steadily in wealth and in political influence, but their spirituality gradually declined as they concentrated on Saint worship, miracle working, magic and superstition. The external religious practices were neglected, morals declined and learning was despised. In many areas Sufi orders succeeded in ruling the ignorant masses through a well organised and power hungry hierarchy. Their local saints were revered by the populace and worshipped after their death as mediators and intercessors. Pilgrim's flocked to the Saint's tombs, willing to pay for a share in the Sheikh's baraka. The orders became rich and powerful, and both politicians and theologians feared to oppose them and preferred to share in the profits.

Some sincere mystics still rose above the general decline. In Egypt, al-Shar'ani (d.1565) lived at the time of the Ottoman conquest and was a serious and comprehensive scholar. In Iran Sadr al-Din Shirazi (d.1640), also known as Mulla Sadra, was a great thinker who continued to develop the theology of illumination founded by Suhrawardi and integrated it with Ibn-'Arabis Unity of Being. His impact is still felt on theologians and philosophers in Iran today. In India in the 18th century Shah Wali-Allah of Delhi tried to integrate the various schools of Sufi thought, whilst Mir Dard contributed much to the formation of Urdu poetry.

In Iran the Safavid order gained political power for two centuries (1499-1720). The Sheikhs of this order claimed descent from 'Ali and they were favourably treated by both the Mongol and the Timurid dynasties. Based in Ardabil in Azerbaijan the order became a local power in the 15th century as it alternatively allied itself with and fought against the rulers of the Turkmen tribal confederations (Ak-Koyunlu, the White Sheep and Kara- Koyunlu, the Black Sheep). The Turkmen Safavids of Anatolia and Azerbaijan were called Kizilbash (Redheads) from the red headgear they wore. In 1501 the Safavid Sheikh Ismail I defeated the Ak-Koyunlu and took the old Mongolian capital of Tabriz where he proclaimed himself as Shah. Later he instituted Twelver Shi'ism as the state religion of Persia and imposed it by force on the population. Many Sunni 'Ulama' and Sheikhs of other Sufi orders were executed.

The Sunni Ottomans felt threatened by Shi'a Persia, and in the ensuing centuries of warfare between these two powers they evolved an aggressive Sunnism within their own Empire. The Sultan Selim I massacred all the Shi'ites that he could lay his hands on, and until modern times the Kizilbash of Anatolia and other Shi'a groups collectively called "Alevis" by the Ottomans were forced to exist as an underground movement. Alevis still number some 8 million people in modern Turkey but they are officially ignored as nonexistent by the authorities. In Arabia the Wahabi puritan revival was extremely anti-Sufi, seeing their practices and doctrines as later pagan additions to pure Islam.

Colonialism, nationalism and secularisation had a negative impact on Sufism in the 19th and 20th centuries. The modern revival of Islamic learning was accompanied by a violent reaction against the superstitions of Sufism. It was accused as being the cause of the Islamic world's backwardness compared to the West. The two great Muslim reformers of the 19th century, Jamal al-Din al-Afghani and Muhammad 'Abduh, both campaigned successfully against Sufi orders helping to diminish their influence. In Turkey, Kemal Ataturk abolished the Sufi orders in 1925 and confiscated their lands and property. He saw them as corrupt and backward forces that hindered the modernisation of Turkish society. In other countries too post-colonial independent central governments were often suspicious of the orders. They were suspected of being cells of political unrest and revolution who held the loyalty of the masses by their superstitions, religious emotionalism and outmoded power structures.

Despite religious and political attempts to eliminate them, the Sufi orders continued to exist, often underground. With the resurgence of fundamental Islam in the second half of the 20th century came also a Sufi revival. Sufism still flourishes in North Africa, Egypt, Sudan, Iran, Central Asia, Pakistan, India and Indonesia. In Soviet Central Asia their underground networks helped Islam survive until the reforms of the late eighties. The disintegration of the Soviet Union has allowed them to return to full public activity in the new republics. Sufism today is still a formidable force in the Islamic world. It still touches and transforms the lives of Muslim people, giving them meaning and emotional support in a world that is increasingly unstable and full of economic woes, suffering and confusion.

Sufi Practice

Initiation into a Sufi order is seen as a necessary ritual that transmits the spiritual grace (barakah, spiritual power) of the guide (murshid) to the disciple (murid). This special grace goes back in an unbroken line to the Prophet himself. In Sufi thought it is likened to a seed planted in the initiate's soul, the equivalent of Christian baptism or new birth. At the initiation ceremony the Master who has experienced union with God and annihilation of self, in addition to giving the disciple the special garment also gives the him a secret word or prayer to help him in his meditation.

Sufis also believe in Spiritual Guides who reveal themselves to the Sufi in visions or dreams and help him on his path. Al-Khidr is one well known such guide who is sometimes identified as the prophet Elijah. The initiate has to learn spiritual poverty (faqr) which means emptying the soul of self in order to make room for God. The illusion of the individual ego must be erased by humility and love of one's neighbour. This is attained by a rigid self discipline that removes all obstacles to the revelation of the Divine Presence.

Path of Pilgrimage

Sufism is seen as a spiritual path of self knowledge that leads to a knowledge of God. God is seen by the "eye of the heart", not by intellectual knowledge or legalistic customs. The outward form of religion is a mere shell which hides the kernel inside it. The kernel is the real Truth, the Sufi's goal on his spiritual path. The Sufi path contains many stages (Maqamat) and states (Ahwal). It begins with repentance when the seeker joins the order and prepares himself for initiation. The guide (Sheikh, Pir) accepts the seeker as his disciple by the ritual of initiation when he imparts his grace, gives him strict ascetic rules to follow and a certain secret word for meditation. The disciple's path is one of continuous struggle against his lower soul. He passes through a number of spiritual stations and states clearly defined by Sufi teaching.

These are the Sufi stations: 1. detachment from the world (zuhd). 2. patience (sabr). 3. gratitude (shukr), for whatever God gives. 4. love (hubb). 5. pleasure (rida) with whatever God desires. Linked to these stations are specific moods or emotions (ahwal) such as fear and hope, sadness and joy, yearning and intimacy, granted to the pilgrim by God's grace for a while with the goal of leading him to on to Ma'rifah (esoteric knowledge, Gnosis), Mahabbah (Love) and to the ultimate goal which is annihilation of personality and unity with God. Beyond this stage the Sufi then enters the state of Baqa', or perseverance in God. He returns from his state of intoxication (Sukr) back into the world completely transformed - reborn. The Sufi path has three ways: Makhafah, the way of fear of God leading to purification. Mahabbah, the way of love leading to sacrifice. Ma'rifah, the way of intuitive knowledge leading to illumination.

Dhikr and Sama

Dhikr and Sama' were based on words attributed to the Prophet: "Whenever men gather together to invoke Allah, they are surrounded by Angels, the Divine Favour envelops them, the Divine Glory (as-Sakinah) descends upon them, and Allah remembers them in His assembly." The hospices became centres where lay people from the countryside would gather together with the members of the order to obey the Quran's injunction to remember God often. This was done in the celebration of the Dhikr, which involved the communal rhythmic repetition of a phrase, usually from the Quran, in which one of the names of God appears. Breath control and body movements were also used as techniques to aid in achieving concentration and control over senses and imagination.

The rosary with 99 or 33 beads was used since the 8th century as an aid to counting the many repetitions (it entered Christian Churches from Sufism via the Crusades). This concentrated meditation can lead to a mystical trance and enlightenment which transforms man's whole being. Sama' was first developed in the mid 9th century in Baghdad. It is another communal ritual practice, defined as a concert of music, poetry recital, singing and dance, which leads the participants to a mystical experience where they seem to hear the music of the heavenly spheres and the voice of God Himself. It attunes the heart to communion with God and is thought to remove all veils hiding God from man's inner vision. Drugs were used by some as an aid to reaching the ecstatic state, coffee by the Shadiliya in the 14th century.

Sufi Saints and Folk Islam

Sheikhs who had reached the highest mystical stage of union with God, were revered by the masses as saints (Awliya') upon whom God had bestowed miraculous supernatural powers and grace. A cult of living and of dead saints developed around them influenced by pagan customs. They were seen as miracle workers, healers, and intercessors for others before God. Their tombs became pilgrimage centres visited by many in order to partake of the Saint's Baraka (blessing, supernatural power) to meet their needs for healing and other help. They would make vows and pray for the saint's intercession on their behalf. Special celebrations which developed into folk festivals were held on the anniversary of their deaths ('urs). They were seen to be mediators between God and man, God answering their prayers on behalf of the supplicants.

Sufism is generally understood to be the inner, mystical dimension of Islam. A practitioner of this tradition is generally known as a cûfî, though some adherents of the tradition reserve this term only for those practitioners who have attained the goals of the Sufi tradition. Another name used for the Sufi seeker is dervish. Classical Sufi scholars have defined Sufism as "a science whose objective is the reparation of the heart and turning it away from all else but God." Alternatively, in the words of the renowned Darqawi Sufi teacher Ahmad ibn Ajiba, "a science through which one can know how to travel into the presence of the Divine, purify one's inner self from filth, and beautify it with a variety of praiseworthy traits."

The Sufi movement has spanned several continents and cultures over a millennium, at first expressed through Arabic, then through Persian, Turkish, and a dozen other languages. Sufi orders, which are either Sunni or Shi'a in doctrine, trace their origins from the Prophet of Islam, Muhammad, through his cousin Ali, or from Abu Bakr. The followers of sufism claim that it is rooted in Muslim culture and tradition, whereas there are factions of Islam — especially Salafism and Wahhabism — that consider Sufism heretical. According to some modern proponents, such as Idries Shah, the Sufi philosophy is universal in nature, its roots predating the arising of Islam and the other modern-day religions; likewise, some Muslims feel that Sufism is outside the sphere of Islam.

The lexical root of Sufi is variously traced to cuf "wool", referring either to the simple cloaks the early Muslim ascetics wore, or possibly to cafâ "purity". The two were combined by al-Rudhabari who said, "The Sufi is the one who wears wool on top of purity." Others suggest the origin of the word cufi is from Ashab as-cuffa "Companions of the Porch", who were a group of impoverished Muslims during the time of Muhammad who spent much of their time on the veranda of the Prophet's mosque, devoted to prayer and eager to memorize each new increment of the Qur'ân as it was revealed. Yet another etymology, advanced by the 10th century Persian historian Abû Rayhân al-Bîrûnî is that the word is linked with Greek word sophia "wisdom".

While all Muslims believe that they are on the pathway to God and will become close to God in Paradise – after death and after the "Final Judgment" – Sufis also believe that it is possible to draw closer to God and to more fully embrace the Divine Presence in this life. The chief aim of all Sufis is to seek the pleasing of God by working to restore within themselves the primordial state of *fitra,* described in the Qur'an and similar to the concept of Buddha nature. In this state nothing one does defies God, and all is undertaken by the single motivation of love of God. A secondary consequence of this is that the seeker may be led to abandon all notions of dualism or multiplicity, including a conception of an individual self, and to realize the Divine Unity.

Thus Sufism has been characterized as the science of the states of the lower self (the ego), and the way of purifying this lower self of its reprehensible traits, while adorning it instead with what is praiseworthy, whether or not this process of cleansing and purifying the heart is in time rewarded by esoteric knowledge of God. This can be conceived in terms of two basic types of law (*fiqh*), an outer law concerned with actions, and an inner law concerned with the human heart. The outer law consists of rules pertaining to worship, transactions, marriage, judicial rulings, and criminal law – what is often referred to, a bit too broadly, as *shariah.* The inner law of Sufism consists of rules about repentance from sin, the purging of contemptible qualities and evil traits of character, and adornment with virtues and good character.

To enter the way of Sufism, the seeker begins by finding a teacher, as the connection to the teacher is considered necessary for the growth of the pupil. The teacher, to be genuine, must have received the authorization to teach (*ijazah*) of another Master of the Way, in an unbroken succession (*silsilah*) leading back to Sufism's origin with the Prophet Muhammad. It is the transmission of the divine light from the teacher's heart to the heart of the student, rather than of worldly knowledge transmitted from mouth to ear, that allows the adept to progress. In addition, the genuine teacher will be utterly strict in his adherence to the Divine Law. Scholars and adherents of Sufism are unanimous in agreeing that Sufism cannot be learned through books. To reach the highest levels of success in Sufism typically requires that the disciple live with and serve the teacher for many, many years.

For instance, Baha-ud-Din Naqshband Bukhari, considered founder of the Naqshbandi Order, served his first teacher, Sayyid Muhammad Baba As-Samasi, for 20 years, until as-Samasi died. He subsequently served several other teachers for lengthy periods of time. The extreme arduousness of his spiritual preparation is illustrated by his service, as directed by his teacher, to the weak and needy members of his community in a state of complete humility and tolerance for many years. When he believed this mission to be concluded, his teacher next directed him to care for animals, curing their sicknesses, cleaning their wounds, and assisting them in finding provision. After many years of this he was next instructed to spend many years in the care of dogs in a state of humility, and to ask them for support.

As a further example, the prospective adherent of the Mevlevi Order would have been ordered to serve in the kitchens of a hospice for the poor for 1,001 days prior to being accepted for spiritual instruction, and a further 1,001 days in solitary retreat as a precondition of completing that instruction. Some teachers, especially when addressing more general audiences, or mixed groups of Muslims and non-Muslims, make extensive use of parable, allegory, and metaphor. Although approaches to teaching vary among different Sufi orders, Sufism as a whole is primarily concerned with direct personal experience, and as such has sometimes been compared to other, non-Islamic forms of mysticism (e.g., as in the books of Seyyed Hossein Nasr).

Sufism, which is a general term for Muslim mysticism, sprang up largely in reaction against the worldliness which infected Islam when its leaders became the powerful and wealthy rulers of multitudes of people and were influenced by foreign cultures. Harun al-Rashid, eating off gold and silver, toying with a harem of scented beauties, surrounded by an impenetrable retinue of officials, eunuchs and slaves, was a far cry from the stern simplicity of an Umar, who lived in the modest house, wore patched clothes and could be approached by any of his followers. The typical early Sufi lived in a cell of in a mosque and taught a small band of disciples. The extent to which Sufism was influenced by Buddhist and Hindu mysticism, and by the example Christian hermits and monks, is disputed, but selfdiscipline and concentration on God quickly led to the belief that by quelling the self and through loving ardour for God it was possible to maintain a union with the divine in which the human self melted away.

In its early stages of development Sufism effectively referred to nothing more than the internalization of Islam. According to one perspective, it is directly from the Qur'an, constantly recited, meditated, and experienced, that Sufism proceeded, in its origin and its development. Others have held that Sufism is the strict emulation of the way of Muhammad, through which the heart's connection to the Divine is strengthened. From the traditional Sufi point of view, the esoteric teachings of Sufism were transmitted from the Prophet Muhammad to those who had the capacity to acquire the direct experiential gnosis of God, which was passed on from teacher to student through the centuries. Some of this transmission is summarized in texts, but most is not. Important contributions in writing are attributed to Uwais al-Qarni, Harrm bin Hian, Hasan Basri and Sayid ibn al-Mussib, who are regarded as the first Sufis in the earliest generations of Islam. Harith al-Muhasibi was the first one to write about moral psychology.

Rabia Basri was a Sufi known for her love and passion for God, expressed through her poetry. Bayazid Bastami was among the first theorists of Sufism; he concerned himself with *fanâ* and *baqâ*, the state of annihilating the self in the presence of the divine, accompanied by clarity concerning worldly phenomena derived from that perspective. Sufism had a long history already before the subsequent institutionalization of Sufi teachings into devotional orders (*tarîqât*) in the early Middle Ages. Almost all extant Sufi orders trace their chains of transmission (*silsila*) back to Prophet Muhammad via his cousin and son-in-law Ali.

The Naqshbandi order is a notable exception to this rule, as it traces the origin of its teachings from the Prophet Muhammad to the first Islamic Caliph Abu Bakr. Different devotional styles and traditions developed over time, reflecting the perspectives of different masters and the accumulated cultural wisdom of the orders. Typically all of these concerned themselves with the understanding of subtle knowledge (gnosis), education of the heart to purify it of baser instincts, the love of God, and approaching God through a well-described hierarchy of enduring spiritual stations (*maqâmât*) and more transient spiritual states (*ahwâl*).

Formalization of Doctrine

Towards the end of the first millennium CE, a number of manuals began to be written summarizing the doctrines of Sufism and describing some typical Sufi practices. Two of the most famous of these are now available in English translation: the *Kashf al-Mahjûb* of Hujwiri, and the *Risâla* of Qushayri. Two of Imam Al Ghazali's greatest treatises, the "Revival of Religious Sciences" and the "Alchemy of Happiness," argued that Sufism originated from the Qur'an and was thus compatible with mainstream Islamic thought, and did not in any way contradict Islamic Law — being instead necessary to its complete fulfillment. This became the mainstream position among Islamic scholars for centuries, challenged only recently on the basis of selective use of a limited body of texts.

Ongoing efforts by both traditionally-trained Muslim scholars and Western academics are making Imam Al-Ghazali's works available in English translation for the first time, allowing readers to judge for themselves the compatibility between Islamic Law and Sufi doctrine. These remarks concern written sources. It is to be remembered that Sufism is transmitted from the heart of the teacher to the heart of the student, not through texts; and also, that texts may not convey everything, or may be read by different seekers on different levels. Therefore the notion of a "formalization of doctrine" in Sufism is not strictly correct.

Growth of Sufi Influence in Islamic Cultures

The spread of Sufism has been considered a definitive factor in the spread of Islam, and in the creation of integrally Islamic cultures, especially in Africa and Asia. Recent academic work on these topics has focused on the role of Sufism in creating and propagating the culture of the Ottoman world, and in resisting European imperialism in Africa and South Asia. Between the 13th and 16th centuries CE, Sufism produced a flourishing intellectual culture throughout the Islamic world, a sort of "Golden Age" whose physical artifacts are still present. In many places, a lodge (known variously as a *zaouia, khanqah,* or *tekke*) would be endowed through a pious foundation in perpetuity (*waqf*) to provide a gathering place for Sufi adepts, as well as lodging for itinerant seekers of knowledge.

The same system of endowments could also be used to pay for a complex of buildings, such as that surrounding the Süleymaniye Mosque in Istanbul, including a lodge for Sufi seekers, a hospice with kitchens where these seekers could serve the poor and/or complete a period of initiation, a library, and other structures. No important domain in the civilization of Islam remained unaffected by Sufism in this period.

Contemporary Sufism

Sufism suffered many setbacks in the modern era, particularly (though not exclusively) at the hands of European imperialists in the colonized nations of Asia and Africa. The life of the Algerian Sufi master Emir Abd al-Qadir is instructive in this regard. Notable as well are the lives of Amadou Bamba and Hajj Umar Tall in sub-Saharan Africa, and Sheikh Mansur Ushurma and Imam Shamil in the Caucasus region. Sufism being the central organizing principle of many traditional Islam cultures, it is not surprising that colonial powers attacked Sufi masters as one means of undermining the forces of indigenous selfdetermination.

In spite of this recent history of official repression, there remain many places in the world with vital Sufi traditions. Sufism is popular in such African countries as Senegal, where it is seen as a mystical expression of Islam. Mbacke suggests that one reason Sufism has taken hold in Senegal is because it can accommodate local beliefs and customs, which tend toward the mystical. In South Asia, four major Sufi orders persist, namely the Chishti Order, the Qadiriyyah, the Naqshbandiyya, and the Suhrawardiyya. The Deobandis (i.e., adherents of the Darul Uloom Deoband) and Barelwi are two significant Islamic movements in this region whose followers often belong to one of these orders.

For a more complete summary of currently active groups and teachers, readers are referred to links in the site of Dr. Alan Godlas of the University of Georgia. A number of Westerners have embarked with varying degrees of success on the path of Sufism. One of the first to return to Europe as an official representative of a Sufi path, and with the specific purpose to spread Sufism in Western Europe, was the Swedish-born wandering Sufi Abd al-Hadi Aqhili. The ideas propagated by such spiritualists may or may not conform to the tenets of Sufism as understood by orthodox Muslims, as for instance with G. I. Gurdjieff and Shawni.

On the other hand, American- and British-born teachers such as Nuh Ha Mim Keller, Hamza Yusuf, and Abdal Hakim Murad have been instrumental in spreading messages that conform fully with the normative tenets of Islam. Other noteworthy Sufi teachers who have been active in the West in recent years include Nader Angha, Hazrat Inayat Khan, Riaz Ahmed Gohar Shahi, Muhammad Emin Er, Nazim al-Qubrusi, Javad Nurbakhsh, and Muzaffer Ozak.

Theoretical Perspectives in Sufism

Traditional Islamic scholars have recognized two major branches within the practice of Sufism, and use this as one key to differentiating among the approaches of different masters and devotional lineages. On the one hand there is the path from the signs to the Signifier (or from the arts to the Artisan). In this branch, the seeker begins by purifying the lower self of every corrupting influence that stands in the way of recognizing all of creation as the work of God, as God's active Self-disclosure or theophany. This is the way of Imam Al-Ghazali and of the majority of the Sufi orders.

On the other hand there is the path from the Signifier to His signs, from the Artisan to His works. In this branch the seeker experiences divine attraction (*jadhba*), and is able to enter the path with a glimpse of its endpoint, of direct apprehension of the Divine Presence towards which all spiritual striving is directed. This does not replace the striving to purify the heart, as in the other branch; it simply stems from a different point of entry into the path. This is the way primarily of the masters of the Naqshbandi and Shadhili orders. Contemporary scholars may also recognize a third branch, attributed to the late Ottoman scholar Said Nursi and explicated in his vast Qur'ân commentary called the Risale-i Nur. This approach entails strict adherence to the way of the Prophet Muhammad, in the understanding that this wont, or *sunnah*, proposes a complete devotional spirituality adequate to those without access to a master of the Sufi way.

Contributions to Other Domains of Scholarship

Sufism has contributed significantly to the elaboration of theoretical perspectives in many domains of intellectual endeavor. For instance, the doctrine of "subtle centers" or centers of subtle cognition (known as *Lataif-e-sitta*) addresses the matter of the awakening of spiritual intuition in ways that some consider similar to certain models of *chakra* in Hinduism. In general, these subtle centers or *latâ'if* are thought of as faculties that are to be purified sequentially in order to bring the seeker's wayfaring to completion. A concise and useful summary of this system from a living exponent of this tradition has been published by Muhammad Emin Er.

Sufi psychology has influenced many areas of thinking both within and outside of Islam, drawing primarily upon three concepts. Ja'far al-Sadiq (both an imam in the Shia tradition and a respected scholar and link in chains of Sufi transmission in all Islamic sects) held that human beings are dominated by a lower self called the *nafs*, a faculty of spiritual intuition called the *qalb* or spiritual heart, and a spirit or soul called *ruh*. These interact in various ways, producing the spiritual types of the tyrant (dominated by *nafs*), the person of faith and moderation (dominated by the spiritual heart), and the person lost in love for God (dominated by the *ruh*).

Of note with regard to the spread of Sufi psychology in the West is Robert Frager, a Sufi teacher authorized in the Halveti Jerrahi order. Frager was a trained psychologist, born in the United States, who converted to Islam in the course of his practice of Sufism and wrote extensively on Sufism and psychology. Sufi cosmology and Sufi metaphysics are also noteworthy areas of intellectual accomplishment.

Sufi Practices

The devotional practices of Sufis vary widely. This is because an acknowledged and authorized master of the Sufi path is in effect a physician of the heart, able to diagnose the seeker's impediments to knowledge and pure intention in serving God, and to prescribe to the seeker a course of treatment appropriate to his or her maladies. The consensus among Sufi scholars is that the seeker cannot self-diagnose, and that it can be extremely harmful to undertake any of these practices alone and without formal authorization. Prerequisites to practice include rigorous adherence to Islamic norms (ritual prayer in its five prescribed times each day, the fast of Ramadan, and so forth).

Additionally, the seeker ought to be firmly grounded in supererogatory practices known from the life of the Prophet Muhammad (such as the so-called "sunna prayers"). This is in accordance with the words, attributed to God, of the following, a famous Hadith Qudsi:

My servant draws near to Me through nothing I love more than that which I have made obligatory for him. My servant never ceases drawing near to Me through supererogatory works until I love him. Then, when I love him, I am his hearing through which he hears, his sight through which he sees, his hand through which he grasps, and his foot through which he walks. It is also necessary for the seeker to have a correct creed (*Aqidah*), and to embrace with certainty its tenets. The seeker must also, of necessity, turn away from sins, love of this world, the love of company and renown, obedience to satanic impulse, and the promptings of the lower self. (The way in which this purification of the heart is achieved is outlined in certain books, but must be prescribed in detail by a Sufi master.)

The seeker must also be trained to prevent the corruption of those good deeds which have accrued to his or her credit by overcoming the traps of ostentation, pride, arrogance, envy, and long hopes (meaning the hope for a long life allowing us to mend our ways later, rather than immediately, here and now). Sufi practices, while attractive to some, are not a *means* for gaining knowledge. The traditional scholars of Sufism hold it as absolutely axiomatic that knowledge of God is not a psychological state generated through breath control. Thus, practice of "techniques" is not the cause, but instead the *occasion* for such knowledge to be obtained (if at all), given proper prerequisites and proper guidance by a master of the way. Furthermore, the emphasis on practices may obscure a far more important fact: The seeker is, in a sense, to become a broken person, stripped of all habits through the practice of (in the words of Imam Al-Ghazali words) solitude, silence, sleeplessness, and hunger.

Dhikr

Dhikr is the remembrance of God commanded in the Qur'an for all Muslims. To engage in dhikr is to practice consciousness of the Divine Presence (some would say "to seek a state of godwariness") according to a variety of means. Some types of dhikr are prescribed for all Muslims, and do not require Sufi initiation or the prescription of a Sufi master because they are deemed to be good for every seeker under every circumstance. Other types of dhikr require specific instruction and permission. Dhikr as a devotional act includes the repetition of divine names, supplications and aphorisms from hadith literature, and sections of the Qur'an. More generally, any activity in which the Muslim maintains awareness of God is considered dhikr.

Some Sufi orders stress and extensive reliance upon Dhikr and termed it the source to attain Divine Love likewise in Qadri Al-Muntahi Sufi tariqa, which was originated by Riaz Ahmed Gohar Shahi. This practice of Dhikr called Dhikr-e-Qulb(remembrance of Allah by Heartbeats). The basic idea of this practice is to visualize the Arabic name of God, Allah as having been written on the disciple's heart. Some Sufi orders engage in ritualized dhikr ceremonies, the liturgy of which may include recitation, singing, instrumental music, dance, costumes, incense, meditation, ecstasy, and trance.

Muraqaba

The practice of *muraqaba* can be likened to the practices of meditation attested in many faith communities. The word *muraqaba* is derived from the same root (*r-q-b*) occurring as one of the 99 Names of God in the Qur'an, al-Raqîb, meaning "the Vigilant" and attested in verse 4: 1 of the Qur'an. Through *muraqaba*, a person watches over or takes care of the spiritual heart, acquires knowledge about it, and becomes attuned to the Divine Presence, which is ever vigilant.

While variation exists, one description of the practice within a Naqshbandi lineage reads as follows:

He is to collect all of his bodily senses in concentration, and to cut himself off from all preoccupation and notions that inflict themselves upon the heart. And thus he is to turn his full consciousness towards God Most High while saying three times: "*Ilahî anta maqsûdî wa-ridâka matlûbî* — my God, you are my Goal and Your good pleasure is what I seek." Then he brings to his heart the Name of the Essence — Allâh — and as it courses through his heart he remains attentive to its meaning, which is "Essence without likeness." The seeker remains aware that He is Present, Watchful, Encompassing of all, thereby exemplifying the meaning of his saying (may God bless him and grant him peace): "Worship God as though you see Him, for if you do not see Him, He sees you." And likewise the prophetic tradition: "The most favored level of faith is to know that God is witness over you, wherever you may be."

Sufi Pilgrimages

In popular Sufism (i.e., devotional practices that have achieved currency in world cultures through Sufi influence), one common practice is to visit the tombs of saints, great scholars, and righteous people. This is a particularly common practice in South Asia, where famous tombs include those of Khoja Afâq, near Kashgar, in China; Sachal Sarmast, in Sindh, Pakistan; and the Darbar-e-Gohar Shahi in Kotri Sharif. Likewise, in Fez, Morocco, a popular destination for such pious visitation is the Zaouia Moulay Idriss II and the yearly visitation to see the current Sheikh of the Qadiri Boutchichi Tariqah, Sheikh Sidi Hamza al Qadiri al Boutchichi to celebrate the Mawlid (which is usually televised on Mocorran National television). Visitors may invoke blessings upon those interred, and seek divine favor and proximity.

Islam and Sufism

Sufism and Islamic Law

Scholars and adherents of Sufism sometimes describe Sufism in terms of a threefold approach to God as explained by a tradition (*hadîth*) attributed to the Prophet Muhammad,"The Shariah is my words, the tariqa is my actions, and the haqiqa is my interior states". Sufis believe the *shariah, tariqa* and *haqiqa* are mutually interdependent. The *tariqa,* the 'path' on which the mystics walk, has been defined as 'the path which comes out of the *Shariah,* for the main road is called *shar,* the path, *tariq.*' No mystical experience can be realized if the binding injunctions of the Shariah are not followed faithfully first. The path, *tariqa,* however, is narrower and more difficult to walk. It leads the adept, called *sâlik* (wayfarer), in his *sulûk* (wayfaring), through different stations (*maqâmât*) until he reaches his goal, the perfect *tawhîd,* the existential confession that God is One.

Traditional Islamic Thought and Sufism

The literature of Sufism emphasizes highly subjective matters that resist outside observation, such as the subtle states of the heart. Often these resist direct reference or description, with the consequence that the authors of various Sufi treatises took recourse to allegorical language. For instance, much Sufi poetry refers to intoxication, which Islam expressly forbids. This usage of indirect language and the existence of interpretations by people who had no training in Islam or Sufism led to doubts being cast over the validity of Sufism as a part of Islam. Also, some groups emerged that considered themselves above the Sharia and discussed Sufism as a method of bypassing the rules of Islam in order to attain salvation directly. This was disapproved of by traditional scholars.

For these and other reasons, the relationship between traditional Islamic scholars and Sufism is complex and a range of scholarly opinion on Sufism in Islam has been the norm. Some scholars, such as Al-Ghazali, helped its propagation while other scholars, such as Ibn Taymiyyah, opposed it. W. Chittick explains the position of Sufism and Sufis this way:

In short, Muslim scholars who focused their energies on understanding the normative guidelines for the body came to be known as jurists, and those who held that the most important task was to train the mind in achieving correct understanding came to be divided into three main schools of thought: theology, philosophy, and Sufism. This leaves us with the third domain of human existence, the spirit. Most Muslims who devoted their major efforts to developing the spiritual dimensions of the human person came to be known as Sufis.

Traditional and Non-traditional Sufi Groups

The traditional Sufi orders, which are in majority, emphasize the role of Sufism as a spiritual discipline within Islam. Therefore, the Sharia (traditional Islamic law) and the Sunnah (customs of the Prophet) are seen as crucial for any Sufi aspirant. One proof traditional orders assert is that almost all the famous Sufi masters of the past Caliphates were experts in Sharia and were renowned as people with great Iman (faith) and excellent practice. Many were also Qadis (Sharia law judges) in courts. They held that Sufism was never distinct from Islam and to fully comprehend and practice Sufism one must be an observant Muslim. In recent decades there has been a growth of non-traditional Sufi movements in the West. Examples include the Universal Sufism movement, the Golden Sufi Center, the Sufi Foundation of America, the neosufism of Idries Shah, and Sufism Reoriented. Rumi has become one of the most widely read poets in the United States, thanks largely to the translations published by Coleman Barks.

Islamic Positions on Non-Islamic Sufi Groups

The use of the title Sufi by non-traditional groups to refer to themselves, and their appropriation of traditional Sufi masters (most notably Jalaluddin Rumi) as sources of authority or inspiration, is not accepted by Muslims who are Sufi adherents. Some traditional Sufis also object to interpretations of classical Sufis texts by writers who have no grounding in the traditional Islamic sciences and therefore no prerequisites for understanding such texts. These are considered by certain conventional Islamic scholars as beyond the pale of the religion. This being said, there are Islamic Sufi groups that are open to non-Muslim participation.

Criticism within Islam

Riaz Ahmed Gohar Shahi was heavily criticized by orthodox theological scholars in Pakistan and abroad. Shahi's books were banned by the Government of Pakistan. Public meetings are not allowed to his followers and no press coverage is allowed to either Gohar Shahi or to his followers due to charges of blasphemy law violations. Many attempts were made on Shahi's life including a petrol bomb attack, thrown into his Manchester residence, and an attack with a hand grenade during the discourse at his home in Kotri, Pakistan.

Gohar Shahi was booked in 1997 on alleged charges of murdering a woman who had come to him for spiritual treatment; Gohar Shahi, and many of his followers, were later convicted under Islamic blasphemy laws by an antiterrorist court in Sindh. Gohar Shahi was convicted in absentia—as then he was in England—resulting in sentences that totaled approximately 59 years. Gohar Shahi died abroad, prior to any decision on appeals filed with the High Court of Sindh.

Perception outside Islam

Sufi mysticism has long exercised a fascination upon the Western world, and especially its orientalist scholars. Figures like Rumi have become household names in the United States, where Sufism is perceived as quietist and less political. The Islamic Institute in Mannheim, Germany, which works towards the integration of Europe and Muslims, sees Sufism as particularly suited for interreligious dialogue and intercultural harmonisation in democratic and pluralist societies; it has described Sufism as a symbol of tolerance and humanism – undogmatic, flexible and non-violent. The Indian government has likewise praised Sufism as the tolerant face of Islam though many believe that Sufis like Naqshbandis have been fanatical and that some of the Sufi traditions like dancing, copied from native Indian traditions help in camouflaging Islamic extremism.

Influence of Sufism on Judaism

A great influence was exercised by Sufism upon the ethical writings of Jews in the middle ages. In the first writing of this kind, we see "Kitab al-Hidayah ila Fara'id al-kulub", Duties of the Heart, of Bahya ibn Pakuda. This book was translated by Judah ibn Tibbon into Hebrew under the title "Hobot ha-Lebabot". The precepts prescribed by the Torah number 613 only; those dictated by the intellect are innumerable. This was precisely the argument used by the Sufis against their adversaries, the Ulamas. The arrangement of the book seems to have been inspired by Sufism. Its ten sections correspond to the ten stages through which the Sufi had to pass in order to attain that true and passionate love of God which is the aim and goal of all ethical self-discipline.

It is noteworthy that in the ethical writings of the Sufis Al-Kusajri and Al-Harawi there are sections which treat of the same subjects as those treated in the "Hobot ha-Lebabot" and which bear the same titles: e.g., "Bab al-Tawakkul"; "Bab al-Taubah"; "Bab al-Muhasabah"; "Bab al-Tawadu'"; "Bab al-Zuhd". In the ninth gate, Bahya directly quotes sayings of the Sufis, whom he calls Perushim. However, the author of the Hobot ha-Lebabot did not go so far as to approve of the asceticism of the Sufis, although he showed a marked predilection for their ethical principles. The Jewish writer Abraham bar $iyya teaches the asceticism of the Sufis.

His distinction with regard to the observance of Jewish law by various classes of men is essentially a Sufic theory. According to it there are four principal degrees of human perfection or sanctity; namely:

1. Of "Shari'ah," i.e., of strict obedience to all ritual laws of Islam, such as prayer, fasting, pilgrimage, almsgiving, ablution, etc., which is the lowest degree of worship, and is attainable by all
2. Of Tariqah, which is accessible only to a higher class of men who, while strictly adhering to the outward or ceremonial injunctions of religion, rise to an inward perception of mental power and virtue necessary for the nearer approach to the Divinity
3. Of "Hakikah," the degree attained by those who, through continuous contemplation and inward devotion, have risen to the true perception of the nature of the visible and invisible; who, in fact, have recognized the Godhead, and through this knowledge have succeeded in establishing an ecstatic relation to it; and
4. Of the "Ma'arifah," in which state man communicates directly with the Deity.

In Popular Culture

The movie Bab'Aziz (2005) directed by Nacer Khemir tells the story of an old and blind dervish who must cross the desert with his little granddaughter during many days and nights to get to his last dervish reunion celebrated every 30 years. The movie is full of Sufi mysticism and even contain quotes of Rumi and other sufi poets and shows an ecstatic sufi dance. Madonna on her record Bedtime Stories (1994) sings a song called Bedtime Story that talks about getting in a high unconsciousness level. The video for the song shows an ecstatic sufi ritual with many dervishes dancing around, Arabic calligraphy and some other Sufi elements. In the year 1998 she recorded the song Bittersweet in which she recites Rumi's poem by the same name.

In the year 2001 Madonna sang the song Secret during her Drowned World Tour showing rituals from many religions including a Sufi dance. Singer/songwritter Loreena McKennit on her record The Mask And Mirror (1994) has a song called The Mystic's Dream clearly influenced by Sufi music and poetry. The band, mewithoutYou, has made references to sufi parables, including the name of their upcoming album "it's all crazy! it's all false! it's all a dream! it's alright!" (2009) Lead singer, Aaron Weiss, claims this influence comes from his parents who are both sufi converts.

5

Nasir Khusraw
Fatimid Intellectual

Abu Mo'in Hamid ad-Din Nasir ibn Khusraw al-Qubadiani or Nâsir Khusraw Qubâdiyânî (1004 - 1088 AD was a Persian poet, philosopher, Isma'ili scholar and a traveler. He was born in Qubadyan, a village in middle-age Bactria in modern Tajikistan and died in Yamagan, a village in Badakhshan province of Afghanistan. He is considered as one of the great poets and writers in Persian literature, the *Safarnama,* an account of his travels, being his most famous work. Nasir Khusraw was born in 1004 AD, in Qubadiyan (Kobadiyan in Balkh a province in present day Afghanistan), then Greater Khorasan. He was well versed in all the branches of natural science, in medicine, mathematics, astronomy and astrology, in Greek philosophy and the writings of al-Kindi, al-Farabi and Ibn Sina; and the interpretation of the Qur'an. He had studied Arabic, Turkish, Greek, the vernacular languages of India and Sind, and perhaps even Hebrew; he had visited Multan and Lahore, and the splendid Ghaznavid court under Sultan Mahmud, Firdousi's patron. Later on he chose Merv for his residence, and was the owner of a house and garden there.

Until A.H. 437 (1046 AD), he worked as financial secretary and revenue collector for the Seljuk sultan Toghrul Beg, or rather of his brother Jaghir Beg, the emir of

Khorasan, who had conquered Merv in 1037. About this time, inspired by a heavenly voice in a dream, he abjured all the luxuries of life, and resolved upon a pilgrimage to the holy shrines of Mecca and Medina, hoping to find there the solution to his spiritual crisis. The graphic description of this journey is contained in the *Safarnama,* which possesses a special value among books of travel, since it contains the most authentic account of the state of the Muslim world in the middle of the 11th century. The minute sketches of Jerusalem and its environs are even today of practical value.

During the seven years of his 19,000-kilometre journey (1046-1052), Nasir visited Mecca four times, and performed all the rites and observances of a zealous pilgrim; but he was far more attracted by Cairo, the capital of Egypt, and the residence of the Fatimid caliph-imam Ma'ad al-Mustansir Billah, the Imam of the Ismaili Shi'a Muslims, which was just then waging a deadly war against the Abbasid caliph of Baghdad, and Toghrul Beg the Seljuk, the great defender of the Sunni creed. At the very time of Nasir's visit to Cairo, the power of the Egyptian Fatimids was in its zenith; Syria, the Hejaz, Africa, and Sicily obeyed al-Mustanir's sway, and the utmost order, security and prosperity reigned in Egypt.

At Cairo, he learned mainly under the Fatimid *dâ'î* ("missionary") Mu'ayyad fid-Din al-Shirazi, and became thoroughly imbued with the Shi'a Isma'ili doctrines of the Fatimids, and their introduction into his native country was henceforth the sole object of his life. He was raised to the position of *dâ'î* "missionary" and appointed as the *Hujjat-i Khorasan,* though the hostility he encountered in the propagation of these new religious ideas after his return to Greater Khorasan in 1052 and Sunnite fanaticism compelled him at last to flee. After many wanderings he found a refuge in Yamgan (about 1060) in the mountains of Badakhshan, where he spent as a hermit the last decades of his life, and gathered round him a considerable number of devoted adherents, who have handed down his doctrines to succeeding generations.

Safarnama (The Book of Travels) is his most famous work. He visited tens of cities in about seven years (1046 March 6 – 1052 October 23) and wrote comprehensively about them: colleges, caravanserais, mosques, area, population, scientists, kings, usual people and his interesting memories. After 1000 years, his *Safarnama* is still readable for Persian-speaking people. Among his other works, most of the lyrical poems in his *Diwan* were composed in his retirement, and their chief topics are an enthusiastic praise of Ali, his descendants, and al-Mustansir in particular; passionate outcries against Khorasan and its rulers, who had driven him from house and home; the highest satisfaction with the quiet solitude of Yumgan; and utter despondency again in seeing himself despised by his former associates and forever excluded from participation in the glorious contest of life. But scattered through all these alternate outbursts of hope and despair we find precious lessons of purest morality, and solemn warnings against the tricks and perfidy of the world, the vanity of all earthly splendour and greatness, the folly and injustice of men, and the hypocrisy, frivolity and viciousness of fashionable society and princely courts in particular.

It is the same strain which runs, although in a somewhat lower key, through his two larger *mathnavis*, the *Rawshana-i-nama* (or Book of Enlightenment, also known as *Shish Fasl*), and the *Sa'datnama* (Book of Felicity). The former is divided into two sections: the first, of a metaphysical character, contains a sort of practical cosmography, chiefly based on Avicenna's theories, but frequently intermixed both with the freer speculations of the well-known philosophical brotherhood of Basra, the Ikhwan al-Safa, and purely Shi'ite or Isma'ili ideas; the second, or ethical section of the poem, abounds in moral maxims and ingenious thoughts on man's good and bad qualities, on the necessity of shunning the company of fools and double-faced friends, on the deceptive allurements of the world and the secret snares of ambitious men craving for rank and wealth. It concludes with an imaginary vision of a beautiful work of spirits who have stripped off the fetters of earthly cares and sorrows and revel in the pure light of divine wisdom and love.

If we compare this with a similar allegory in Nasir's *Diwan*, which culminates in the praise of Mustansir, we are fairly entitled to look upon it as a covert allusion to the eminent men who revealed to the poet in Cairo the secrets of the Isma'ili faith, and showed him what he considered the heavenly ladder to superior knowledge and spiritual bliss. A similar series of excellent teachings on practical wisdom and the blessings of a virtuous life, only of a more severe and uncompromising character, is contained in the *Sa'datnama*; and, judging from the extreme bitterness of tone manifested in the reproaches of kings and emirs, we should be inclined to consider it a protest against the vile aspersions poured out upon Nasir's moral and religious attitude during those persecutions which drove him at last to Yumgan.

Of all other works of the author, the *Zaad al-Musafirin* (or Travelling Provisions of Pilgrims) and the *Wajh-i-Din* (or The Face of Religion) are theoretical descriptions of his religious and philosophical principles; the rest of them can be dismissed as being probably just as apocryphal as Nasir's famous autobiography (found in several Persian *tadhkiras* or biographies of poets), a mere forgery of the most extravagant description, which is mainly responsible for the confusion in names and dates in older accounts of our author. Another work of Nasir Khusraw is the Persian philosophical work "Gushayis wa Rahayish" which has been translated to English by F.M. Hunzai under the title "Knowledge and Liberation".

The poetry of Nasir Khusraw is replete with advice and wisdom. Being the representative of the Fatimid Imams in Khorasan, Nasir guided his followers through his poetry. His Persian poetry is enjoyed by the average Persian speaker of today and is taught in grade school. The great and-well-known lsmaili Missionary Hakim Nasir Khusraw was the celebrated medieval erudite poet, philosopher, traveller and Hujjat of Khurasan. Nasir Khusraw was one of the most important figures of llth century Iran - an era which has produced such men of prominence as Omar Khayyam, Hasan bin Sabbah. and al-Mua'yyid ash-Shirazi.

Nasir Khusraw, who is considered as the Real Wisdom of the East came from Qubadiyan in Balkh. The full name of this most attractive and remarkable personality of Persian Literary History was Abu Muin'id-Din-Nasir-i-Khusraw. He called himself Marwazi Qubandiyani, as the capital of state of which Qubadiyan belonged was Marw. His father was a small land-owner in the vicinity of Balkh. He was born in the month of Dhelqad 394 A.H./1003-4 C.E. during the time of Sultan Mahmood Ghaznavi. He was seeking education from his early childhood and devoted about thirty years in achieving it. He became all in all in every field of knowledge, in intellectual, as well as traditional.

He memorised the Holy Quran and became an expert in tradition and in interpretation of Holy Ouran. Besides Islamic literature. he also studied the new and the old testament and books of other religions thoroughly. He studied the al-Magisty of Ptolemy, geometry of Euclid, alchemy, physics, logic, music, mathematics, medicine astronomy, astrology etc. He was profound in literature and knew Hebrew, Sanskirit besides Arabic, Persian, Turkey and Greek languages. He studied the philosophy of Socrates, Plato, Aristotle and the epistles of Kindi, Farabi and Avicenna (Abu Ali Sina). He refers to his high status of knowledge in his Diwan.

"Na mond az heech goon danish kih manzan na kardam-istifadat beesh-o-kamtar. No knowledge remained in the world from which I was not benefited more or less". About his original religion it is said that he was Shia, Nasir calls himself an Alawi in two of his couplets in his Diwans, from which Dr. lvanow concludes that "Alawi" does not only mean, Shiite but there is quite enough reason to believe that

Nasir was really a "Sayyid". But it is difficult to prove this for he exercised modesty and religious self-effacement in this connection.

The inhabitants of Yamgan valley, where Nasir lived his last days and died, consider themselves as Sayyids and the descendants of Nasir Khusraw. They are fanatical Sunnis and they believe their ancestor Nasir was a Sufic Pir. Being born in the family belonging to the government officials' class, he followed the custom of that time and entered the government service of Ghaznavid and Saljuq administrations. Nasir was employed as a government secretary and a revenue officer.

Mr. Taqi-zada in his book "Ham majlis wa ham piyala" of kings has accused him of being participant of the assemblies of drunken orgies of princes and so forth. Scrutinizing Nasir's own statements, says Ivanow, one can see that all this is based on misunderstanding. As a gifted and mentally alert youth, he undoubtedly took much real interest in many things, though this never amounted to anything like his poetry's years - a long search for Truth. He himself has said in his Diwan, he would hardly have devoted his time to composing indecent or frivolous poetry and practising such vices, that when you remember these, your face becomes dark and mind becomes depressed. This is of course, expressed in poetry in which hyperbolism, exaggeration is often the fundamental law. Most probably this simply means that he enjoyed his life and composed ordinary love songs, which in the strictly religious outlook of his old age appeared to him as shameful frivolity. The change of dynasty took place in his mother country in 429 A.H./1038 C.E. When he was 35 years old. Eight years later he set out on his great journey.

Change in his Life and Approach to Imam

It is generally accepted that Nasir went on to the pilgrimage as an orthodox Muslim and became converted to Ismailism in Egypt through which he had to pass on his way to Meçca. He returned to his native land after some time as an Ismaili missionary of such a high rank as a Hujjat. According to Dr. Ivanow "for him (Nasir Khusraw) obviously the truth was only Islam and it may be easily realized that the truth was the authentic interpretation of religion which can be received only from the Imam. It is quite possible, that he might have been shiite, perhaps a change of dynasty, if it upset his career, the frustation of his youthful ambitions, even his probable contacts with Ismailis - all these together possibly inspired him to espouse the cause of the Fatimids whose star had never risen so high as at that particular time,".

Nasir Khusraw has given two statements pertaining to his conversion in his Safarnama. One is the oftcited story of his religious dream at the beginning of the journey and the second one is his "confession" in the form of the lengthiest of his qasidas. About his dream he has written in his Safarnama that on a certain night he saw in his dream some one saying to him "How long shall you go on drinking the wine that ruins the human reason? It is high time for thee to become sober". He answered in the following words: "The wise have not invented any better means for the purpose of reducing sorrows of the world", the addresser of the dream said, "Senselessness and unconsciousness do not bring peace of mind. One cannot be called a wise man if one leads people to unconsciousness. It is necessary to search for something that flourishes reason and increases wisdom. He asked,"Where can I find that?" The addresser replied: "Those who search will find, and waved his hand in the direction of Qibla saying nothing more.

This was the sign indicating the Fatimid Imams who were in Cairo in Egypt. After seeing this dream he resigned from his services and set out on his great journey. "Nasir", says Ivanow, "himself well knew the harm that he was causing to himself but obviously the speaker in the dream was someone of especial importance, the Prophet or the Imam, not named by him out of peculiar modesty. It is generally believed that the Prophet may " appear in the dream" only to deserving and pious people and would not visit others. Thus the mention of a holy visitor is equivalent to the narrator's claim to exceptional piety and virtue. So his sincere devotion to religion of Shiite type caused Nasir Khusraw to be converted to Ismailism where he could recover from his chronic drunkness i.e. practising religious life without knowing its real meaning and implications. He was awakened from his intoxication, i.e. he was convinced of the Ismaili faith and later he went to Cairo for higher training and instructions:

"In the autumn of the 1045 C.E., says E.G. Browne 'Nasir Khusraw being warned by dream, determined to renounce the wine and to undertake the pilgrimage to Mecca. He was about 40 years old at that time. He performed a complete ablution, repaired to the mosque of Jazjanan, where he then happened to have registered a solemn vow of repentence, and set out on his journey in 437 A.H./1045 C.E."

Nasir Khusraw after seeing a dream resigned from his services and set out on the great journey with his younger brother Abu-Saeed and an Indian servant. He travelled by the way of Shaburqan to Merv, then proceeded to Nishapur and visiting the tomb of Sufi saint Bayazid of Bistan at Qumis, came by way of Demghan to Samnan. where he met ustad Ali Nisai, a pupil of Avicenna and lecturer on arithmetic, geometry and medicine. Passing onwards through Qazwin he reached Tabriz on Safar 20th, 438 A.H./1046 C.E. and there he made the acquaintance of the poet Qatran, to whom he explained passages in poems of Daqiqi and Maujik. Then he made his way successively to Van, Akhiat, Bittis, Arzan, Mayfaraqin, Amid, Aleppo, and Ma'arratun-Nu'man, where he met great Arabic philosophical poet Abul-ala-af-Ma'arri of whose character and attainment he speaks in warmest terms. Then he visited Hama, Tripoli, Bayrout, Sidon, Tyre, Acre, and Hayfa.

He spent some time in Syria in visiting the tombs of Prophets and other holy places, including Jerusalem and

Bethlehem, he made his first pilgrimage to Mecca in 1047 C.E. From Mecca by the way of Damascus to Jerusalem, he proceeded by land to Egypt and finally arrived in Cairo on Safar 7th, 439 A.H./1047. C.E.

"Nasir Khusraw," says E.G. Browne "Attracted by the fame of al-Mustansir, came from Khurasan to Egypt, where he lived seven years, performing the pilgrimage and returning to Egypt every year."

Dr. Ivanow says that "it would be strange that if he remained a Sunni until his arrival in Cairo, he should have been converted by no less a figure than al-Mua'yyid himself and at once accepted into the service."

His stay in Cairo marks an epoch in his life, for it was here he became acquainted with the splendour, justice and wise administration of Fatimid Caliph and Imam al-Mustansir billah and here it was that he was initiated into esoteric doctrine of Ismaili creed, received the commission to carry on their propaganda. The star of the Fatimid had never risen so high as at this particular period. Nasir Khusraw in his Safarnama has described the city of Cairo, the excellent administration of Imams of Fatimid Caliphs and the wealth, contentment and security of their subjects. His description of Cairo, its mosques, its gardens, buildings and suburbs is admirable. The details of Fatimid administration given by him are most valuable. He was much impressed with the discipline of the army, maintenance of laws peace and order in the country. Describing the excellent administration in beautiful words, he says, "it seems that Fatimids are the only lawful authorities and the protectors of the garden of Allah."

According to Encyclopaedia of Islam, Nasir Khusraw left Persia at the difficult period, when the country was being laid waste by the continued wars between the various princes. He found the same wretched picture in all the Muslim countries which he had to traverse on his journey. Only Egypt proved a pleasing exception, where he saw prosperity, rich bazars, harmony and tranquility. As the Ismaili dynasty of

Fatimids were ruling in Egypt at that time, Nasir concluded that Islam had diverged from the true path and that only Ismailism could save the true believers from inevitable ruin.

When Nasir Khusraw visited Cairo in 439 A.H., he went to the court of Fatimid Caliph, Al-Imam Mustansir billah. There he met Khawaja al-Muayyid Fiddin al-Shirazi, who was then one of the twelve 'Hujjats' of the Imam. He discussed with him about the allegories of the Holy Ouran and other secrets of the Shariat (religious law) and he found the rightfullness of the Fatimid Caliph al-imam-al-Mustansir billah and accepted him as his Imam. He says, "I searched in the world for Tawel-e-mutashabihat (The meaning of allegories of Holy Ouran) but I could not find them anywhere except with Fatimid Caliphs".

He praised his teacher Al-Muayyid in his Diwan for his superiority in knowledge.

"Kih kard az khtir-i-khwaja Muayyid Dar-i-Hikmat kushada bar tu yazdan shab-i-man rooz-i raushan kard Khawaja za burhanha-i-choon khurshid-ipakhshan.

Mara binamood hazir har do aakm ba yak ja dar tanam paida pinhan."

"From the heart of Al-Muayyid, God has opened for thee the doors of wisdom. Khawaja changed my night into a shiny day by his arguments right like sun. He showed me both the worlds in my person, he made me behold them openly as well as secretly in one in my person."

In Noorum Mubin with reference of Rawzatus Safa. Habibus-Siyar, Dabistanul Mazahib it is written that Nasir Khusraw acquired the knowledge of Philosophy at Jama-Azhar. He made vast studies at Darul-Hikmat, held discussions with Khawaja Al-Muayyid a diplomat and Intelligent Dai-ud-Duwa't, from him acquired deep knowledge of Philosophy. Later on, he was brought before the Imam Mustansir billah by Vazir Abu Nastre Sadka Ibn Yusuf, where he received the blessings of Imam. Later on he was bestowed with the title of Dai-ud-Duwa't by Imam. He was then sent to various tours prior to his departure to his native country, where he was designated to carry on the work of preaching. Thus Sayyidna Nasir Khusraw spent three or five years in the service of Imam and was appointed to the propagation of Da'wah in Khurasan. He was given the title of Hujjut-i-Khurasan and he became one of the twelve Hujjuts of the court of Imam.

Beginning of Da'wah:-in 444 A.H. when he returned to Khurasan, he had already given up all the luxuries and he began to propagate the Da'wah with great enthusiasm and ambition. He started his mission from Balkh and used to send 'Daees' 'Madhoons' (missionaries and their assistants) to the provinces of the country. Besides being well versed in the different fields of knowledge he had a great ability and power of eloquence and discussions with 'ulemas' and praised the glory of Fatimide Caliphs and asserted their Imamat very efficiently and took pride in being a follower of the Fatimid Imams and used to call himself a Fatimi. This caused Abbasid minded Ulema to agitate the public to rise against him in enemity because they were the enemies of the Fatimids. Soon the Saljuqs ruled the land, became convinced that Nasir's activity was a serious threat to them. So he was persecuted and had to flee from Balkh. He took refuge in Mazindaran.

The fact that he visited Mazindaran, is alluded in some of Nasir's poems, and is attested by his contemporary Abul-Maali in Bayanil-adyan. He also tried to propagate the Da'wah but unfortunately was confronted with the same enmity as he had to face in Balkh. Once again he directed his feet towards Balkh and entered Nishapur, where he once again tried his luck at the preaching but had to face the same bitter enemity, so he left for Badakhsan and settled in Yamgan, and started his mission vigorously. He made Yamgan his seat of Dawat, from where he used to send every year a book written by himself in the provinces, in support of his propagation besides missionaries. Most of his work was done at Yamgan. Professor Ivanow says that the political situations of that time did not let him out of this narrow valley which proved to be his prison and from which only death released him. But then too he had some means of communication with the outer world, even with Egypt, otherwise he would not have written his qasidas and perhaps other books.

He also received Da'wat books from Egypt, where as according to local tradition of Badakhshan, Shah Sayyid was busy with converting local inhabitants and even undertook extensive journeys in the East, during which he visited India. All this is narrated in the book called Gawhar-raz written by Nasir Khusraw. It is due to his tireless endeavours that there are lakhs of lsmailis in Afghanistan, Russia, China. Chitral, Hunza, Gilgit and even in the world like Pamir-the roof of the world. He often used to go to neighbouring countries for preaching. It is said that once he went to a place called Munjgan (Lutkoh) in Chitral where he stayed for a short time. The natives of that place today consider the place where he stayed as a Holy Shrine and claim that they possess some books written by him in Arabic which are translated into Persian and Turkish. They also claim that they have a cloak and sandals of the celebrated Hujjat.

His works:- "Except with the spiritual help of the descendants of the Prophet (Tayid-i-al-Rasul). I would have neither had any book to my credit nor anything to teach others. (From Diwan of Nasir Khusraw). Many Persians are poets by nature but the poems of Nasir Khusraw are moral, Philosophical and religious. Nasir Khusraw has written numerous works of the hightest values and interest both in verse and Prose. Most of the works of this great author have been the objects of very careful study by many eminent Western scholars like Bland, Dorn, Ethe, Fagnan, Noldeke, Pertsch, Riev, Schefer and many others. His religious and philosophical views are abundantly illustrated in his verses.

His great works include the most important great Philosophical 'Diwan' which was composed in the miserable years of his exile. The artistic value of his poems is not especially high, but the philosophical matter which still awaits its investigator is of very great importance for the history of Persian Literature. It is a complete encyclopaedia of lsmaili teaching but ofcourse unsystematic one. From linguistic stand point also the work is of extra ordinary interest. A good edition of Persian text appeared in Teheran in 1928 C.E. in which two not very long didactic poems were appended to. Rushanai-nama or the book of felicity which sharply criticises the aristocracy of the Kingdom and praises the peasants is "The nourisher of every living creature".

The best known of Nasir's Prose works is the SafarNama, a description of his pilgrimage to Mecca, which is an exceedingly valuable source of the most varied information. As he appears in his best work Safar Nama, he was by his outlook a country squire, always with keen eyes on matters which belonged to the usual circle of interest of his native land. He pays special attention to land, irrigation facilities, bazars (markets) trade and industry. But unfortunately this work has come down to us only in a very mutilated form and has probably been edited by a Sunni hand. The other works of Nasir are mainly Ismaili text books. Among them first place should be given to Zad-al Musafrin. It is an encyclopaedia of a special character which deals with the most varied questions of a metaphysical and cosmographical nature. The doctrine of Tawil or allegorical interpretation is clearly explained by him such as Paradise, hell, the Resurrection, the torment of tombs, the rising of sun from the west are all allegorically explained in his work.

No less important is the Wadjh-i-Din an introduction to lsmailism, which gradually initiates the reader in lsmaili belief by means of quotations from the Holy Ouran, clearly put together. A number of similar pamphlets like Umm-al-Kitab, which were quite recently fairly widely disseminated among lsmailis of the Pamirs are sometimes credited to our author Sayyidna Nasir Khusraw. He also wrote more than a dozen treatises expounding the doctrines of the lsmailis, among them the Jami al-Hikmatain in which he attempted a harmony between theology and philosophy. His other works are: Khwanal lkhwan, Shish-Fasi, Gushaish wa-Rihaish, Bustanul-uqul, Dalili-Mutahhareen etc. Nasir's works were numerous but many have not survived in perfect form.

Modern lsmaili researcher Nasir Hunzai, has done vast studies of his works and has also translated most of them into Urdu, says that although a considerable portions of Nasir's work is now available in good editions, one cannot yet assert that sufficient light has been thrown upon his striking personality. It would be particularly valuable if his philoso-phical system could be studied as it is of far-reaching impor-tance for the history of thought in Persia and history of lsmailis. Although Hakim Nasir Khusraw was a great philosopher and poet, his main subject remained religion. He used his poetry and philosophy for the propagation of lsmaili dawat. He always took pride in spiritual elevation by Taid-i-lmam (the spiritual help of Imam). To him philosophy was nothing in comparison to the spiritual elevation. He says:

Karkunan-j-khudai ra chubibeeni,
Dil nadihi bazbah flasafah marhooh,
Rui chu soui kouda-odin haq aari,
Zoor-i-tan-o-noor-i-dilat gardad afzoon.

(Translation): "When you will behold the personals of God then you will never be pawned by philosophy. When you will proceed towards God and follow the right path your phybical power and spiritual enlightenment will increase."

The death of Nasir Khusraw:-There is a controversy about the death of Hakim Nasir Khusraw. Some say that he died at the age of 140, but the modern researchers in history are of the opinion that he died between the age of 87 and 100. The great savant Taqi Zadah, in his introduction to the Safarnama holds in support to Haji Khalifa who has mentioned in his book Taqeen-ut-Tawareekh that the great Hakim's death occured in the year 481 A.H. Hakim Nasir Khusraw died at Yamgan and was buried there. His mausoleum is looked upon as a holy shrine by the natives of Badakhshan. Nasir Khusraw was that man of wisdom whose memory would never fade out with time but would live for centuries.

6

Intellectual Life among the Ismailis

In less than a hundred pages Heinz Halm looks at the Fatimid caliphate from an angle that allows readers to appreciate, more than ever before, the intellectual traditions prevalent and encouraged during the Fatimid epoch. He offers a panoramic perspective on the working of the da'wa, the promotion of learning through the establishment of the al-Azhar and the Dar al-'Ilm (House of Knowledge), and the majalis al-hikma (sessions of wisdom) held for instruction in Ismaili doctrines. He discusses intellectual endeavours of the Fatimids both in the context of the sociopolitical conditions of the times as well as in the light of the Shi'i emphasis on knowledge going back to the period of the early Imams. For those interested in history, and especially the history of the Ismailis, this book is highly recommended. The emphasis on teaching and learning will appeal to teachers and educators, particularly those concerned with religious education and the history of education. With a jargonfree, lucid writing style, the book can make an educative reading for any one with an interest in Ismaili thought and history.

The Fatimid Caliphate

The intellectual activities of the Ismailis during the Fatimid period have been described by one author as analogous to that which took place in Europe in the 18th century. This, no doubt, leads one to ask what was it about the Fatimids that led to this flowering of intellectual life? The history of the Ismailis can be understood as the embodiment of one response, among others, to the message contained in the Islamic revelation. While in the Ismaili community's own tradition, the attitudes and beliefs that characterise the Ismailis can be traced back to the lifetime of the Prophet Muhammad, the name 'Ismaili' came to be used in later centuries for the body of followers of Imam Ja'far al-Sadiq "who remained faithful to the line of his descendants through his elder son and designated heir, Imam Isma'il."

The next four Imams succeeding Imam Isma'il evolved an intricate network of agents and emissaries, which came to be known as the da'wa. The movement paved the way for the creation of the Fatimid caliphate in the early part of the tenth century, in North Africa during the time of the Imam al-Mahdi. The Fatimid caliphate remained in North Africa during the reign of the first four Imams al-Mahdi, al-Qa'im, al-Mansur and al-Mu'izz - a period of 64 years from 909 CE to 973 CE. During their time, the Fatimids established and maintained a powerful army and navy. The Imams al-Mahdi and al-Mansur founded the cities of al-Mahdiyya on the Tunisian coast and al-Mansuriyya just south of Qayrawan, respectively, which were named after them. ...al-Mahdi went in person to Tunis; he visited Carthage and other places, and he went along the entire coast, looking along the sea for a site for a city which might make him and his sons after him invulnerable. ...He looked for a long time, and found no better location that that of [what is now] al-Mahdiyya. He therefore built the city there, and made it his capital.

The city of Mahdiyya was a palace city which was inhabited by the royal family and also housed the administration and a naval base. One can still find traces of Fatimid grandeur in the city, including the mosque Imam al-Mahdi built for himself and which was restored in the 1960s. During the reigns of the Imams al-Mansur, the capital city of the Fatimids was moved from Mahdiyya to Mansuriyya, which was to later become a model for the city of Cairo. In 969 CE, Imam al-Mu'izz, "an excellent planner, an efficient organiser and a statesman amply talented in diplomacy," with the help of his general Jawhar, acquired Egypt peacefully. Jawhar, under the Fatimids, took up the governorship of Egypt from 969 CE to 973 CE. During this time the building of the new city of Cairo began and in 970 CE the foundation for the al-Azhar mosque was laid. Around the same time the two holy cities of Makkah and Medina came under Fatimid control. The Imam himself arrived in Cairo in 973 CE.

All the delegations which had greeted him, as well as his sons, brothers and uncles, and the other descendants of al-Mahdi made their entrance with him; he brought with him the coffins of his forebears al-Mahdi, al-Qa'im and al- Mansur .... Stanley Lane-Poole's description of Imam al-Mu'izz may aid one to understand his successful reign: He was a ...born statesman, able to grasp the conditions of success and to take advantage of every point in his favour. He was also highly educated, and not only wrote Arabic poetry and delighted in its literature, but studied Greek, mastered Berber and Sudani dialects, and is even said to have taught himself Salvonic ... His eloquence was such as to move his audience to tears. To prudent statesmanship he added a large generosity, and his love of justice was among his noble qualities. While the Fatimid period led to a flourishing commerce, agricultural advancements and political stability in Egypt and other areas under their influence, it was "in the sphere of intellectual life that Fatimid achievement seems most brilliant and outstanding."

Intellectual Traditions in Fatimid Egypt

In the Shi'i interpretation of Islam and particularly in the Ismaili Tariqah there is a great importance placed on knowledge. The Fatimids' support for learning was a reflection of this importance. Further, in Shi'a theology the

Imam is believed to be the possessor of a special 'ilm, by way of which he interprets the Islamic revelation for his followers. This intimate link between the status of the Imam and knowledge provided a spiritual motivation for the encouragement of intellectual life. The Fatimids came to power through a movement with complex intellectual doctrines. The close relationship between the Fatimid state and the Ismaili da'wa provided another impetus for teaching and learning. Furthermore, the Fatimids were vying against the Abbasids for the leadership of the Muslims.

A part of this competition was to patronise the best minds within Muslim societies. Thus, their rivalry with the Abbasids as well as with the Umayyad rulers of Spain provided another reason for their patronage of intellectual endeavours. The al-Azhar mosque became the primary centre of learning in Fatimid Cairo. The author questions the generally held view that it was a centre for Ismaili da'wa teachings. Instead, he argues that al-Azhar was the place where the external meaning of the law (shar'ia) was taught according to the Ismaili interpretation. These sessions were open to everyone, including women. The inner meaning of the law was taught at the majalis al- hikma which were held in the Imam's palace. These sessions were open only "to initiates who had already pledged their allegiance to the Imam."

All the lectures in 'sessions of wisdom' were reviewed and approved by the Imam prior to their presentation. The sessions were not only for teaching purposes, but they also provided an occasion for submitting charitable dues. The Dar al-'Ilm was founded by the Imam al-Hakim in 1005 CE. The breadth of disciplines studied there was its unique feature and made it stand out from other institutions of learning in its time. The facilities at the Dar al-'Ilm were accessible to all people. "...Lectures were held there by the Qur'an readers, astronomers, grammarians and philologists, as well as physicians." There was tremendous scientific activity as well under the Fatimids. It is best reflected in the life of Ibn al-Haytham.

Born in Basra (in present-day Iraq) in 965 CE, he was polymath and a master of all the scientific fields of his time. He was invited to Cairo by Imam al-Hakim to lead the construction of a dam across the Nile. While this project did not materialise, Ibn al-Haytham went on to compose many works on physics, philosophy, astronomy, mathematics and medicine, including his greatest work the Kitab al-manzir (Treatise on Optics). In this work, Ibn al-Haytham refuted the theory of Euclid and Ptolemy that the eye sends out visual rays to the object of vision, arguing that the form of the perceived object passes into the eye through a transparent body (lens). The correctness of this theory was established several centuries later among European scientists.

The Da'wa Organisation

In common with the other Shi'i groups, the Ismailis hold that spiritual knowledge and wisdom are revealed to humanity through Prophets, who imparted the exoteric law (shar'ia). Thereafter, the knowledge is imparted through the Imam, who is always present to provide the esoteric meaning of the revealed law. "It was on account of his superior 'ilm that the 'Alid Imam was regarded by the Shi'a as the sole instrument through whom the divine purpose could be fulfilled on earth." As is evident from the work of Ismaili scholars, the principle of receiving knowledge from the Imam, however, did not rule out the use of rational or intellectual faculties on the part of the believer. Thus, the acceptance of authority was not simply an act of blind obedience but of human reasoning, recognising its limitations in discovering spiritual mysteries and thus seeking to apprehend them through the mediation of the Imam.

The dialectic of reason and spiritual authority thus underlies the intellectual history of the Ismailis. The Imam used a network of da'is, headed by a chief da'i, to "summon people to follow the true Imam and instruct the individual who 'responds to the summons'...in wisdom." The da'i Ahmad al-Naysaburi offers a concise outline of the talents, characteristics and qualities possessed by an ideal da'i: ...The good qualities of an expert lawyer patience, good theoretical education, intelligence, psychological insight, honesty, high moral character, sound judgement. ...a strong will, generosity, administrative talent, tact and tolerance. ...honest and reliable. ...ready to sacrifice his life and everything for the religion.

The da'i was not only to be well versed in "the Qur'an, the commentary on the Qur'an, the Traditions of the Prophet, stories of the prophets and the Ismaili interpretation of these writings" but he was equally required to be knowledgeable in "logic and philosophy, history and geography." The da'is had special methods that they tended to use during the propagation of the faith. According to the book, Kitab al-'Alim wal-gulam (The Book of the Master and the Disciple) this method included finding a worthy initiate, conducting the oath of secrecy and carrying out a step-by-step induction into wisdom.

The sources tell us that the da'is chose their examples, metaphors and arguments according to their audience. Thus, it is said about a da'i that, To the artisan he spoke about his respective trade: to the tailor, for instance, about needle and thread, eyelet and scissors; to the shepherd about his staff and wrap, and the flock and shepherd's pouch. Thus, the da'is followed a pedagogical principle enunciated in the Qur'an where the Prophet is asked to speak to each person according to his or her abilities. The traditions of teaching and learning in the Fatimid period should be seen as an integral part of Muslim intellectual traditions. On the one hand, they shared many aspects of learning with other Muslim societies.

On the other hand, the Fatimid approach to knowledge had its distinctive features as well, which arose both from the particular socio-political conditions at that time as well as from the status of the Imam in Shi'i theology as the ultimate authority in religious knowledge. These distinctive features included, among others, its da'wa organisation, and its emphasis on batin and ta'wil. The intellectual life in Fatimid times, along with such traditions in other periods of the Ismaili history, is a clear testimony that Ismailism does provide a balanced and integrated approach to reason and faith.

In its bold diversity of intellectual endeavours, the period provides a beacon of hope in a time when need for the appreciation of diversity of intellectual approaches is required perhaps more than in any other time. As the book demonstrates, the thinkers of the Fatimid times engaged with the cutting edge issues of their time and utilised the most advanced forms of thought available to them in this engagement. This venturesome spirit to the issues faced by the community is yet another form of inspiration that makes the period of the Fatimids relevant to our times.

His Highness the Aga Khan became Imam (spiritual leader) of the Shia Imami Ismaili Muslims on July 11, 1957 at the age of 20, succeeding his grandfather, Sir Sultan Mahomed Shah Aga Khan. He is the 49th hereditary Imam of the Shia Imami Ismaili Muslims and a direct descendant of the Prophet Muhammad (peace be upon him and his family) through his cousin and son-in-law, Ali, the first Imam, and his wife Fatima, the Prophet's daughter. Son of Prince Aly Khan and Princess Tajuddawlah Aly Khan, the Aga Khan was born on December 13, 1936, in Geneva. He spent his early childhood in Nairobi, Kenya, and then attended Le Rosey School in Switzerland for nine years. He graduated from Harvard University in 1959 with a BA Honors Degree in Islamic history.

Like his grandfather Sir Sultan Mahomed Shah Aga Khan before him, the Aga Khan has, since assuming the office of Imamat in 1957, been concerned about the well-being of all Muslims, particularly in the face of the challenges of rapid historical changes. Today, the Ismailis live in some 25 countries, mainly in West and Central Asia, Africa and the Middle East, as well as in North America and Western

Europe. Over the five decades since the present Aga Khan became Imam, there have been major political and economic changes in most of these areas. He has adapted the complex system of administering the Ismaili community, pioneered by his grandfather during the colonial era, to a new world of nation-states, which has grown in size and complexity following the independence of the Central Asian Republics of the former Soviet Union.

The Aga Khan has emphasised the view of Islam as a thinking, spiritual faith: one that teaches compassion and tolerance and that upholds the dignity of man, Allah's noblest creation. In the Shia tradition of Islam, it is the mandate of the Imam of the time to safeguard the individual's right to personal intellectual search and to give practical expression to the ethical vision of society that the Islamic message inspires. Addressing as Chairman, the International Conference on the Example (Seerat) of the Prophet Muhammad in Karachi in 1976, the Aga Khan said that the wisdom of Allah's final Prophet in seeking new solutions for problems which could not be solved by traditional methods, provides the inspiration for Muslims to conceive a truly modern and dynamic society, without affecting the fundamental concepts of Islam.

During the course of history, the Ismailis have, under the guidance of their Imams, made major contributions to the growth of Islamic civilisation. The University of Al-Azhar and the Academy of Science, Dar al-Ilm, in Cairo and indeed the city of Cairo itself, exemplify their contributions to the cultural, religious and intellectual life of Muslims. Among the renowned philosophers, jurists, physicians, mathematicians, astronomers and scientists of the past who flourished under the patronage of Ismaili Imams are Qadi al-Numan, al-Kirmani, Ibn al-Haytham (al-Hazen), Nasir eKhusraw and Nasir al-Din Tusi. Achievements of the Fatimid Empire dominate accounts of the early period of Ismaili history, roughly from the beginnings of Islam through the 11th century. Named after the Prophet's daughter Fatima, the Fatimid dynasty created a state that stimulated the development of art, science, and trade in the Mediterranean Near East over two centuries.

Its centre was Cairo, founded by the Fatimids as their capital. Following the Fatimid period, the Ismaili Muslims' geographical centre shifted from Egypt to Syria and Persia. After their centre Alamut (in Persia), fell to Mongol conquerors in the 13th century, Ismailis lived for several centuries in dispersed communities, mainly in Persia and Central Asia but also in Syria, India and elsewhere. In the 1830s, Aga Hassanaly Shah, the 46th Ismaili Imam, was granted the honorary hereditary title of Aga Khan by the Shah of Persia. In 1843, the first Aga Khan left Persia for India, which already had a large Ismaili community. Aga Khan II died in 1885, only four years after assuming the Imamat. He was succeeded by the present Aga Khan's grandfather, and predecessor as Imam, Sir Sultan Mahomed Shah Aga Khan.

In recent generations, the Aga Khan's family has followed a tradition of service in international affairs. The Aga Khan's grandfather was President of the League of Nations and his father, Prince Aly Khan, was Pakistan's Ambassador to the United Nations. His uncle, Prince Sadruddin Aga Khan, was the United Nations' High Commissioner for Refugees, United Nations' Coordinator for assistance to Afghanistan and United Nations' Executive Delegate of Iraq-Turkey border areas. The Aga Khan's brother, Prince Amyn, joined the United Nations Secretariat, Department of Economic and Social Affairs following his graduation from Harvard in 1965. Since 1968, Prince Amyn has been closely involved with the governance of the principal development institutions of the Imamat.

He is Director of the Aga Khan Foundation (AKF) and a member of the Board of the Aga Khan Fund for Economic Development (AKFED) and Chairman of its Executive Committee. Prince Amyn was also deeply involved in the establishment and the development of the Tourism

Promotion Services (TPS). He is also a Director of the Aga Khan Trust for Culture (AKTC). The Aga Khan's eldest child and daughter, Princess Zahra, graduated from Harvard in 1994 with a BA (Honours) Degree in Development Studies, and is the Head of the Social Welfare Department (SWD) located within the Secretariat of the Aga Khan in France. She has policy and management responsibility for the health, education, and planning and building service companies of the Aga Khan Development Network (AKDN). She also plays a key policy role with respect to the other social development institutions of the Network.

His eldest son, Prince Rahim, serves as Executive Director of the Aga Khan Fund for Economic Development (AKFED) and has particular responsibility for the Fund's activities in West Africa. He holds a Bachelor of Arts degree in Comparative Literature from Brown University, Rhode Island, USA, and has attended an executive development programme in Management and Administration at the University of Navarra IESE Business School in Barcelona, Spain. The Aga Khan's second son, Prince Hussain, graduated from Williams College (USA) with a Bachelor of Arts degree and has a Master of International Affairs degree from Columbia's School of International and Public Affairs (SIPA) where his main area of study was Economic and Political Development with a regional focus on the Middle East and North Africa. His youngest son Prince Aly Muhammad was born in 2000.

In consonance with this vision of Islam and a longstanding tradition of service to humanity, the Ismailis have elaborated a well-defined institutional framework to build capacity and improve the quality of life within the communities in which they live. Under the Aga Khan's leadership, this framework expanded and evolved into the Aga Khan Development Network, a group of institutions working to improve living conditions and opportunities in specific regions of the developing world. In every country, these institutions work for the common good of all citizens regardless of their origin or religion. Their individual mandates range from architecture, education and health to the promotion of private sector enterprise, the enhancement of non-government organisations and rural development.

As part of the commemoration of His Highness the Aga Khan's Golden Jubilee which began on 11th July 2007, he has been paying official visits to some 35 countries, using these occasions to recognise the friendship and longstanding support of leaders of state, government and other partners in the work of the Ismaili Imamat, and to set the direction for the future, including the launching and laying of foundations for major initiatives and programmes.

The Ismaili Community

The Shia Imami Ismaili Muslims, generally known as the Ismailis, belong to the Shia branch of Islam. The Shia form one of the two major branches of Islam, the Sunni being the other. The Ismailis live in over 25 different countries, mainly in Central and South Asia, Africa and the Middle East, as well as in Europe, North America and Australia. As Muslims, the Ismailis affirm the fundamental Islamic testimony of truth, the Shahada, that there is no God but Allah and that Muhammad (peace be upon him and his family) is His Messenger. They believe that Muhammad was the last and final Prophet of Allah, and that the Holy Quran, Allah's final message to mankind, was revealed through him. Muslims hold this revelation to be the culmination of the message that had been revealed through other Prophets of the Abrahamic tradition before Muhammad, including Abraham, Moses and Jesus, all of whom Muslims revere as Prophets of Allah.

In common with other Shia Muslims, the Ismailis affirm that after the Prophet's death, Hazrat Ali, the Prophet's cousin and son-in-law, became the first Imam – the spiritual leader – of the Muslim community and that this spiritual leadership (known as Imamat) continues thereafter by hereditary succession through Ali and his wife Fatima, the

Prophet's daughter. Succession to Imamat, according to Shia doctrine and tradition, is by way of *Nass* (Designation), it being the absolute prerogative of the Imam of the Time to appoint his successor from amongst any of his male descendants. His Highness Prince Karim Aga Khan is the 49th hereditary Imam of the Shia Imami Ismaili Muslims. He was born on 13 December 1936 in Geneva, son of Prince Aly Khan and Princess Tajuddawlah Aly Khan and spent his early childhood in Nairobi, Kenya. He attended Le Rosey School in Switzerland for nine years and graduated from Harvard in 1959 with a BA (Honours) in Islamic History. He succeeded his grandfather Sir Sultan Mahomed Shah Aga Khan on 11 July 1957 at the age of 20.

Spiritual allegiance to the Imam and adherence to the Shia Imami Ismaili *tariqah* (persuasion) of Islam according to the guidance of the Imam of the Time, have engendered in the Ismaili Community an ethos of self-reliance, unity, and a common identity. In a number of the countries where they live, the Ismailis have evolved a well-defined institutional framework through which they have, under the leadership and guidance of the Imam, established schools, hospitals, health centres, housing societies and a variety of social and economic development institutions for the common good of all citizens regardless of their race or religion. During the course of history, the Ismailis have, under the guidance of their Imams, made significant contributions to Islamic civilisations, the cultural, intellectual and religious life of Muslims. The University of al-Azhar and the Academy of Science, Dar al-Ilm, in Egypt and indeed the city of Cairo itself, are testimony to this contribution. Among the renowned philosophers, jurists, physicians, mathematicians, astronomers and scientists of the past who flourished under the patronage of Ismaili Imams are Qadi al-Numan, al-Kirmani, Ibn al-Haytham (al-Hazen), Nasir e-Khusraw and Nasir al-Din Tusi.

The Aga Khan, like his grandfather before him, has always been concerned about the wellbeing of all Muslims, particularly the impact on them of the challenges of the rapidly evolving world. Addressing as Chairman, the International Conference on the Example (*Seerat*) of the Prophet Muhammad in Karachi in 1976, he noted that the wisdom of Allah's final Prophet in seeking new solutions for problems which could not be solved by traditional methods, provides the inspiration for Muslims to conceive a truly modern and dynamic society, without affecting the fundamental concepts of Islam.

Since the present Aga Khan assumed the office of Imamat in 1957, there have been major political and economic changes in most of the countries where Ismailis live. He has adapted the complex system of administering the various Ismaili communities, pioneered by his grandfather during the colonial era, to a world of nation states. In the course of that process, Sir Sultan Mahomed Shah Aga Khan, who was twice President of the League of Nations, had already provided a contemporary articulation of the public international role of the Imamat. The Imamat today, under the present Aga Khan, continues this tradition of strict political neutrality.

In designating his successor to the Imamat in 1957, Sir Sultan Mahomed Shah Aga Khan stated in his will:

"In view of the fundamentally altered conditions in the world...due to the great changes which have taken place...I am convinced that it is in the best interests of the Shia Muslim Ismailia Community that I should be succeeded by a young man who has been brought up in the midst of the new age and who brings a new outlook on life to his office of Imam".

Upon succeeding to the leadership of the Ismaili Muslims, the immediate concern of the Aga Khan was therefore to prepare his community, wherever they lived, for the changes that lay ahead. This rapidly evolving situation called for bolder initiatives and new programmes to reflect developing national aspirations. In Africa, Asia and the Middle East, a major objective of the Community's social welfare and economic programmes, until the mid-fifties, had been to create a broad base of businessmen, farmers and professionals. The educational facilities of the Community tended to emphasise secondary-level education. With the coming of independence, each nation's economic aspirations took on new dimensions, focusing on industrialisation and modernisation of agriculture.

The Community's educational priorities had to be reassessed in the context of new national goals. Throughout much of the developing world, Ismailis were affected by radical changes in their respective countries. On the Indian subcontinent, and in South East Asia, major political changes followed the advent of independence, which gave rise to new nation states often followed by dislocation of populations. In certain African countries, the Ismaili community was similarly affected. In 1972, under the regime of the then President Idi Amin, Ismailis and other Asians, despite being citizens of the country and having lived there for generations, were expelled.

The Aga Khan had to take urgent steps to facilitate their resettlement elsewhere, and owing to his personal efforts most found homes, not only in Asia, but also in Europe and North America. Most of the basic resettlement problems were overcome remarkably rapidly. This was due to the adaptability of the Ismailis themselves and in particular to their educational background and their linguistic abilities, as well as the efforts of the host countries and the moral and material support from Community programmes. Such programmes have continued and have, in fact, been given a new orientation so that the Community continues to play a fuller part in the development and progress of the countries of its adoption.

Sir Sultan Mahomed Shah Aga Khan established social development institutions in the subcontinent of India and Pakistan, "for the relief of humanity". They include institutions such as the Diamond Jubilee Investment Trust and the Platinum Jubilee Investments Limited which in turn assisted the growth of various types of co-operative societies. Diamond Jubilee Schools for girls were set up throughout the remote Northern Areas of Pakistan. In addition, scholarship programmes established at the time of the Golden Jubilee to give assistance to needy students were progre-ssively expanded. In East Africa, major social welfare institutions were created, including the Aga Khan Hospital in Nairobi.

Economic development institutions were also established in East Africa. Companies such as the Diamond Jubilee Investment Trust (now Diamond Trust Bank of Kenya) and the Jubilee Insurance company, which are today quoted on the Nairobi Stock Exchange, have become important national economic institutions. In the early 1980s many new social and economic development projects were launched. These range from the establishment of the US$ 300 million international Aga Khan University with its Faculty of Health Sciences and teaching hospital based in Karachi, and the creation of a girls school and a medical centre in the Hunza region, in one of the remote parts of Northern Pakistan bordering on China and Afghanistan, to the establishment of the Aga Khan Rural Support Programme in Gujarat, India, and the extension of existing urban hospitals and primary health care centres in Tanzania and Kenya, in East Africa.

These initiatives form part of an international network of institutions involved in fields that range from education, health and rural development, to architecture and the promotion of private sector enterprise. Known as the Aga Khan Development Network, its constituent institutions, all founded over the past thirty years, include the Aga Khan Foundation, Aga Khan University, Aga Khan Fund for Economic Development and the Aga Khan Trust for Culture, comprising the Aga Khan Program for Islamic Architecture at Harvard University and the Massachusetts Institute of Technology, the Aga Khan Award for Architecture and the

Historic Cities Support Programme. The Network also includes the Aga Khan Health Services and the Aga Khan Education Services, providers of health care, schooling and other educational services in South Asia and East Africa since the beginning of the twentieth century.

These institutions which are open to all, regardless of origin or creed, are described in greater detail in the brochure on the Aga Khan Development Network. In view of the importance that Islam places on maintaining a balance between the spiritual wellbeing of the individual and the quality of his or her life, the Imam's guidance deals with both aspects of the life of his followers. The Aga Khan has encouraged Ismaili Muslims, settled in the industrialised world, to contribute towards the progress of communities in the developing world through various development programmes.

In recent years, Ismaili Muslims, who went to the U.S. and Canada, often as refugees from Asia and Africa, have readily settled into the social, educational and economic fabric of urban and rural centres across the continent. As in the developing world, the Ismaili Muslim Community's settlement and the establishment of community institutions in the developed world have been characterised by an ethos of self-reliance, an emphasis on education and a pervasive spirit of philanthropy. It is this commitment to man's dignity and the relief of humanity that inspires the Ismaili Imamat's philanthropic institutions. Giving of one's competence, sharing one's time, material or intellectual wherewithal with those among whom one lives, for the relief of hardship, pain or ignorance is a deeply ingrained tradition which shapes the social conscience of the Ismaili Muslim community.

7

The Limit of Islamic Orthodoxy

The role that Islam plays in the economic circumstances and development of Muslim nations has been the subject of intense debate among Muslims and non-Muslims alike. Western critics of Islam or "Islamic civilization," such as Bernard Lewis (1990) and Samuel Huntington (1993), have decried its economic irrationality, incompatibility with democracy, and failure to separate religion and state; while scholars such as Edward Said (2001:11) have denounced such thinking as Orientalist essentialism that ignores "the internal dynamics and plurality" of Muslim nations. The debate is not just academic. Today, there are over 1.3 billion Muslims in the world and more than 50 predominantly Muslim nations. Some of the governments of these nations are meeting their citizens' economic needs, while many others are unable or unwilling to address them. The United Nations (2001) ranks countries on a Human Development Index (HDI), based on their life expectancy, literacy rate, school enrollments, and per capita gross domestic product (GDP). Five Muslim-majority nations are rated as having "high" human development, 27 as "medium," and 21 as "low."

Even in Muslim nations with medium standards of living, many citizens live in poverty: one-fifth to one-quarter of the populations of Algeria, Indonesia, and Egypt are poor, as defined by local standards. In the poorest Muslim nations, the bulk of the population suffers from economic deprivation, the gap between rich and poor is wide, unemployment and underemployment are high, educational opportunities are limited, and life expectancies are low. What to do about the depressed economic conditions in which many Muslims live is the subject of much private concern, public discussion, and movement activism throughout the Muslim world. Since the mid-nineteenth century, the debate and mobilization on economic issues often centered on whether socialism or nationalism was the solution.

Islamist (or Islamic fundamentalist) movements seeking the implementation of Islamic law (the shari'a) in an Islamic state as the solution to economic problems began to form in the late 1920s, but public interest in such movements did not take off until most secular, putatively socialist, and/or nationalist regimes failed to solve these problems during the 1960s, 1970s, and 1980s. Today, Islamists vie with Islamic modernists (or reformists), who see the best hope for economic progress in keeping Islam out of legal codes and maintaining strict separation of mosque and state. In this chapter, we move away from the public discourse and skirmishes of movement leaders, academics, and media pundits to explore how moral cosmology—Islamic orthodoxy versus modernism—affects the economic beliefs of ordinary Muslims.

Most scholarly accounts of religion and politics in predominantly Muslim countries have been historical or observational, relying on careful analyses of the speeches and writings of leaders of Islamist and modernist movements, of archival materials on the formation, political activities, and platforms of movement organizations, and, in many cases, on the author's direct experience with the Muslim world. While much has been learned from this work, it is often not based on analyses of interviews with representative samples of Muslims, and we therefore know relatively little about how ordinary Muslim citizens make linkages between their faith and economic preferences. Throughout the world, religious traditionalists are commonly characterized as being to the political right of modernists.

Yet, despite the conventional wisdom, our research in the United States, 21 European countries, and Israel has uncovered a surprising relationship: in many countries where Catholicism, Eastern Orthodoxy, Judaism, or Protestantism predominate, the religiously orthodox are to the right of modernists on cultural issues of abortion, sexuality, family, and gender, but to the left of modernists on issues of economic justice. In this chapter, we examine whether the less recognized element of this pattern—the tendency for the religiously orthodox to be more economically progressive than modernists— holds in countries where Islam, another Abrahamic faith tradition, predominates. We analyze newly available national surveys of seven Muslim-majority nations (Algeria, Bangladesh, Egypt, Indonesia, Jordan, Pakistan, and Saudi Arabia) to test two alternate arguments to explain how orthodoxy versus modernism affects attitudes toward economic justice among Muslims.

Our own Moral Cosmology theory, which, we argue, applies to all of the Abrahamic faith traditions, regardless of their specific theological tenets, posits that because the religiously orthodox are theologically communitarian in seeing individuals as subsumed by a larger community of believers and as subject to the timeless laws and greater plan of God, they are disposed toward economic communitarianism, whereby it is the society's responsibility to provide for those in need, reduce inequality, and intervene in the economy to meet community needs. Modernists, because they are theologically individualistic in that they see individuals themselves as responsible for their destinies and as having to make moral decisions in the context of the times, are inclined toward laissez-faire economic individualism, which sees the poor as responsible for their fates, supports wider income differences to pro- mote individual initiative, and wants government to keep out of the economy. We test this theory, which does not depend on the specific content of faith traditions, against a logical counter thesis, based on what Islamic scripture says about economic matters, that limits the effect of Islamic orthodoxy versus modernism only to government responsibility for the poor.

We find that Islamic orthodoxy—measured as the desire to establish Islamic law—is associated in these countries with the broad economic communitarianism expected by Moral Cosmology theory. In The Protestant Ethic and the Spirit of Capitalism and his other works on religion, Weber was primarily concerned with differences among faith traditions (e.g, Catholicism, Protestantism, ancient Judaism) and their effects on economic beliefs and practices. Our Moral Cosmology theory, with its emphasis on differences within faith traditions among individuals holding different moral cosmologies, complements Weber's. Our argument is that cosmological differences between the religiously orthodox and modernists that had only just begun to appear when Weber wrote The Protestant Ethic (1904–05) exist today within all of the Abrahamic traditions and have similar effects, regardless of the specific tenets of these traditions, on economic and cultural beliefs.

Because differentiation between the orthodox and modernist cosmologies is required for these cosmologies to affect political beliefs, our argument should hold only since modernist and orthodox theological strands became separate within each of the religions of the Book— that is, the development of Reform Judaism, which grew out of Enlightenment ideas and was formalized in documents like the Pittsburgh Platform of 1885; the rise of Islamic "modernism" in the late-nineteenth century; the appearance at the turn of the twentieth century of the "modernist" movement in Catholicism that nearly caused a schism in the Church; and the split between mainline and fundamentalist churches in U.S. and British Protestantism in the early twentieth century. In discussing the effect of moral cosmology on cultural and economic attitudes, we begin with Hunter's (1991:49) distinction between two "fundamentally different con-ceptions of moral authority." The religiously orthodox impulse views God as the ultimate judge of good and evil, regards sacred texts as divinely revealed and hence inerrant and timeless, and sees the deity as playing an active role in people's everyday lives.

In contrast, the modernist 1 impulse views individuals as having to make moral decisions in the con- text of the times, sees religious texts and teachings as human creations that should be considered in cultural context along with other moral precepts, and regards individuals as largely determining their own fates. Note that the modernist impulse encompasses both believers and nonbelievers or secularists. Drawing out the theological and political orientations of these ideal-typical visions of moral authority—or what we prefer to call moral cosmologies, we argue that the religiously orthodox cosmology is theologically communitarian in that it regards individuals as subsumed by a larger community of like-minded believers who are all subject to the laws and greater plan of God. In the orthodox cosmology, timeless religious truths, standards, and laws are seen as having been laid down once and for all by God—laws that the community must uphold and that everyone is obliged to obey.

The theological communitarianism of the orthodox, we argue, inclines them to an authoritarian strand of cultural communitarianism, in which the community must enforce divinely mandated moral standards on abortion, sexuality, family, and gender. Theological communitarianism, however, also inclines the orthodox to economic communitarianism or egalitarianism, whereby it is the state's responsibility to provide for those in needs, reduce the gap between rich and poor, and intervene in the economy so that community needs are met. The communitarianism of orthodoxy entails watching over community members, giving it both a strict side and a caring one, and inclining its adherents toward cultural authoritarianism and economic egalitarianism. Orthodoxy, as we conceive it, does not refer to "doctrinal" orthodoxy or belief in the specific tenets of a faith tradition (e.g., the existence of heaven and hell, the divinity of Jesus), but to a broad theological orientation toward the locus of moral authority with which the orthodox of all of the Abrahamic faith traditions would agree.

In other words, orthodox Catholics, Jews (with a small "o" to distinguish their cosmology from formal membership in the Orthodox branch of Judaism), Muslims, and Protestants adhere to different religious tenets, but they share the broad worldview that the locus of moral authority is God and that legal codes should reflect absolute and timeless divine law. We argue that modernists, in contrast to the orthodox, are theologically individualistic in that they see individuals as largely responsible for their own moral decisions and fates. The modernist cosmology combines support for individual choice and freedom with an expectation of individual responsibility, inclining its adherents to cultural individualism or libertarianism, where- by the resolution of a pregnancy is seen as a woman's private decision, individual freedom in sexual expression is allowed, and husbands and wives should decide for themselves how to divide their labor or structure their partnership.

The theological individualism of modernists also inclines them to laissez-faire economic individualism or inegalitarianism, whereby individuals are held responsible for their economic fortunes—good or bad—and the solution to poverty and inequality is greater effort and initiative by the poor themselves rather than government efforts to improve their lot, equalize incomes, or redistribute economic resources by nationalizing businesses. Our argument is, of course, probabilistic, not deterministic, and some modernists hold communitarian economic beliefs, such as socialism or communism. We argue and will show that the individualism that characterizes both the modernist moral cosmology and laissez-faire economics inclines modernists toward such economic individualism more than toward economic communitarianism.

While orthodoxy and modernism are ideal types, representing polar extremes, our Moral Cosmology theory treats cosmology as a matter of degree, with people's cultural and economic attitudes tending to reflect where they are on the continuum of orthodoxy/modernism. In this chapter, we focus on the economic consequences of the continuum of moral cosmology for Muslims— the tendency for the Islamic orthodox to be more economically egalitarian than Islamic modernists. Islam, a religion of the Book along with Judaism and Christianity, has a sacred text that is taken by Muslims as divine revelation. The vast majority of Muslims—some scholars would say all— regard the Qur'an as divinely revealed, inerrant, and to be taken literally. In this sense, (nearly) all Muslims are "orthodox," and a question about the liter- al truth of the Qur'an, such as that which we used to help distinguish the orthodox from modernists among Catholics, Jews, and Protestants based on their beliefs about the Bible, probably would not distinguish among Muslims.

Yet one dimension of orthodoxy/modernism that does differentiate among Muslims is the extent to which they believe that the Qur'an and other sacred texts of Islam should be the sole basis of the legal system and the state. The establishment of Islamic law, which is based on sacred Islamic texts, would be the fulfillment of the orthodox belief that it is the responsibility of the community to uphold timeless divine law. Orthodox Muslims differ from modernist Muslims in wanting Islamic law to constitute the sole legal foundation of the state, and it is this distinction and its consequences for economic attitudes that is our focus here. The distinction between Muslims who would apply Islamic law in all realms of life and those who would not is central both to divisions within Muslim publics at large and to the agendas of many of the major political and intellectual movements of Muslims of the last century and a quarter. Since the Egyptian Hasan al-Banna founded the Society of Muslim Brothers in 1928, the goal of Islamists has been the implementation of the shari'a in all realms of life as the sine qua non of an Islamic state.

The primacy of this goal reflects the fact that religion and state were once one in the first Islamic state of the seventh century, where the Prophet Muhammad was both the religious and political leader. While orthodox Muslims are not monolithic in their interpretation of the shari'a, they share the desire to implement Islamic law as the sole legal foundation, rather than allow legal codes to emerge through pluralistic political negotiation and compromise between competing interests, including secular ones. The economic communitarianism that Moral Cosmology theory expects among the orthodox of all of the Abrahamic faith traditions manifested itself historically and still does today in many Muslim countries in practices of patrimonialism, whereby the clan or tribal leaders were/are responsible for the well-being of the community's needy. It can also be seen in "Islamic economics," which was developed in late-colonial India of the 1940s by Sayyid Abul A'la Mawdudi (1903–79), the Islamist founder of Jamaat-i-Islami.

Apart from prohibiting riba (excessive interest) and collecting and distributing zakat (an obligatory charitable contribution to the poor), the details of Islamic economics are vague, although it appears that this would not involve as extensive control of the economy by the state as in socialist command economies, but would require a greater commitment—much of it voluntary on the part of believers—to looking out for the poor and to maintaining more equitable economic dealings than is true in laissez-faire capitalism. Islamic "modernism," as the movement came to be called, emerged during the late nineteenth century, especially in India and Egypt.

The theological individualism that Moral Cosmology theory assumes of modernists in all Abrahamic traditions can be seen in an important theological distinction made by early Islamic modernists. Moulavi Chiragh Ali (1844–95), a noted Indian modernist, distinguished between the revealed law of the Qur'an, which is immutable and timeless, and the common law, which is the product of Muslim history and reflects the circumstances of each age. He argued that since Islamic law was, in part, a product of the times, it could not constitute a timeless moral code for Muslims, thus necessitating a new legal frame in accord with the standards of modernity. A distinction with similar implications was made by the Egyptian modernist, Muhammad Abduh (1849–1905), between ibadat (acts of worship) and mu-amalat (commercial or civil acts related to the affairs of the world).

According to 'Abduh, while Islamic texts mandated specific rules regarding the worship of Allah, they included only broad principles on how humans should relate to each other, thus leaving it up to humans to apply these in specific circumstances. This not only allowed but also required the application of ijtihad (independent reasoning) in the development of legal codes. The distinction made by Chiragh Ali and Abduh allows humans much discretion in organizing their affairs, including their economic structures and individual economic behavior. An essay by an anonymous Indian modernist, originally published in 1877–80 and included in Moaddel and Talattof's (2000:123–35) anthology, argued that Islamic laws prohibiting the taking of interest and limiting individual discretion in passing on estates were breeding "listlessness and inactivity" among Muslims in India, throwing many into poverty.

The solution was not for government to provide free education, which only "lower[s] our character by rendering weaker the motives for the exercise of our energies and by diminishing our prudence or responsibility to ourselves," but to understand that "there is no connection whatsoever, either necessary or even contingent, between Religion in its pure sense and civil and juridical laws." Only the separation of mosque and state would result in "wider diffusion of habits of energy and patience, self-exertion and self-dependence." The essay concludes with an homage to the Indian modernist leader, Sir Sayyid Ahmad Khan (1817–98), who sought to reconcile Enlightenment values and natural law with Islamic belief through the application of ijtihad to sacred texts, and who was a strong advocate of laissez-faire capitalism and a limited role of government.

Muslim modernists today seek a strict separation of mosque and state and resist the implementation of Islamic law. Kurzman (1998:19, 1999) notes that such Muslims object to the implementation of the shari'a on several grounds, including that "divine revelation has left the form of government for human construction," that political power would corrupt religious rulers, and that "the Qur'an refers to the shari'a as a path, not as a ready-made system of law, waiting to be put in practice." While the writings of orthodox and modernist thinkers and the political positions of the movements they inspired seem to be in accord with Moral Cosmology theory, whether these movements represent the sentiments of ordinary Muslims is an empirical question that can be resolved only with data for individuals. We have found, for example, that in the United States, where the most visible movements and leaders appearing to represent the religiously orthodox have a conservative, laissez-faire economic agenda, the orthodox are to the left of modernists on economic issues in a General Social Survey (GSS) of Americans.

Thus, in accord with Moral Cosmology theory, which expects similar effects of orthodoxy/modernism on economic attitudes in all of the Abrahamic faith traditions, we test the following hypothesis on nationally representative samples of Muslims:

Hypothesis 1: Religiously orthodox Muslims, as indicated by their desire to implement Islamic law as the sole law of the land in their country, will be more economically communitarian or egalitarian than their modernist counterparts in supporting (1) government efforts to improve the lot of the poor and needy, (2) greater equality of incomes, and (3) government nationalization of private business and industry. Moral Cosmology theory is not denomination- specific in that it does not depend on the content of religious texts. It assumes that the orthodox of all of the Abrahamic faith traditions differ from modernists in their economic orientations, regardless of the specific doctrinal positions on economic matters in their religious texts. In our earlier analyses of Judeo-Christian traditions, we argued that the Torah and the Bible are ambiguous regarding economic matters.

Yet are there clear economic messages in Islam that might impel those who seek to build a state around it to endorse communitarian economic relations? We test Moral Cosmology theory against the logical counter-thesis that the tenets of Islam on economic matters can explain any tendency for the more text-bound Islamic orthodox to be more communitarian than Islamic modernists. In contrast to the sacred texts of Judaism and Christianity, the Qur'an is very specific about the obligation of every Muslim to give to the poor, orphaned, and widowed, "so that wealth may not merely make a circuit among the wealthy". The third of five pillars of the faith, zakat (purification), requires Muslims with the financial means to give at least 2.5 percent of their net assets (not just their income) annually to the needy. The institution of zakat changed during Muhammad's lifetime from voluntary private charity in Mecca, where he and his followers were in a minority and powerless, to a compulsory obligation of the faith, with specific rates, collected and distributed by state-run institutions, once Muhammad and his followers migrated to Medina in 622 and established the first Islamic state.

The Hadith (2:24:537), the sacred text that records the sayings of the Prophet, reports Muhammad as saying, "Allah has made it obligatory for them to pay zakat from their property; it is to be taken from the wealthy among them and given to the poor" (emphasis added). Among the countries considered here, zakat is collected and distributed by the state in Pakistan and Saudi Arabia; in the other countries, because they are largely secular states, it is left to individuals to make contributions directly to the needy or to organizations serving them. While the Qur'an is clear in requiring those with financial means to give to the poor and in providing mechanisms whereby the state will look out for the needy, it neither enjoins economic equality nor questions the right of individuals to hold private property. State ownership of property is not directly addressed; contemporary proponents and opponents of government ownership alike cite scripture to support their stances, suggesting that Islam takes no clear position on this.

In the Qur'an (20:131), differences in wealth and property are viewed as a test by Allah of the charitableness of the wealthy but as unimportant after death. While there is a spiritual equality of believers before Allah, there is no assumption that such equality does or should hold in human societies. A well- known proverb attributed to the Prophet states, "Men are equals like the teeth of a comb; one has precedence over another only in well-being". We conclude that while Islamic texts mandate efforts to provide for those in need, they do not enjoin equality of income or wealth, nor sanction violation of the private property of others, nor take a clear position on government ownership of industry as a means of meeting community needs.

Thus, we test Moral Cosmology theory (H 1), which posits broad egalitarian/communitarian effects of orthodoxy in all religions of the Book, against a hypothesis based strictly on the economic directives of Islamic texts, which limits the effect of orthodoxy vs. modernism to the one clear economic directive of Islam, which is the state's responsibility to care for the needy:

Hypothesis 2: Religiously orthodox Muslims, as indicated by their desire to implement Islamic law as the sole law of the land in their country, will be more supportive than their modernist counterparts of government efforts to care for the needy, but will not differ from modernists in their desire for more equal incomes or their willingness to nationalize private property or businesses. Governments of Muslim-majority nations differ in their ability or willingness to meet the economic needs of their citizens. We expect that failure to meet material, educational, and health needs will increase popular demand for economic reform, while maintenance of a high standard of living will reduce the desire for such reform. Hashmi (2004), for example, has shown that the failure of Bangladesh's "socialist-secular-Bengali-nationalist" government during the 1970s to bring about the promised socialist utopia increased the popularity of Islamist groups calling for social justice and economic reform.

Thus we hypothesize, Hypothesis 3: The lower a country's standard of living (life expectancy, literacy, school enrollments, and per capita GDP), the greater will be support for government efforts to improve the lot of the poor and needy, reduce inequality of incomes, and nationalize private business and industry. How strong an effect that support for implementation of Islamic law has on the desire for egalitarian economic reforms should depend on the country's standard of living. In countries where people's basic needs are not being met by the state, the desire to implement the shari'a will be more strongly associated with egalitarian positions than in countries where these needs are being met; the general condition of the population in the former countries more seriously fails to meet communitarian economic norms.

Thus we hypothesize, Hypothesis 4: In countries with low standards of living (life expectancy, literacy, school enrollments, and per capita GDP), support for implementing Islamic law will be more strongly associated with support for government efforts to improve the lot of the poor and needy, reduce inequality of incomes, and nationalize private business and industry than in countries with higher standards of living.

Contrasting the economic rationality or self-interest assumed by free market economists with the voluntary communitarianism on the part of Muslims of all classes assumed by Islamic economics, Kuran (2004:42) describes the task of Islamic economics as "to transform selfish and acquisitive Homo economicus into a paragon of virtue, Homo Islamicus." Kuran's argument is that Islamic economics, not Islamic theology, assumes this communitarianism on everyone's part; a classic study of the terms used in the Qur'an argued that Islamic theology is couched in the language of commerce, trade, and economic rationalism: "The mutual relations between God and man are of a strictly commercial nature. Allah is the ideal merchant. Life is a business, for gain or loss. He who does a good or an evil work ("earns" good or evil), receives his pay for it, even in this life". We contrast the assumption in Islamic economics of voluntary communitarianism by all classes with a rational choice, "underdog principle" that posits that the advantaged will be less economically communitarian than the disadvantaged, each class reflecting its economic self-interest.

Since we see the assumption of Islamic economics that advantaged Muslims will voluntarily support egalitarian economic arrangements as ignoring the effect of class on communitarianism, we hypothesize, Hypothesis 5: Muslims with more education, higher income, or who are in the middle or upper class will be less supportive of government efforts to care for the needy, of efforts to equalize incomes, and of government nationalization of businesses and industry than those who are less educated, poorly paid, and in the working class or unemployed. If, however, there are no class differences in Muslims' economic attitudes and if these attitudes are communitarian, this would support the assumption of Islamic economics that the advantaged can be counted on in the establishment of a more just Islamic state.

Seven Muslim- Majority Nations

The seven countries examined here are among the most

populous and influential Muslim nations in the world. They include Indonesia, with the world's largest Muslim population, Pakistan with the second largest, and Bangladesh, Egypt, and Algeria, with the fourth, fifth and ninth largest Muslim populations. Including Jordan and Saudi Arabia, just under half of the world's 1.3 billion Muslims lives in these countries. While there are religious minorities of Coptic Christians in Egypt, Hindus in Bangladesh, and Christians, Hindus, and Buddhists in Indonesia, these nations are overwhelmingly Muslim, ranging from 88 percent in Bangladesh to 99 percent in Algeria and Saudi Arabia. Most of these populations are predominantly Sunni, with Shi'a making up about 20 percent of Pakistanis and 15 percent of Saudi citizens. Standards of living in these countries range from low to moderate.

The United Nations' (2001) HDI ranges from .47 in Bangladesh (the same as Haiti, the poorest country in the Western Hemisphere) to .75 in Saudi Arabia. Four of these countries—Algeria, Egypt, Indonesia, and Saudi Arabia—are what Mahdavi (1970) calls "rentier states," whose government and economy depend on substantial rents from oil and hydrocarbon sales (Saudi Arabia and Algeria), transit charges (Egypt, from the Suez Canal), or revenue from tourism (Bali in Indonesia, and, to a lesser extent, Egypt). In rentier states, only a small proportion of the population is involved in the enterprises creating most of the nation's wealth, making most people's income less dependent on their own efforts and skills than on who they know (personal relationships and crony capitalism), their ethnicity, or their citizenship.

Islam is the state religion of Saudi Arabia, and this is nominally the case in Algeria, Bangladesh, Jordan, and Pakistan. The legal systems of these countries generally incorporate Islamic law in some form; the only exception is Bangladesh, which has no shari'a courts. Saudi Arabia has had the shari'a as the sole basis of its legal code and the Qur'an as its constitution since its founding in 1932. In the remaining five nations, the shari'a is applied only to family matters (e.g., divorce, marriage, child custody, inheritance); criminal and civil law are based on non-Islamic legal codes. Whether the shari'a should be the sole basis of all law, should apply to specific realms of life, or should not apply at all is a matter of intense discussion and activism in all seven countries. Islamist movements seeking to implement Islamic law in all realms of life and condemning the current, more limited applications of this—ranging from those endorsing violence to those working within the political system to effect gradual change—exist in each of the seven nations considered here.

Among the more prominent Islamist movements are the Society of Muslim Brothers in Egypt and Jordan, the Islamic Salvation Front (FIS) in Algeria, Laksar Jihad (Holy War Brigade) in Indonesia, and Jamaat-i-Islami in Bangladesh and Pakistan. Islamists in Saudi Arabia challenge both the monarchy and the religious establishment that supports it, seeking to rid the kingdom's laws of anything that they consider to be inconsistent with the shari'a and thus establish a truly Islamic state. Modernist thinkers and movements, including Muhammadiyah in Indonesia, resist the agenda of the Islamists in each of these societies.

The data with which we test our hypotheses are from the fourth wave of the World Values Surveys (WVS), conducted from 1999 to 2003, which surveyed 81 societies. Our sample consists of Muslims living in seven Muslim-majority countries: Algeria, Bangladesh, Egypt, Indonesia, Jordan, Pakistan, and Saudi Arabia. The surveys of six other Muslim-majority nations in the WVS (Albania, Azerbaijan, Bosnia- Herzegovina, Iran, Morocco, and Turkey) did not include our key independent variable—support for Islamic law. Analyses are limited to respondents ages 18 years and older who self-identify as Muslim. In Algeria, which is 99 percent Muslim, the respondent's religion was not asked; thus we include every respondent. In some of our analyses, we pool the samples for all seven countries into a single sample, weighting each sample proportional to the size of the country's Muslim population.

The surveys of the seven nations considered here are among the first to assess public opinion in predominantly Muslim countries. Some of the surveys were conducted under difficult circumstances, including the temporary firing of Mustafa Hamarneh by the University of Jordan. Did the politically repressive climate in some of these countries affect the candor with which respondents answered questions? While it undoubtedly did affect some respondents, Inglehart and Norris (2003) found that respondents in Muslim nations surveyed in the WVS were no different from respondents in Western nations in their willingness to express support for democracy. To partly take into account the possibility that political repression in a country affected respondents' willingness to voice opinions on the establishment of Islamic law and economic matters, we control for "repression" (described in the next section) in analyses of the pooled sample. To measure the orthodoxy/modernism continuum among Muslims we use a question on support for establishing Islamic law as the sole basis of jurisprudence: We recode responses so that high values indicate support for implementing the shari'a while low values indicate opposition to this (1 = 5, 2 = 4, 4 = 2, 5 = 1).

The response categories, because they differ from the standard Likert scale (i.e., strongly agree, somewhat agree, neither agree nor disagree, somewhat disagree, strongly disagree), may have resulted in some acquiescence bias, although other surveys of some of the same countries, using Likert scales, found similar high levels of support for implementing Islamic law as we find. Because popular discourse and Islamist movements in each of these countries center on whether the shari'a should be the sole basis of all law, should be limited to family matters, or should have no influence on legal codes, the question should be easily interpretable as referring to the application of Islamic law in all realms of life. Using the degree of support for implementing the shari'a to measure Islamic orthodoxy/modernism is consistent with the orthodox desire to establish and uphold what they see as divinely ordained eternal laws that apply to all members of the community, and with the contrary modernist belief that legal codes should reflect the times and draw upon multiple sources, including secular ones. In our research on Judeo-Christian nations, we used agreement with the statement "Right and wrong should be based on God's laws," among other items, to distinguish the orthodox from modernists.

While implementation of the shari'a has both religious and political implications, this is not surprising in the case of Islam since Muhammad unified religion and the state in the first Islamic state of the seventh century. Nonetheless, under the possibility that the most politicized Muslims might be both more supportive of establishing Islamic law solely for political motives and more favorable toward economically progressive policies, we control for discusses politics, based on the question: "When you get together with your friends, would you say you discuss political matters (3) frequently, (2) occasionally, or (1) never?" We use this to indicate the most rudimentary level of politicization—debating political issues with others—in the absence of measures of higher levels of political involvement (e.g., membership in political organizations, participation in protest). If support for implementing the shari'a is merely capturing politicization, then inclusion of this variable should reduce its effects on economic attitudes.

It could also be argued that any effect of support for implementing the shari'a on economic attitudes may be due to an underlying nationalism or rejection of the West (including Western jurisprudence, foreign domination of the economy, debt dependency on the West, neoliberal economic restructuring required by the IMF or World Bank, and globalization), which could produce egalitarian economic stances. Thus, we control for national pride, the best indicator of nationalistic values in the WVS, and strongly linked, in a recent survey of nationalism in Iraq, to oppositional attitudes toward foreign occupation. Respondents were asked, "How proud are you to be [nationality]," and responses are coded (1) not at all proud, (2) not very proud, (3) quite proud, or (4) very proud. We also test whether advantaged Muslims are less egalitarian than disadvantaged Muslims, as (H5) posits following the underdog principle, or whether Muslims of all classes are equally willing to support egalitarian economic arrangements, as the voluntary communitarianism assumed by Islamic economics implies. In our models, education is in eight ordered categories ranging from (1) no formal education to (8) university- level education, with degree.

Household income before taxes, counting all wages, salaries, pensions, and other income, is coded in deciles by the local investigators in each country—with (1) as the lowest decile and (10) as the highest. Occupation/employment status is a dummy variable series identifying owner/manager, professional, white collar, blue collar, army, student, housewife/retired, and unemployed (reference category). Mosque attendance is how often, apart from weddings and funerals, the respondent attends religious services, and ranges from (1) never or practically never to (7) more than once a week. We make no prediction for the effect of mosque attendance since it is an indicator of orthopraxy (engaging in the rituals and practices of a faith tradition) rather than of orthodoxy, the focus of our theory. While for Muslims, orthopraxy is at least as important as orthodoxy, we later show that it is generally not contact with fellow worshipers in itself but whether the individual holds the orthodox moral cosmology that leads to communitarian economic stances.

Nonetheless, following Brooks (2002), we test with an interaction term whether support for Islamic law, coupled with frequent mosque attendance, leads to exceptionally high economic communitarianism because exposure to clergy, sacred texts, and fellow worshipers may intensify the effects of the respondent's moral cosmology. The highest correlation between support for the shari'a and mosque attendance is .261 in Algeria, but to reduce multicollinearity in analyses including the interaction of these, we centered each of them on its country mean (or the pooled mean for analyses of the pooled sample) before creating the interactions. We also control for age coded in years; gender, coded as (1) male and (0) female; marital status, coded as (1) single and (0) married, widowed, or divorced; and urban, measured as size of town in eight categories from (1) under 2,000 to (8) 500,000 or more. In analyses of the pooled sample of seven countries, we test for the additive effect of standard of living (under H3) and the interactive effect of this with support for Islamic law (under H4). The United Nation's (2001) HDI is used as a measure of standard of living. We also control for repression, measured as the country's 2000–01 rating by Freedom House.

To test for the interactive effects of support for Islamic law with HDI and repression, we include interactions of these variables, computed after centering each variable. While the Gini coefficient, a measure of economic inequality, might also be expected to affect economic attitudes, this is unavailable for Saudi Arabia and has far less effect on economic attitudes than HDI in the remaining countries. We analyze the effect of moral cosmology and socioeconomic characteristics on three economic attitudes that contrast communitarian/ egalitarian economic policies with individualistic policies. Both our Moral Cosmology theory (H1), which applies to all of the Abrahamic traditions, and the alternate hypothesis (H2), which is based specifically on the tenets of Islam, lead us to expect an association between cosmology and support for government efforts to care for the needy. Everyone provided for is the respondent's self-placement on a 1 to 10 scale, where (1) indicates complete agreement that "people should take more responsibility to provide for themselves" and (10) complete agreement that "the government should take more responsibility to ensure that everyone is provided for."

Moral Cosmology theory (H 1) posits that support for the shari'a should also be positively associated with a desire for greater income equality. Because Islamic texts do not enjoin economic equality, the alternate hypothesis, (H 2), posits no effect of support for the shari'a on the belief that incomes should be equalized. We test these hypotheses using the variable more equal incomes, where (1) is complete agreement that "we need larger income differences as incentives for individual effort" and that "incomes should be made more equal." Finally, while Moral Cosmology theory expects support for Islamic law also to be positively associated with a desire for government nationalization of businesses as a means to meet community needs (H), Islamic sacred texts appear to regard private property as inviolable and take no clear position on government ownership, leading us to hypothesize under the alternate hypothesis, (H 2), that orthodox Muslims will not differ from modernist Muslims on nationalization of businesses.

We test these hypotheses using more government ownership, where (1) indicates complete agreement that "private ownership of business and industry should be increased" and that "government ownership of business and industry should be increased." Because Moral Cosmology theory and the alternate hypothesis differ on which economic attitudes are linked with support for Islamic law, we analyze these attitudes separately. We use ordinary least squares (OLS) regression to estimate the effect of support for Islamic law, socioeconomic characteristics, and control variables on economic attitudes in each country. Since direction is predicted for most independent variables (positive for shari'a and negative for socioeconomic variables and HDI), we use one-tailed tests of significance for these variables and two-tailed tests when direction is not predicted (mosque attendance, age, gender, marital status, and urban). In our analyses of the pooled sample of all countries, we cannot use hierarchical linear modeling (HLM) to estimate the effects of individual-level vs. country-level variables on economic attitudes, because the small number of countries precludes this. In our OLS analyses of the pooled samples, we include the additive effects of HDI and repression and the interactive effects of each of these with support for the shari'a.

Note that because we limit our analyses to self-identified Muslims and in no country do more than 0.7 percent of respondents report that they do *not* believe in God, there are almost no secularists or nonbelievers in the samples. The desire to implement Islamic law is widely held among Muslims in the seven Muslim- majority nations considered here. There is, however, considerable variation across countries, with Saudi Arabians showing the strongest support and Indonesians the least. Popular support for implementing Islamic law in all realms of life is loosely connected to which domains the *shari'a* currently covers in each country. In Saudi Arabia, where the *shari'a* is the sole basis of the legal code, nearly three-fourths of the population (73.8 percent) regards implementation of this as "very important" to good government.

In countries where Islamic law applies only to family matters, lower levels of support are found for instituting the *shari'a* as a total system of law (53.7 percent in Jordan, 48.0 percent in Egypt, 36.7 percent in Algeria, 36.4 percent in Pakistan, and 15.0 percent in Indonesia). In Bangladesh, where Islamic law has no role in the legal system, 21.7 percent regard establishing the *shari'a* in all realms of life as "very important." The strong popular support in Saudi Arabia, Jordan, and Egypt for implementing the *shari'a* suggests that were these countries to become less repressive, the democracies established might not resemble what Western promoters of democracy in the Muslim world would envision. While very few respondents say that implementation of the *shari'a* is "not important," disinterest in implementing this is highest in Bangladesh and Indonesia (9.2 and 9.3 percent, respectively), perhaps due to the presence and influence of Hindus in the former and of Christians, Hindus, and Buddhists in the latter, and the resulting syncretic nature of Islam in these countries.

The distinction among Muslims in these nations is not between equal-sized groups of the religiously orthodox and modernists. As we found in our analyses of predominantly Christian and Jewish nations, populations rarely fall into polarized camps along cosmological lines. Instead, there is a continuum of belief, and in some countries the distribution is skewed toward the orthodox pole, in others it is approximately normal, while in still others it is skewed toward the modernist pole. Moral cosmology is a matter of degree, and we will show that the strongest advocates of the *shari'a* are more communitarian in their economic positions than those who are less enthusiastic, or not at all, about implementing this.

Recall that responses range from (1) economically individualistic to (10) economically communitarian, making the midpoint 5.5. Among Muslims in these countries, popular support is greatest for government taking more responsibility to ensure that everyone is provided for, as opposed to individuals taking more responsibility for themselves (6.06 in the pooled sample). Preferences between making incomes more equal and increasing income differences as an incentive to individual effort lean toward the latter (4.24 in the pooled sample). The relative disinterest in equalizing incomes may be because the Qur'an does not enjoin economic equality but does mandate *zakat* to care for those in needs.

Yet surprisingly, since the Qur'an also appears to hold private property as inviolable and takes no clear position on nationalization of businesses, Muslims support increasing government ownership of economic resources (5.64) almost as much as they support increasing government efforts to care for the needy. Muslims living in countries with higher living standards tend to be less supportive of increasing government efforts to care for the poor (the correlation is –.21) and equalizing incomes (–.45), as expected under (H), but more supportive of increasing government ownership (.34). We explore these relationships through multivariate analyses of the pooled sample.

To put the economic stances of Muslims in a global context, Norris and Inglehart report that residents of predominantly Muslim nations surveyed in the WVS are more likely than residents of predominantly Catholic, Eastern Orthodox, or Eastern (Asian) nations, but not Protestant nations, to favor increased government responsibility for everyone, more likely to support greater government ownership than the residents of all except Eastern Orthodox and Eastern nations, but less likely to favor equalizing incomes than residents of all except Eastern Orthodox nations. From our Moral Cosmology theory (H1), we expect support for implementing the *shari'a,* as an indicator of religious orthodoxy among Muslims, to be associated with communitarian economic attitudes, including support for the government taking more responsibility to provide for everyone, for a more equal income distribution, and for greater government ownership of businesses and industries.

The alternate hypothesis (H 2), based on the specific economic tenets of Islam, posits a narrower effect of orthodoxy, only on support for increased government responsibility for everyone. We find strong confirmation in the bivariate associations for the broad communitarian effects expected under Moral Cosmology theory. The desire to implement Islamic law as the sole legal foundation of the state is positively and significantly associated with support for greater government effort to provide for everyone in six of the seven countries (the exception being Saudi Arabia), with wanting to equalize incomes in three countries (Pakistan, Indonesia, and Algeria), and with support for increased government ownership in six countries (the exception being Indonesia). The effects of orthodoxy on support for greater government effort to care for the needy could be explained by both hypotheses, but the totality of effects, including those on support for equalizing incomes and greater government ownership of businesses, can be explained only by Moral Cosmology theory.

Effects of support for Islamic law on the desire for increased government responsibility for all and nationalization of businesses are stronger in countries with low standards of living (especially Bangladesh) than in those with higher living standards (Saudi Arabia and Jordan); the correlations of HDI with these coefficients across countries are –.49 and –.32, respectively. HDI has little effect on the strength of the relationship between support for the *shari'a* and equalizing incomes (.13). We explore these relationships further in analyses of the pooled sample. We estimate the probability of obtaining this number of significant coefficients by chance very conservatively at .0000176. Had we posited an opposite effect of orthodoxy among Muslims, we would have found no support for this in any of the seven nations. We conclude from these analyses of each country that there is strong support for the broad effects of religious orthodoxy on egalitarian economic beliefs that our Moral Cosmology theory posits.

To examine further the economic effects of support for Islamic law and how these vary depending on country-level factors (e.g., standard of living, political repression), we conduct OLS analyses on the pooled sample for the seven countries. Support for establishing the *shari'a* is positively associated in the pooled sample with wanting greater government responsibility for everyone, more equal incomes, and increased government ownership of businesses and industries. Thus, supporters of Islamic law who go to the mosque frequently are especially likely to favor equalizing incomes, perhaps because they are receiving reinforcement for their communitarian beliefs from like-minded clergy and fellow worshipers.

With all controls added, the standardized coefficients indicate that support for establishing Islamic law is the single-most important factor in support for greater government responsibility to care for everyone and the third-most important factor (after education and HDI) in support for increased government ownership of businesses. We made no prediction as to the effect of mosque attendance on economic communitarianism. The inconsistent effects of mosque attendance—positive on equalizing incomes but negative on greater government ownership—may arise for a number of reasons. Mosques differ in type from government-controlled to independent, in theological orientation, in whether a political message is delivered, and in the content of that message. Attendance may occur for nonreligious reasons (e.g., out of a desire to appear faithful or socially acceptable to others, to make business or political contacts, or for purely social reasons).

Nonattendance need not indicate a lack of religious commitment; it can arise from distrust of the religious leadership, for example, because this is appointed by, accommodates to, or colludes with a largely secular and/or corrupt regime. Most important, while the communitarianism of orthodoxy is a broad worldview that is not limited in its implications to the narrow community of fellow worshipers, the sense of community created through mosque attendance may be limited to the specific congregation. In a U.S. study, Ryle and Robinson (2006) found that the orthodox cosmology was the strongest predictor of a sense of community with neighbors, friends, fellow congregants, co-workers/fellow students, and ethnic group members, while frequent attendance at religious services had no effect in promoting such feelings beyond attachment to fellow congregants. The Islamist economic program of "Islamic economics" assumes that even advantaged Muslims will voluntarily opt for more egalitarian economic relations. From the underdog principle, we hypothesized (H) to the contrary, that class matters in economic attitudes; advantaged Muslims will be less supportive of government efforts to care for the needy, equalize incomes, and nationalize businesses.

The economic self-interest expected by the underdog principle is evident in these models, with highly educated people and those with high household incomes being less supportive of progressive economic reforms, with one exception, which we later discuss. Contrary to this principle, unemployed people are less supportive of increasing government responsibility for everyone and equalizing incomes than almost any other occupational category, although otherwise there is no systematic effect of occupation (e.g., between owners/managers and blue-collar workers) on economic attitudes. Overall, there is more support for the rational choice, underdog principle than for the assumption of Islamic economics that advantaged Muslims can be counted on to support communitarian economic arrangements.

Discussing politics frequently or having a strong sense of national pride, do not diminish the effects of support for Islamic law on economic attitudes. Muslims who discuss politics frequently are less likely to want greater government responsibility for the needy and greater government ownership but more likely to want incomes to be equalized. An interaction term, testing the possibility that supporters of Islamic law who are politicized are exceptionally egalitarian, is not significant for any of the economic attitudes (details available on request). Nor are the effects of orthodoxy due to any tendency for nationalistic Muslims to be both more supportive of Islamic law out of an anti-West sentiment, and more egalitarian or anti-capitalist in their economic views. Muslims with strong pride in their country are actually less favorable toward increasing government responsibility for everyone and equalizing incomes.

As we hypothesized under (H), high standards of living (HDI) are negatively related to support for government taking more responsibility for everyone and for equalizing incomes, apparently reflecting the feeling that when the country as a whole is doing reasonably well economically, there are fewer needy to take care of (or that they are less deserving of help) and less necessity for government to support the poor or equalize incomes. Interestingly, with a two-tailed test, HDI is *positively* related to support for increased government ownership of businesses, suggesting that Muslims in high- HDI countries may feel that state ownership ensures prosperity. High income and white- collar occupation are also positively associated with support for government ownership (had we used two-tailed tests). This may indicate support among high-status groups for the crony capitalism and family patronage systems that characterize the *rentier* economies of some of the nations (Algeria, Egypt, Indonesia, and Saudi Arabia) in our study. Those who are better off in such states are likely to benefit directly from state control of productive resources through their association with government elites.

To test whether support for Islamic law has a stronger effect on economic egalitarianism in countries with lower standards of living, as we hypothesized under (H4). The significant negative effects of these interactions indicate that, as expected, the lower the country's standard of living, the greater the effect that support for Islamic law has on all three economic attitudes. Failing to meet the needs of the citizenry strengthens effects of Islamic orthodoxy on the desire for egalitarian economic reform. Political repression, which is only modestly correlated with HDI (–.079), is associated with a desire for greater government responsibility for everyone and more equal incomes, possibly because repressive governments are less likely to look out for those in need. Interestingly, the more repressive the government, the less effect that support for the *shari'a* has on wanting greater government responsibility for everyone and more equal incomes. In politically repressive regimes, orthodox Muslims, who are the objects of government repression in some of these countries, may prefer those Islamic non- governmental organizations (NGOs), rather than the state, provide for the poor and needy. As we later discuss, this is the strategy that most Islamist movements have adopted when faced with government repression and corruption.

Through analyses of seven Muslim-majority nations, we tested two alternate hypotheses linking orthodoxy vs. modernism in Islam with economic attitudes. Our Moral Cosmology theory assumes similar effects of moral cosmology on economic (and cultural) attitudes within all of the Abrahamic faith traditions. Specifically, we argue that the theological communitarianism of the religiously orthodox inclines them to favor communitarian/egalitarian economic arrangements (and communitarian/authoritarian cultural policies that seek to impose what they see as divinely ordained standards on abortion, sexuality, family, and gender). In contrast, the theological individualism of modernists disposes them toward individualistic, laissez-faire economic arrangements (and individualistic/libertarian cultural policies). While Moral Cosmology theory does not depend on the specific content of Islam, the alternate hypothesis, based on tenets of Islam with regard to economic matters, limits the effect of orthodoxy only to government aid to the needy, which is supported by the Islamic pillar of *zakat,* and posits no effects on equalizing incomes or government ownership of businesses.

We found that in all seven nations, orthodoxy—measured as support for the implementation of Islamic law (the *shari'a*) as the sole legal foundation of the state—is associated with support for one or more of the following economic reforms: greater government responsibility to provide for everyone, equalization of incomes, or increased government ownership of business. That orthodoxy is linked in these countries, not only with support for government provision for those in need, but with support for other progressive economic policies that are not enjoined by Islamic texts, supports our Moral Cosmology theory linking orthodoxy to communitarian economic policies in all of the Abrahamic traditions.

In additional analyses not reported in this chapter but available on request, we tested the argument of Moral

Cosmology theory that orthodoxy is associated with cultural communitarianism or authoritarianism, and found that support for the implementation of Islamic law is significantly related in each of the seven countries to two or more of the following: (1) agreement that "men make better political leaders than women do," (2) agreement that abortion is never justifiable, (3) agreement that homosexuality is never justifiable, and (4) agreement that divorce is never justifiable. Thus, the link between religious orthodoxy and economic communitarianism that we found earlier in societies that are predominantly Protestant, mixed Protestant and Catholic (West Germany), Catholic (Austria, Ireland, Italy, Poland, Portugal), Eastern Orthodox (Bulgaria, Romania), and Jewish holds in seven predominantly Muslim societies as well—18 societies in all. We caution, however, that economic conditions or unique historical circumstances may affect whether Moral Cosmology theory holds in a specific context.

As we found for the seven Muslim-majority nations considered here, depressed economic conditions may strengthen the link between orthodoxy and economic communitarianism, while better economic conditions weaken this. Historical contingencies may also matter. In our earlier analyses of European countries, we found that modernists in France are actually to the left of the orthodox on economic issues— the reverse of the expected pattern. In explaining this, we noted Percheron's (1982:8) observation that "left and right in France today coincide in large part with the 'red' and 'white' of the Revolution," the red referring to anticlerical revolutionary Republicans and the white to Catholic loyalists. While we found evidence of economic communitarianism among ordinary orthodox Muslims, is there also evidence of this in Islamist movements in Muslim-majority nations?

We noted above that in politically repressive societies, support for Islamic law is less strongly related to a desire for greater government responsibility for everyone and equalizing incomes, and we suggested that orthodox

Muslims may, in such states, prefer that economic needs of the citizenry be addressed by Islamic NGOs rather than the secular state. In highly repressive Egypt of the 1930s, the Muslim Brotherhood began to establish a broad network of welfare agencies, clinics, factories offering good wages and benefits, daycare centers, youth clubs, unemployment agencies, and so forth. After the 1992 Cairo earthquake, it was the Brotherhood, not the government that stepped in to provide medical assistance, shelter, food, and clothing for the victims. This "state within a state", while not the first choice of Islamists seeking to establish an Islamic state became a model for "re-Islamization from below" that has been widely adopted throughout the Muslim world.

Eschewing government funds and drawing on *zakat* contributions (as would an Islamic state), these welfare networks demonstrate that Islamist organizations can outperform secular governments in providing social services to citizens. The cosmological and class differences that we found among Muslims in support for communitarian economic measures suggest that an Islamist call for progressive economic change would draw support from orthodox Muslims and from those at the bottom of educational and income hierarchies. One of the attractions of Islamist movements arguably is their emphasis on economic reform and their efforts to address, with varying degrees of success, human needs that established governments have been unwilling or unable to meet.

The landslide victory in the 2005 Iranian presidential election of Islamist Mahmoud Ahmadinejad over Akbar Hasmeni Rafsanjani, a reformist/modernist, stunned Western observers, who had assumed that cultural liberties initiated by outgoing reformist president, Muhammad Khatami, would continue. In a country where the official jobless rate is 11 percent and inflation 14 percent, Ahmadinejad promised to put the poor at the top of his agenda, pledged to renationalize the oil industry and redistribute its wealth, and condemned the reformists' reintroduction of private banks and privatization of state-owned industries for increasing the gap between rich and poor.

The *New York Times* (Slackman 2005) reported that, "while [Ahmadinejad] often invoked God and his faith, he has usually done so in the context of populist proposals to lower prices, raise salaries, and create jobs." Ahmadinejad's critique of corruption and cronyism in Iran's *rentier* economy and his social conservatism contrasted sharply with Rafsanjani's neoliberalism (ending subsidies for bread, gas, and utilities; accelerating privatization; and encouraging foreign investment) and cultural progressivism. While some might view Ahmadinejad's populism as strictly instrumental, he garnered 62 percent of the vote, drawing especially on the orthodox Muslim poor and unemployed.

Yet encouraging as Ahmadinejad's victory may be for Islamists throughout the Muslim world, the weaker commitment to economic communitarianism that we found among well-educated and highly paid Muslims suggests a problem for proponents of "Islamic economics," who assume that an Islamic state could rely on advantaged classes to willingly build an economically just society. We conclude that while *zakat*, the pillar of Islam requiring Muslims to provide for those in need, may reinforce the tendency for Muslims who support implementation of the *shari'a* in all realms of life to be more economically egalitarian, the tendency for such Muslims to go beyond the tenets of their faith in supporting equalization of incomes or nationalization of businesses and industries cannot be attributed to Islam per se, but rather to the economic communitarianism that we have argued characterizes the orthodox of all of the Abrahamic faith traditions. The culturally authoritarian impulse of orthodox Islam regarding the position of women, abortion, sexuality, and family has been well documented by other scholars, but as we have shown, among Muslims who want religion to be at the core of the state, there is an economically egalitarian face as well.

Both the Moroccan *qadi* in Dale F. Eickelman2 s book *Knowledge and Power in Morocco* , as well as the Jordanian preacher described by Richard Antoun in his book *Muslim Preacher in the Modern World* deal with the complicated task of bridging the gap between localised traditions of their own villages and the more standardised traditions of the literate elite, in the context of the 20th century, a time characterised by changes in the political order as well as far-reaching economic and social transformations. The 'organisation of traditions and the education of religious men of learning is the primary focus of my essay. However, this comparison of two ethnographies also alludes to the wider topic of new methods of ethnographic writing in general, as both ethnographies contain biographical elements of lives of particular individuals. Given this less conventional genre in anthropological writing which Eickelman designates 'social biography and the background of the ongoing debate within Anthropology about questions of power and authority in ethnographic writing, which has been going on since the early 19802 s, this essay will first present an overview of the current debate before comparing aspects of the two life-histories, as described by Eickelman and Antoun.

Beginning with an outline of the recent discussions about methodological concerns about the common forms of anthropological writing and a broad classification of the two works within this debate, one can say that the 'traditional ethnography, characterised by its attempts at a holistic analysis and a rigid dichotomy between 'Us and Them' has increasingly been challenged. Critics claim that the distinction between the processes of fieldwork and the writing of ethnographies has often been blurred, and ethnography has been presented as if the results of the first inevitably necessitated the outcome of the second, disguising that ethnographies, though claiming to represent certain cultures, are in fact literary products themselves, dependent on the social, political and historical circumstances in which they are created.

This form of authoritative representation of other cultures alludes to structures of superiority and inferiority, reflecting the hegemony of the coloniser over the colonised. In speaking for the other, the anthropologist not only claim to know which parts of a culture are important, worth discussing and characteristic, but he also largely excludes his 'subjects from the possibility of speaking for themselves. Nevertheless, the seemingly objective stance of the anthropologist that allows him to generalise from his own experiences onto the field of an entire society is embedded in a perspective that is set by the authors relation to his home as well as to his host society. One of the problems that stems from this fact is that the ethnographer, unable to completely exclude his personal point of view from his perception, fails to accurately interpret the other culture within its context and is thereby likely to exoticise what seems perfectly familiar in the local setting.

Likewise, critics maintain that holistic descriptions of culture in anthropology, in their attempt to find overarching characteristics, instead produce culture and tradition rather than analysing them. In the search for general rules of social conduct within a given society, the anthropologist is always in danger of seeing homogeneity and fixed boundaries between people in a society, when actually there is no such thing:

"The effort to produce general ethnographic descriptions of peoples beliefs or actions risks smoothing over contradictions, conflicts of interest, doubts, and arguments, not to mention changing motivations and historical circumstances."

In tackling the problems of conventional ethnographies, only a few of which are presented here , it has been argued that anthropological writing requires a style that is more self-reflective. Instead of exclusively focusing on the presentations of other cultures, the specific instance of the anthropological encounter and the relationship between author and 'subject should be made explicit and incorporated into the process of the writing itself, giving a more prominent voice to the anthropologist and his motives, as well as to the people he studies. In other words, the impersonal and authoritative style should be superseded by the establishment of a narrative presence, taking account of the fluid character of society that resists all efforts of being authoritatively textualised.

As a result of that, the last two decades have witnessed an increased diversification in anthropological writing. Abu-Lughod, for example, attempts to counter stereotyping by concentrating on the narratives of individual members of the society. To elicit claims of authority and objectivity, she makes her own perspective as a native Palestinian explicit, and tackles the muting of local voices, thus far prevalent in anthropological writing, by leaving the women the space to tell their own stories, attempting to capture the "life as lived" among the Awlad Ali. By writing - as she calls it - against culture, she dismisses the common assumptions made on the basis of the term `culture , such as timelessness, coherence and homogeneity, and concentrates instead on how social life within a society does in fact proceed.

Nancy Lindisfarne, engaging in yet another innovation in anthropological literature by writing up her fieldwork in Syria in the form of short-stories, gives similar reasons for her endeavour : with the presentation of the results of her field-research in the form of fiction, she attempts to evade claims of scholarly authority, as well as the 'orientalist trap, and to convey a more realistic and lively picture of everyday life. Furthermore, in refraining from writing her account in the established academic language and style, Lindisfarne endeavours to sustain a dialogue between the anthropologist and her 'subjects, and to thereby break down the unequal relation between them.

In American anthropology in particular, attempts have been made from the 1980s onward to confront the problem of exoticising the other in anthropological writing, by employing person-centred ethnographies or life histories, in order to convey the subtlety of individual stories, without seeing them as completely determined by their respective cultural setting. In his rather controversial ethnography *Tuhami: Portrait of a Moroccan* , the life history of a Moroccan tilemaker from Meknes, Crapanzano takes this approach further by asserting that genres of writing are cultural constructs themselves, which means that the subjective realities of life stories can not always be communicated in the (Western) genre of biography. Based on this, Crapanzano does not make the attempt to write up his accounts as a conventional biography, but instead tries to make sense of Tuhami's life story as he himself relates it, neglecting aspects like chronology and logical coherence.

At the same, time the presence of the ethnographer is always made explicit, hence putting the telling of the life history into context. In using this sort of approach, Crapanzano aims at bridging the discrepancy between the anthropologists and his subject's perception of reality, which he feels ethnographies have so far failed to communicate:

"The ethnography comes to represent a sort of allegorical anti-world, similar to the anti-worlds of the insane and the child. The ethnographic encounter is lost in timeless description; the anguished search for comprehension in the theoretical explanation; the particular in the general; the character in the stereotype."

Regardless of the question of whether Crapanzano really evades the problem of the willy-nilly creation of stereotypes and a static and unchanging culture, '*Tuhami* is in fact an profound innovation, as the author refrains from imposing pre-made categories on the ethnographical account, even so fundamental a distinction as between dream and reality.

In an attempt to classify the two ethnographies that are the focus of this essay, one can state that both Eickelman and Antoun, by making use of idiosyncratic life-histories, seek to make their informants voices heard. Eickelman in particular explicitly considers the circumstances under which his book was written, giving an in depth account of the reciprocal perception of the qadi and himself. However, both ethnographies seem to remain in many ways on the firm ground of conventional ethnographic writing, as they remain relatively modest in scope and do not stretch the limits of conventional anthropological writing in any great way.

Whereas anthropologists like Abu-Lughod strive to question notions of conformity within a given society, focusing on individual experiences as a way to transcend the cultural setting in which these individuals live, and to take on a perspective that does not explain the actions of individuals solely in terms of their social roles, but gives them a voice treating them as individuals in their own right , Eickelman and - even more so - Antoun approach their particular subjects as proponents of a particular social group. Their accounts remain case studies for the analysis of a broader phenomenon, that is religious learning and the organisation of religious traditions. Both anthropologists stress the peculiarities of the singular instance, refraining from presenting them as stereotypical. However, their aim is not to capture 'the life as it is lived, but to view them as the particular case of the carrier of a particular social role which is embedded in a wider context, which the authors wish to explore.

Between conventional 'authoritative ethnographies and the post-modern idea of writing *against* culture , Eickelman and Antoun take a midway stance. In explaining his approach Eickelman states : "His [the *qadi's*] voice is present throughout the text, but so is mine."

Having discussed some aspects of the idea of writing ethnographies as social biographies or life histories, I shall now explore some similarities and differences between the two ethnographies, concerning the organisation of religious traditions in different settings. Although I think that individual cases sometimes allude to wider social contexts and thus allow more general statements on a moderate scale about these circumstances, in my comparison of the

Moroccan *qadi* and the Jordanian preacher, I will confine myself to comparing them as individual instances and only generalise where this seems unproblematic. Within the recent debate about the Anthropology of Islam, there has been major dissent concerning the notion of 'Little and 'Great traditions, that were first introduced in the 1940s , signifying the discrepancy between the overarching beliefs and rituals of the literate elite throughout the Islamic world, as opposed to the localised, often syncretic practices that widely differ amongst Muslims.

Some scholars, including Richard Antoun, view this concept valuable in exploring the accommodation of the high tradition within a local context. Others reject this analytical distinction, asserting a variety of Islams instead of a single monolithic religion and dismiss the notion of 'great traditions as stipulating an essential core of the Islamic religion, which can be transcended from the particular circumstances in which it is practised. Since both Abd ar-Rahman, the Moroccan *qadi* in the centre of Eickelman's book, and Luqman, the Jordanian preacher described by Antoun, in their functions as judge and preacher are the proponents of Islamic orthodoxy in their respective surroundings, a comparison may also illuminate how far the notion of a normative essence of Islam can be maintained.

To begin with the case of Abd ar-Rahman, a *qadi* in a medium-sized Moroccan town which is also a centre of pilgrimage, his education in the religious sciences is characterised by a relatively high degree of organisation and the straight-forward path he follows in his educational career. Beginning his education with the memorisation of the Quran in the local mosque-school and subsequently in a nearby tent-school , he finally proceeds to study at the renowned Yusufiya-madrasa of Marrakesh. The different stages of Abd ar-Rahman's and his elder brothers career education, show that the idea of 'travelling for study, characteristic for Islamic education since the Middle Ages, still played quite an important role for religious students in Morocco at the beginning of the 20th century.

Although there seems to be quite a high degree of organisation in religious learning, the networks of local mosque-schools and madrasas all through the country were characterised by a lack of institutionalisation. There were no overarching structures whatsoever, no clearly identifiable body of students or teachers nor did the institutions of higher learning have distinct entry qualifications or exams. Instead, religious learning was embedded in the social environment of the particular institution, as the different forms of patronage and financial support for colleges and their students shows. This lack of institutionalisation is not only evident in the sphere of religious learning, but also in the organisation of the Moroccan Ulama as a whole, who were far less a corporate group than the accumulation of individual *alims*, lacking an overarching organisation as well as a collective self-identification.

Eickelman's study also suggests that Islamic knowledge in the Moroccan context is signified by a strong emphasis on mnemonic knowledge, reflecting the alleged unchanging character of the Quranic Revelation. One of the striking features of Abd ar-Rahman's early formation is therefore the separation of understanding (*fahm*) and exegesis (*tafsir*), although this altered in Morocco under the influence of modernist thought in the 1920s. Despite its relatively fixed contents however, to interpret this way of learning as being static and uncritical would be misleading. Although in the particular case, Abd ar-Rahman's education in the religious sciences led to a career as a jurisconsult, by far not all graduates from the *madrasas* pursued a career in Islamic law. This alludes to some wider implications of Islamic education and knowledge in the Moroccan context as it presented itself at the beginning of the 20th century.

As already mentioned, the colleges hardly ever provided formal certificates for their graduates. Rather, the study at a renowned institution such as the Yusufiya brought with it increased recognition by the social environment and served as a status-marker. Beyond being an institution for the formation of judges or preachers, these colleges helped the establishment of personal networks that could be used in subsequent political or entrepreneurial careers. Finishing his religious education, Abd ar-Rahman first became assistant *qadi* in his hometown following the patronage of his elder brother, where he had a number of different duties, including being the imam and holding the Friday sermons. Progressing to be the *qadi* of the pilgrimage town of Boujad some twenty years later, his duties became more responsible but also more limited in scope, as he was now chiefly engaged with settling disputes concerning marriages, inheritance and land transactions in and around Boujad. However, the case of Abd ar-Rahman likewise shows that the rural notables also made their living as landowners.

According to Eickelman's analysis, the role of the qadi in the context of rural Morocco was twofold, in that it consisted on the one hand of the implementation of Islamic law, but on the other hand had to take into account the local concepts of justice, which made an intimate knowledge of the society indispensable. Furthermore, Abd ar-Rahman's perception of the role of the *ulama* is illuminating since he considers them to be responsible for distinguishing between the accepted Islamic practices and (*bida*), such as the worshipping at local shrines, thereby defending what they regard as Islamic orthodoxy. Abd ar-Rahman's role therefore can be described as that of a cultural broker, mediating the between the rural environment and the wider sphere of society.

Another aspect worth mentioning in Eickelman's account is the relation between the *ulama* and the centres of political power, a crucial issue in Islamic history up until the present day. In relation to French colonial rule, the Moroccan *ulama* seems to have taken a non-confrontational stance, sometimes even overtly co-operating with them following the course of their monarch. Only with the escalation of the struggle for independence following the Berber decree in

1930 , the learned men began to resist the French rule, without ever becoming a revolutionary vanguard as the Iranian *ulama* was in the struggle against the shah. Always underlying the Moroccan *ulama's* resistance was a constant weighing of two factors: which means of resistance were reasonable in the situation (*aql*) and what was required by Islamic law (*shra*).

Turning now to Luqman, the Jordanian preacher central to Antoun's book, the case shows a distinctly different path to becoming a local representative of Islamic orthodoxy. Being from a landowners family in a Jordanian village, Luqman attended primary education, which also included the memorisation of the Quran, although mnemonic learning did not play as important a role as in Abd ar-Rahman's education. Disregarding his father's wishes, Luqman subsequently pursued his religious studies under the tutelage of the local preacher. His entire education took place in the setting of his local village with no organisational background whatsoever, rather being driven solely by his private impulse. Furthermore, Luqmans education was a private and individual endeavour, rather than the socially accepted and indeed bolstered offered by the networks of *madrasas* in Morocco.

This meant that he had to work as a teacher to make a living while studying. The lack of institutionalisation of religious life in Jordan is also reflected in the way Luqman installed himself as preacher in his native village, first without any formal designation and solely on the ground of the acknowledgement of his expertise by the villagers. Also, the notion of religious knowledge as a status-marker is largely absent from Luqman's case. Although Islamic knowledge was valued, the vocation of the village preacher was anything but prestigious. Being funded directly by his village rather than by a central institution, the preacher frequently had to demand his payment from the peasants which negatively affected the preachers status.

The scope of the preachers duties however went far beyond leading the daily prayers and delivering the Friday sermon: he also served as marriage officer, religious teacher and religious and ethical counsellor, settling disputes and more remarkably - writing Quranic amulets - a practice regarded as 'un-Islamic in more conservative settings. According to Antoun, the multiple roles played by the preacher display the "organic" character of religious life in the local setting, where it can hardly be separated from other social spheres, such as kinship, economy and politics. It also shows that religious life on the local level was more or less autonomous of influences from the outside. In the light of this, Luqman too sees his role as the village preacher as twofold: "To organise relations of people with the Lord and to organise the relations of people with one another in all matters."

Concerning the relation between the carriers of religious knowledge and politics, Luqman's case seems to suggest the reluctance of the rural educated to actively engage in political matters. In a fashion similar to that of Abd ar-Rahman in the Moroccan case, the preacher sees himself primarily as the guardian of orthopraxy and the agent for the implementation of religious ethics in everyday life. Only when the consensus of society and thereby the basis of Islamic solidarity is seen as being threatened, as in the case of Jordan with the emergence of political parties in the 50s and 60s, did the preacher take a more active stance, dismissing party politics as hypocrisy and a threat to traditional family and kinshipties.

In this brief discussion of the two ethnographies, I hope to have pointed out some of the differences and similarities of two particular cases. From the prior discussion about biographies as an alternative mode of ethnographic writing however, I think it becomes clear that neither Abd ar-Rahman nor Luqman must be seen as characteristic proponents of the Moroccan and Jordanian *ulama*. Unquestionably, the juxtaposition of the two cases shows some similarities, such as the overall absence of political engagement as long as the proper conduct of religious life is not endangered. Besides, in both cases, the learned men seem to play the role of brokers between the rural context and the wider world of the Islamic *Ummah*. At the same time however, their specific role requires an intimate knowledge of their community, which means that they lack the basic features of what Simmel had called 'the stranger, a representative of the wider society in the local context, who does not organically belong to it, but can be "near and far at the same time."

Despite these similarities, the consideration of the two cases more than anything else displays the great variety of religious life throughout the Islamic world. In our concrete case, this becomes particularly clear in the completely different forms of transmitting religious knowledge, the different connotations that are attached to acquiring this knowledge and the differing valuation by the rest of the society. In the light of this, it becomes increasingly hard to uphold the dichotomy of 'little and 'great traditions. Not only does such a distinction contain the assumption of a normative and unchanging core of Islam but it also seems to stipulate an overarching orthodoxy that - parallel to High-Arabic as the overarching religious language - transcends regional diversities and is never affected by local practices.

Although the two cases both display the prevalent emphasis on orthopraxy rather than on orthodoxy that somewhat masks the regional differences, the comparison of two *alims* from different rural settings rather suggests the absence of a normative core of Islam and seems to underline al-Zein's proposal of analysing each 'Islam in its specific context, taking into account the interdependencies with other spheres of social life and to examine how meanings are produced for each instance individually. Briefly summing up, one can state that the two ethnographies give accounts of the unrestricted diversity of social life on different levels. Firstly, by the describing the make up of religious life in specific settings, both works convey a sense of the variety of religious expressions throughout the Islamic world that resist clear-cut classifications.

Furthermore, although both Eickelman's and Antoun's ethnographic writings are still deemed rather conventional, in that they maintain the aims of description and interpretation, they do not present their 'main characters as stereotypical carriers of their specific roles, that is proponents of Islamic knowledge in a rural setting, but rather see them as the result of their particular life-stories and individual circumstances. In the concluding sentence of his book, Antoun states: "To put it another way, all of the above was an accident of biography, social position, and individual inclination."

8

Rational Tradition in Islam

Most of the Arabian Peninsula is a dry sandy desert. The early inhabitants lived a nomadic lifestyle, breeding camels and herding goats and sheep in the scrublands on the borders of the desert. The first settlements appeared around 2000 BC along the coastlines and in the rocky oasis regions along the coast of the Red Sea. Arab society was organized into tribes, with each person depending on their tribe for survival. Each tribe attempted to maintain control over an oasis, and wars frequently broke out between tribes over access to fertile land and water. Battles between the tribes often led to cycles of murder and vengeance that lasted for centuries.

Trade between Persia and Egypt was carried by camel trains across the Arabian desert. Desert oasis towns grew into regional trading centers where Arab merchants traded spices and other commodities with the Syrians, Egyptians, and Persians. Merchants along the southern coast also traded goods with African merchants across the Red Sea. A variety of religious beliefs existed throughout the Arabian peninsula before Islam. Some desert tribes believed in ancestral spirits and practiced human sacrifice, others worshipped the ancient goddess of fertility. Many believed in a supreme god and also in a number of lesser gods and goddesses who were his children.

Jewish tribes had long been settling throughout the peninsula. They owned some of the best land and maintained their wealth and power by controlling much of the trade, especially in metals and weapons. Christian missionaries were busy establishing churches in Arab cities, and many Arab tribes had converted to Christianity. Arab kingdoms in Syria and Egypt were devoutly Christian. For over one thousand years, the Greek and Roman empires had battled against the Persian Empire for control of the Middle East. After the fall of Rome, the Greeks formed an alliance with Christian Arabs in order to defeat a series of Persian invasions. The Persians also formed alliances with Arab tribes, paying them to join the fight.

The Greeks believed that God was the Trinity, but Arab Christians rejected this idea, believing that God was a single entity. This dispute led to persecutions and assassinations and eventually the Arabs broke off their alliance with the Greeks. Regional power was now beginning to favor the Arabs, but in order for them to realize this power, they first needed to unite behind a common cause. Mecca was an important religious center long before the appearance of Islam. Pilgrims journeyed from all over the region to worship the idols contained in its many sacred shrines. The most sacred shrine contained a black meteorite that was believed to have supernatural powers because it had fallen from the heavens.

Muhammad

Muhammad was born around the year 570 in Mecca. His father died before he was born and his mother died when he was still a child, leaving him to be brought up by his grandfather and later by his uncle. As a young man, he traveled with the trading caravans from Mecca to Syria. When he was 25, he married a wealthy older widow and became the manager of her business interests. Muhammad developed a passion for religion. For years he studied and discussed the Jewish and Christian scriptures and spent much of his time contemplating God in the hillside caves outside of Mecca. He formulated his own uniquely Arab interpretation of religion, based loosely on the biblical scriptures but also incorporating Persian ideas.

Abraham was the mythical forefather of the Jews. His faith in one universal God was said to have been so strong that God promised his descendents possession of the land of Israel. But the Jews had twice been removed from the land, supposedly because of their disobedience to God, and the Christians were guilty of corrupting the faith by claiming that God had a son. Muhammad believed that the Arab people were also the descendents of Abraham through his first son to an Egyptian slave girl. Muhammad figured that if he could teach the Arabs to embrace Abraham's original faith in one God, then the Arabs could claim to be the rightful heirs to Abraham's religious tradition.

When Muhammad was about forty years old, he started preaching to his family and friends. He called his new religion Islam (meaning "surrender to God"). He claimed that it was not a new religion but rather an old one that had freed itself from the corruptions of Judaism and Christianity. Muhammad declared himself to be the last of the biblical prophets. Those who accepted Islam would be called Muslims. Muhammad preached that there is only one God and that he is almighty and all-knowing, and that he represents justice and fairness, kindness to orphans and widows, and charity to the poor. And although God is compassionate, he will inflict harsh punishment upon those who defy him. Muhammad's words had the power to stir the emotions of those who listened ...

The righteous are those who believe in God, and the Day of Judgment, and in the angels, and the holy book, and the prophets. They share their wealth with their family, and with orphans, and the helpless, and with travelers in need, and with beggars. They attend to their prayers and give to charity. They are true to their promises, and are steadfast in trial and adversity and in times of war. Such are the true believers. Such are the God fearing. They will be blessed and forgiven by God, and a generous provision shall be made for them. As for the unbelievers, it is the same whether you warn them or not, they will not have faith. God has closed their hearts and ears. Their sight is dimmed and an agonizing punishment awaits them.

The Day of Judgment

The Day of Judgment was invented by the Persian prophet Zoroaster around 700 BC and it became the central theme of Persian religion. It was an effective way of instilling the fear of God into people, allowing priests to more easily control the minds of believers, even convincing them to sacrifice their lives for the sake of a heavenly reward. The ancient Egyptians were obsessed with life after death, but the early Jewish prophets made no mention of it. They did not seem so eager to drag their religion into deeper superstition for the sake of a cheap morality. Although many early Christians were opposed to the Book of Revelations, its description of the Day of Judgment was eventually adopted by the Christian religion.

With the Persians and Christians both believing in heaven and hell, and with most other people being naturally superstitious about death, Muhammad embraced the Day of Judgment as the foundation of his new religion. Hope for reward and fear of punishment in the afterlife became his only solid argument for believing in God. He said ... Every soul will get what it deserves on the Day of Judgment. On that day, a trumpet shall sound and the dead will rise up from their graves. The gates of heaven shall swing open and angels will surround the throne giving glory to the Lord. The earth will shine with the light of the Lord, and the book will be laid open.

It will be a day of disaster for the unbelievers. They will find their deeds written down in the book. Nothing will be missing from the greatest to the smallest detail. Every soul shall know what it has done and what it has failed to do, and every soul shall be treated accordingly, for God knows everything, even the innermost thoughts of men. The righteous will return to the Garden of Eden, whose gates will open wide to receive them. They will be adorned with gold and precious jewels and dressed in robes of silk. Resting comfortably with modest virgins for companions, they will feast on abundant food and drink. This shall be your reward on the Day of Judgment. Our gifts can have no end.

But a terrible fate awaits the evildoers. A voice will cry, "Cast into hell every hardened unbeliever, every opponent of charity, every doubting sinner. Hurl him into the fierce, tormenting flames!" Here boiling water shall be poured on their heads. Their bodies will be immersed in fire until their skin is thoroughly burned. They will burn here in hell, a miserable resting place, where they will drink boiling water, rotten blood, and other horrible things. After Muhammad began preaching, many of his friends became enemies, despising him for speaking out against the shrines and other objects of worship that were attracting visitors to Mecca. "Are we to renounce our gods for the sake of a mad poet?" they asked. Over the next ten years, Muhammad continued to preach in Mecca, gathering around him a small but dedicated band of followers.

The Qur'an

There were no important works of literature written in Arabic before Muhammad's time. Most stories were passed down by word of mouth. Muhammad composed verses which were at first committed to memory by his followers and were later written down by scribes to form chapters of his holy book, the Qur'an . He claimed to have been given his revelations by an angel named Gabriel, although references to the angel in the Qur'an are vague and open to interpretation. Muhammad summarized the Jewish and Christian scriptures, adapting them to Arab ways. He offered the Arabs a simple interpretation of the Bible written in a style that was easy to understand. The Qur'an uses colorful language, switching rapidly from one subject to the next, repeating the same stories over and over with slight variations each time. Muhammad said ...

The Qur'an has been revealed to you in Arab language so that you may spread the word to other men, and so that they may give thought.

In this way, we have inspired you with knowledge of righteousness when you knew nothing about faith or scripture. We have made it a light to guide those who we wish to serve us. They shall now be guided along the right path, the path of God. All that is in the heavens and on the earth belong to him, and all things shall return to him in the end. The Qur'an mentions most of the Bible's main characters from Adam and Eve to Jesus and Mary. Muhammad regarded Jesus as an important prophet but was outraged by claims that he was the son of God ...

Those who say that the Lord has fathered a son are preaching an outright falsehood. The very heavens above would crack open, the earth would break apart, and the mountains would crumble to dust before the merciful Lord ever fathered a son, because it is not in his nature to have one. Muhammad rejected the importance of Christian forgiveness, instead preaching that revenge was the proper form of justice. He reasoned that crime would be discouraged by the fear of revenge. He failed to acknowledge that forgiveness is always the conclusion of careful thought, whereas revenge is only an expression of blind instinct.

War against Mecca

The authorities in Mecca grew increasingly hostile towards Muhammad's new religion. Persecution against his followers became so intense that many of them were forced to flee. When the citizens of Mecca finally threatened to kill Muhammad, he fled north to the oasis town of Medina, where he was soon joined by hundreds of his followers. An uneasy balance of power existed between Arab and Jewish tribes for control of Medina. Muhammad and his followers joined this power struggle by forming strategic alliances with other tribes. His position was strengthened by gaining converts.

Muhammad's conflict with Mecca intensified over the following years. His followers attacked Meccan trading caravans and Meccan forces lay siege to Medina. The Arab tribes in Medina forgot their old rivalries and united behind Muhammad. He promised them a reward in heaven if they undertook to protect him with their lives and accept him as their leader. He said ...

He who is prepared to die fighting for the cause of God, whether he dies or triumphs, he shall be richly rewarded. Do you fear the heat of combat? Hell is hotter! Paradise is waiting for you! Muhammad continued adding new chapters to the Qur'an , but the nature of his religion was changing. New verses reflected the thoughts of a warlord engaged in constant battle ... Those who attack God and his apostle and spread disorder in the land must be put to death or crucified, or have their hands and feet cut off on opposite sides, or be banished from the land. They will be shamed in this world and harshly punished in the next, except for those who repent before you destroy them. For you know that God is merciful and forgiving.

The Jewish tribes in Medina were naturally skeptical about his claim to be one of their prophets. They ridiculed him and later conspired against him. His early respect for the Jews turned into bitter resentment. He used his growing power to banish one Jewish tribe from the city. He later accused the remaining tribe of treachery in his war against the Meccans and the men of the tribe were slaughtered. Believers, do not take the Jews or the Christians for friends. They are friends only to each other. Whoever of you seeks their friendship shall be treated like one of them. God does not guide such wrongdoers.

Having established an Islamic government in Medina, Muhammad introduced new laws and punishments which covered everything from ownership of property to marriage and divorce. Some laws promoted equality and social justice, while others were simply reflections of the existing culture of tribal warfare and harsh desert justice. The Muslims formed alliances with desert tribes and battled for control of the surrounding countryside. Jewish tribes offered fierce resistance against the growing Muslim army but were eventually defeated. Those who did not convert to Islam were put to the sword and their women and children enslaved.

Believers, make war on the infidels who dwell around you. Deal firmly with them. Know that God is with the righteous. God has sent forth his apostle with guidance and the true faith to make it triumphant over all religions, however much the idolaters may dislike it. No longer able to defeat the Muslims, the Meccans signed a peace treaty. But Muhammad was dissatisfied with the terms of the treaty and his army eventually marched into Mecca and its people and places of worship were converted to Islam. As a concession to the old religions, Muhammad embraced existing religious traditions such as the feast of Ramadan and the pilgrimage to Mecca to see the sacred meteorite.

Muhammad's Final Years

Muhammad preached that it was the duty of all Muslim men to fight for the establishment of an Islamic world empire. He said that defeated populations must accept Islam or be put to the sword. Jews and Christians were to be offered the alternative of paying a special tax for being non-Muslims. Muhammad later decreed that there should be no other religion in Arabia than Islam. Faced with a choice between conversion and death, some Christians chose to die, while many others converted their churches into mosques. The Qur'an contains laws for managing slaves. Muslim men were permitted to keep any number of female sex slaves. This provided a strong motivation for his followers to go out and conquer in the name of Islam.

Arab men were traditionally allowed to take as many wives as they pleased. But Muhammad limited each man to only four wives. Muhammad said that God made men superior to women, and so women must always obey the commands and satisfy the needs of their husbands. After the death of his first wife, Muhammad married ten other women. In one of the last chapters of the Qur'an , he admonished two of his wives for being jealous of his intimacy with a Christian slave girl. Before he died, he issued a special revelation forbidding any of his wives from marrying again. In the years following Muhammad's death, there was some confusion about the contents of the Qur'an , with several different versions in circulation. An authoritative version was eventually issued by the ruling clerics and all other copies were burned. Those who compiled the Qur'an were unsure of the original order of the chapters, so they were arranged in order of length, with the longest chapter first and the shortest last.

Early Arab Conquest

Muhammad had succeeded in unifying the Arab tribes under a single leadership. He sent messengers to warn neighboring kings and emperors to embrace Islam, but he died before he could undertake any further conquests. Convinced that God and history were on their side, an army of warriors on horseback set out to complete Muhammad's mission to bring the entire world under the political control of Islam. Any gold or other riches taken from the conquered lands were to be shared among the Arab tribes, encouraging them to stay in the federation.

The Muslims easily forced the Greeks out of Palestine, Syria, and Egypt. The largely Christian populations were tired of paying taxes to the Greeks. The Arabs among them welcomed their brothers and embraced the new faith, which was much less complicated than Christianity and much easier to believe. The Persian Empire was also easily conquered. It had been weakened by decades of war and the inhabitants hated their corrupt and oppressive rulers. A rapidly expanding Arab empire based on equality and social justice promised to be a much more favorable place to live.

Sunni and Shiite

After Muhammad's death, the leadership of the federation passed on to his closest friends and companions. But after the assassination of their third leader, the authorities in Mecca argued over how to choose the next leader. Civil war broke out and Islam splintered into two main factions, the Sunnis and the Shiites. The Shiites wanted the leadership to pass down to Muhammad's descendents. They believed that the highest religious leader is God's representative on earth with the authority to add to the message of the Qur'an.

The Sunnis wanted the new leader to be elected by the ruling clerics. They believed that the Qur'an is the final authority and that there must be no further revelation. Muhammad's son-in-law ruled briefly before the commander of the Arab forces in Syria defeated the Shiites and gained control of the empire. He moved the capital to Damascus and his family ruled there for the next hundred years.

Late Arab Conquest

The enormous riches gained from the early conquest had given the Arabs a luxurious standard of living. For the next few decades they feasted and made love to their slave girls until the population had increased sufficiently to make further conquest possible. Arab armies were soon pushing onwards in every direction. They captured all of North Africa and then moved north into parts of Spain and Portugal. The Spanish lived under severe oppression and were happy to see their king defeated. A large Muslim army then crossed the mountains into the south of France before being pushed back by French forces.

Arab armies conquered Afghanistan, Pakistan, and parts of India before moving north into central Asia, finally being stopped by the Chinese. By now the Arabs were less interested in converting foreigners to Islam. Defeated armies were either killed or enslaved. Breeding with captured slave girls was a more effective way to spread Islam. Those foreigners who saved themselves by converting to Islam were treated as second class citizens by the Arabs. The infidels to the east were mainly Buddhists and Hindus. The godless Buddhists were pacifists and offered no resistance to the invading Muslim armies.

The invaders destroyed the Buddhist monasteries and burned their books. Wherever they went, they killed the men and took the women and children as slaves. The Hindus were able to offer some resistance, but were unable to prevent the establishment of Muslim rule over large parts of India. The defenders knew what they were up against. If it appeared that a battle could not be won then the men would kill their own women and children and carry on fighting to the death.

New Muslim Empire

By around the year 750, a considerable tension had grown throughout the Muslim empire. The Arab tribes were no longer receiving their share of the profits from conquest. The Meccans accused the leadership in Damascus of abandoning Islam. The Shiites opposed the Sunni leadership. And those who had converted to Islam in conquered lands were demanding the same rights as Arabs. Tensions erupted into a violent revolution which began in Persia and quickly spread throughout the rest of the empire. The Persian rebels fought to establish a new leadership which represented the aspirations of all Muslims, not just Arabs. After successfully overthrowing the old ruling dynasty, the capital of the empire was moved to Baghdad, and it was here that Islam reached the height of its power and prosperity.

The Hadith

Around 150 years after Muhammad's death, a number of books were written containing stories that were supposedly passed down by word of mouth to the descendents of Muhammad's companions. These books, known as the Hadith, quickly became the authorative explanation of the Qur'an . Despite their questionable authenticity, they are still used today to clarify the details of the religion and its laws. A collection of laws from both the Qur'an and the Hadith were compiled into a basic legal system known as Sharia. Sharia is a complete package, intended to be easily implemented in any conquered country. Islamic values were never meant to change, and so the laws were never meant to change either.

Science and Philosophy

Arabic became the common language of the Islamic Empire, and the surviving works of Greek science and philosophy were translated into Arabic. The Muslims established schools and libraries throughout their empire, and while the Church was prohibiting scientific enquiry in Europe, Muslim scholars were busy making important contributions to astronomy and medicine. While European mathematics was being held back by the use of unwieldy Roman numerals, Muslim scholars had adopted the decimal number system and were busy making progress in the development of new mathematical techniques like algebra.

Some Islamic thinkers tried to introduce elements of science and philosophy into Islam. They wrote that although there can only be one truth, there may be two ways of looking at the truth, religion for the uneducated masses and philosophy for the educated elite. There should be no conflict between religious revelation and philosophical reasoning as long as they both reach the same conclusions about the existence of God. Other Islamic thinkers rejected science and philosophy. They quite rightly observed that philosophical enquiry tends to drift towards atheism, and that the scientific viewpoint is not compatible with life after death. Permitting free inquiry might inevitably lead to the rejection of Islam.

Other Sects

Over the centuries, cultural differences forced some groups to break away from mainstream Islam. They formed new religious sects, each with their own unique interpretation of Islam, differing on issues such as monogamous marriage, head dress for women, and variations of Islamic law. Some sects became more progressive while others became more conservative. The Qur'an may be good at instilling the fear of hell, but it does not offer thinking people any easy path to spiritual enlightenment. After the spread of Islam, many open minded spiritual thinkers living under its influence were driven to look beyond conventional Islam for better ways of understanding God.

Some used drugs to expand their consciousness. Others achieved spiritual euphoria by dancing around in circles for hours on end. Many left their homes to seek solitude in the mountains and deserts. Through quiet contemplation, they attempted to transcend this worldly life and develop a sense of oneness with God. The search for spiritual enlightenment under Islam led many to join a sect known as Sufism. Seeing religion as a liberating force instead of a moral burden, Sufi thinkers stressed that true religion was less about having blind faith in scripture and tradition, and more about developing an ever deepening appreciation of God through open minded contemplation of nature.

Jalaladin Rumi was an orthodox cleric in the 1200s who had his mind opened to Sufi wisdom by a vagabond preacher. Rumi embraced peace and love and became perhaps the most respected poet and philosopher in Islamic history. His words were compiled into a book in which he wrote ...

There are two worlds. There is the outer world which appears to exist, and seems solid and permanent, but in truth is an illusion. And there is the inner world that many people deny, and is invisible to the senses, and yet is real and eternal. Once your heart becomes pure and clear, it will become a mirror on which pictures will appear from beyond this earthly realm. Not only will such pictures appear, but also the image of the one who painted them. Sometimes God shows us the way to go. Sometimes he shows us the opposite way. The work of religion is full of confusion. But it is not a confusion that turns us away from God, it is a confusion that leads us to drink from his love and become utterly intoxicated.

Knowledge about religion is bad for the spirit. Such knowledge is like borrowed money; it does not belong to the one who possesses it. Yet those who study religion wrongly believe that they are acquiring spiritual knowledge. You must become ignorant about religion. You must become ignorant about worldly matters too. In fact you must become completely insane. Whatever may be profitable to you, flee from it. Whatever may advance your interests, shun it. If anyone wants to keep you, curse them. Lend money to those who have no hope of returning it. Ignore danger and walk freely through places that others avoid. Throw away your reputation and be free from shame. Only when you can do all this will you have obtained true spiritual knowledge.

No human behavior is entirely right or wrong, whether it be anger or patience, innocence or deceit. Nothing is absolutely good or absolutely evil. The benefit or harm of everything depends on the situation. For this reason, knowledge is useful and wisdom is vital. Although Sufism was based upon Islam and Sufi teachers often quoted from the Qur'an , those who strayed too far from the teachings of Muhammad were accused of blasphemy by conservative clerics and were either persecuted or killed. Rumi's writings are now banned in many Islamic countries.

Decline of Islam

The Mongol invasion of Persia in the 1200s marked the beginning of the decline of Islamic culture. Baghdad was conquered by the Mongols, its people were slaughtered, its wealth was plundered, and its libraries were destroyed. Central government came to an end and the Islamic Empire splintered into regional kingdoms. Around the same time, new techniques in the production of paper made the Qur'an easier to copy, and as copies became more widely available, more Muslims were able to read and interpret it for themselves. Science and philosophy were soon denounced as heresy. For a growing number of believers, the truth had already been revealed in the Qur'an and anything not conforming to Islamic teachings must be condemned.

The Turks

After recovering from the Christian crusades, the Mongol invasions, and the bubonic plague, Turkish tribes began battling to establish a new Islamic empire. They gained control over much of the old empire, and in 1453, they captured the Greek city of Constantinople and made it their capital. For the next few hundred years, Turkish armies fought an almost continuous holy war against the Christians, capturing Greece, Serbia, Hungary, and much of south eastern Europe. Twice they invaded Austria, laying siege to its capital, Vienna. But each time they were beaten back by an alliance of European forces using superior heavy artillery.

End of the Empire

After seeing the revolutionary effect that the printing press was having in Europe, it was banned by Muslim authorities as a potential instrument of sacrilege and heresy. Without the free flow of information and ideas, the Islamic world soon became an intellectual, technological, and economic backwater. As Europe emerged from the Christian Dark Ages, the Islamic world plunged deeper into its own darkness. Without modern technology, the Muslims suffered a long series of defeats against the Europeans. The Islamic Empire was eventually conquered and carved up after being defeated alongside the Germans in the First World War.

Dream Traditions of Islam

Few Western dream researchers have any familiarity with the rich dream traditions of Islam. The Muslim faith first emerged in seventh century B.C.E. Arabia as a profound revisioning of early Jewish and Christian beliefs and practices. One theme the Prophet Muhammad drew from the scriptures of those two religions was a reverence for dreaming. In the Qur'an, as in the Jewish Torah and the Christian New Testament, dreams serve as a vital medium by which God communicates with humans. Dreams offer divine guidance and comfort, warn people of impending danger, and offer prophetic glimpses of the future. Although the three religions drastically differ on many other topics, they find substantial agreement on this particular point: dreaming is a valuable source of wisdom, understanding, and inspiration. Indeed, as I will propose in this brief essay, Islam has historically shown greater interest in dreams than either of the other two traditions, and has done more to weave dreaming into the daily lives of its members.

From the first revelatory visions of Muhammed to the myriad dream practices of present-day Muslims, Islam has developed and sustained a complex, multifaceted tradition of active engagement with the dreaming imagination. For scholars trained in Western psychology, the dream traditions of Islam may appear alien, unapproachable, and perhaps not even relevant to the primary concerns of their research. This attitude is unfortunate, because there is great potential here for crosscultural dialogue, with the benefit of greatly enhanced knowledge on both sides. The admittedly formidable linguistic and cultural chasm between Islamic and Western traditions should not deter people from making the effort to build bridges across that chasm. The simple fact is that all humans dream, and thus dreaming itself is a bridging phenomenon between the two traditions.

Muslims have been paying close attention to their dreams for nearly 1500 years, and their insights and observations have many significant points of contact with the theories developed by Western psychologists over the past 150 years. The aim of this essay is to highlight those points of contact and show where further conversation between Muslims and Westerners can promote a deeper mutual understanding of the origins, functions, and meanings of dreaming. The horrific eruption of violence, fear, and destruction in the past several weeks has been awful to behold, and I know I am not alone in feeling an urgent desire to find some way of ending the bloodshed and creating a better relationship between Muslims and Westerners. In that broader historical context, this essay is intended as one small contribution to the cause of creative reconciliation between people who have been warring against each other for far too long.

Dreams in the Qur'An

Muhammed recorded the Qur'an between the years 610 and 632 C.E. Tradition has it that the first revelation of the Qur'an was given to Muhammed by the angel Gabriel in a dream. The text of the Qur'an contains 114 chapters (suras) of varying length and content. Unlike Jewish and Christian scriptures, which were produced by multiple authors from different historical times and cultural backgrounds, the Qur'an is the work of a single man, in a single lifetime. The text thus bears a strong stamp of that man's personality-Muhammed is the Prophet of Allah, the human medium of God's ultimate revelation. To learn about Islam is inevitably to learn about the Prophet Muhammed. Several passages of the Qur'an contain discussions of dreams and dreaming, and because of the absolute centrality of the Qur'an to Muslim faith these passages have become fundamental to all later Islamic dream traditions. What follows are brief synopses of four suras in which dreams play a significant role.

12: Joseph. In this chapter Muhammed gives a condensed version of the story of Joseph (following the essential outline found in the Torah's Genesis 37-50). While much of the material from the Genesis version has been removed, the three major dream episodes in Joseph's life all remain, and these episodes combine to make a clear point: dreams, and the ability to interpret them, are an important sign of God's favor. Muhammed starts sura 12 with the young Joseph telling his father he had a dream in which "eleven stars and the sun and the moon were prostrating themselves before me." Joseph's father warns the boy not to tell the dream to his older brothers, who jealously harbor murderous intentions toward him (in Genesis the dream is interpreted to mean that one day Joseph's eleven brothers, mother, and father will all bow down to him-a prospect that enrages his brothers). Joseph's father prophesizes that his youngest son "shall be chosen by your Lord. He will teach you to interpret visions."

The prophecy is borne out later in the sura when Joseph, unjustly imprisoned in Egypt, is asked to interpret the dreams of two fellow prisoners: "One of them said: 'I dreamt that I was pressing grapes.' And the other said: 'I dreamt that I was carrying a loaf upon my head, and that the birds came and ate of it. Tell us the meaning of these dreams, for we can see you are a man of learning.' Joseph replied: 'I can interpret them long before they are fulfilled. This knowledge my lord has given me, for I have left the faith of those that disbelieve in Allah and deny the life to come. I follow the faith of my forefathers, Abraham, Isaac, and Jacob.'" Joseph tells the first man his dream means he will be released and serve the king wine, while the second man's dream means he will be crucified, and the birds will peck at his head.

When these predictions come true, Joseph's skill as a dream interpreter comes to the attention of Egypt's king, who has been troubled by two dreams of his own, one in which seven fatted cows devour seven lean ones, and the other in which seven green ears of corn devour seven dry ones. The king asks his royal advisors to tell him the meaning of these dreams, but they cannot do so, saying "It is but an idle dream; nor can we interpret dreams." Joseph, however, is able to interpret the dreams accurately as anticipations of the future welfare of the land and its people, when seven years of plenty will be followed by seven years of famine. The king is pleased with this interpretation, and as a reward makes Joseph his personal servant. Very much like the Genesis version, the Qur'an portrays Joseph as an exemplary man of faith and piety, and one clear sign of his close relationship with God is his ability to have and interpret revelatory dreams.

The Ranks. Like sura 12, this one also retells a story found in the book of Genesis. Here the main subject is Abraham, whose life is recounted in Genesis 12-25. The Qur'anic version focuses specifically on God's command to Abraham to sacrifice his only son, Isaac (cf. Genesis 22): "[Abraham said] 'Grant me a son, Lord, and let him be a righteous man.' We [Allah] gave him news of a gentle son. And when he reached the age when he could work with him his father said to him: 'My son, I dreamt that I was sacrificing you. Tell me what you think.' He replied: 'Father, do as you are bidden. Allah willing, you shall find me faithful.' And when they had both surrendered themselves to Allah's will, and Abraham had laid down his son prostrate upon his face, We called out to him, saying: 'Abraham, you have fulfilled your vision.' Thus did We reward the righteous. That was indeed a bitter test."

Several points are worth noting here. First is the explicit reference to a dream as the means by which Abraham receives this command; the Genesis version does not emphasize the dream provenance as clearly. Second is the unquestioned assumption by both Abraham and his son that the dream is a command from Allah. The dream as Abraham describes it has no special markers of divine origin, and yet he and his son immediately agree that what Abraham has envisioned is ordained by God and must be done. This leads to the third and theologically most important point: the dream and their interpretation of it lead Abraham and his son to "surrender themselves to Allah's will."

This humble obedience is the very heart of the Muslim faith-the absolute trust in God, even to the point of sacrificing one's most cherished human attachments ("That was indeed a bitter test"). Muhammad's retelling of the story of Abraham and Isaac in many ways encapsulates the whole of the Qur'an. A fourth and final point to note here is the interesting twist at the end of the story, which differs quite dramatically from the Genesis version. In sura 37, Abraham is stopped in the sacrifice of his son by God's sudden words, "Abraham, you have fulfilled your vision." Abraham is true to his dream not by literally enacting it in the physical sacrifice of his son; rather, he "fulfills his vision" by a symbolic demonstration of his absolute obedience to God. As I will discuss later, this emphasis on the symbolic rather than the literal will pave the way for later Muslim philosophical and theological thinking about what kinds of truth can be discerned via the dreaming imagination.

8: The Spoils - This sura describes two of Muhammad's own dream experiences. He mentions them in the context of telling how in the early years of his mission he struggled to lead his followers in battle against their opponents" some of the faithful were reluctant. They argued with you [Muhammad] about the truth that had been revealed, as though they were being led to certain death." Muhammad says he prayed to God for help, and God responded as follows: "You [Muhammad] were overcome by sleep, a token of His [Allah's] protection. He sent down water from the sky to cleanse you and to purify you of Satan's filth, to strengthen your hearts and to steady your footsteps. Allah revealed His will to the angels, saying: 'I shall be with you. Give courage to the believers. I shall cast terror into the hearts of the infidels. Strike off their heads, maim them in every limb!'"

A little further on, Muhammad describes his experience the night before a particular battle, when he and his army were encamped across a valley from a gathering of hostile warriors: "Allah made them appear to you in a dream as a small band. Had He showed them to you as a great army, your courage would have failed you and discord would have triumphed in your ranks. But this Allah spared you. He knows your inmost thoughts." The two dreams reflect the warlike environment in which Muhammad and his followers first established the Muslim faith. Although Muhammad spent much time alone in desert caves praying and meditating, he was also a charismatic warrior who led his troops through several harrowing battles. The dream experiences reported in this sura express Muhammad's faith in God's rousing presence during times of violent struggle. In this way the two dreams are similar to many passages in the Torah and the New Testament, where God appears to the faithful in times of danger, violence, and despair to offer reassurance and heavenly comfort.

An unusual feature in this sura is the frank acknowledgment that God may use dreams to deceive the faithful for their own good. Muhammad is grateful that Allah knew his "inmost thoughts," i.e., his secret fear that his army would be defeated, and sent a dream that reassured him. The value of the dream is clearly not in the accuracy of its representation of physical reality, but rather in its inspiring emotional effect on Muhammad-the dream emboldens him to ignore any "realistic" appraisal of his chances and to continue fighting in total confidence of ultimate victory.

17: The Night Journey - This sura begins with the following lines: "Glory be to Him who made His servants go by night from the Sacred Temple [of Mecca] to the farther temple [the Throne of Allah] whose surroundings we have blessed, that we might show him some of Our signs. He alone hears all and observes all." The remainder of the chapter consists of a lengthy revelation to Muhammad regarding the creation of the world, resurrection and the afterlife, ritual practice, ethical precepts, warnings against unbelief, and several other key principles of the Muslim faith. The text does not specifically say whether Muhammad's journey occurred in a waking or dreaming state.

The visionary quality of the experience and the fact that it happened at night support the belief that it was a dream, but later Muslim commentators have argued that it was not a dream but an actual physical transportation to heaven. Here we run into the difficult methodological problem of trying to distinguish dreams from other types of extraordinary visionary experience. How to tell the difference between dreams, visions, hallucinations, out-of-body experiences, and so forth is a major challenge for the cross-cultural study of dreams. I will return to this issue at the end of the essay; for the moment, I simply want to highlight the fact that this sura, one of the most mystically evocative narratives in the whole Qur'an, is decidedly ambiguous about whether or not Muhammad's "Night Journey" was a dream.

Dreams in the Hadith

Both during and after Muhammad's death a number of accounts were written of his words and deeds, and these accounts are gathered in the hadith. Among the various sayings of the hadith are several detailed discussions of dreams and dreaming. Although secondary in theological importance to the passages from the Qur'an, the references to dreaming in the hadith are extremely significant historically, and they have added important conceptual and technical elements to the dream traditions of Islam. In particular, the hadith contain abundant references to the practice of dream interpretation, and many of the interpretive principles enunciated in these passages continue to guide the dream practices of present-day Muslims in countries around the world.

The legitimacy of dream interpretation as a religious activity receives strong endorsement from the hadith, most directly in the verses that state: "When the companions of the Messenger of God [Muhammad] saw dreams while he was still alive they would tell him of their dreams and he, for his part, would interpret them as God willed." Many hadith describe Muhammad's interpretations of particular images and symbols in the dreams of his followers, while other verses tell of Muhammad's own dreams and his interpretations of them. For example, the hadith report several dreams Muhammad had of his friend 'Umar, who later became one of his successors. The dreams express Muhammad's respect and admiration for the power of 'Umar's faith, and this provided 'Umar with a kind of divine sanction for the day when he assumed religious authority following the death of Muhammad.

According to these texts, Muhammad was sensitive to the practical difficulties encountered by many of his followers who were trying to interpret their own dreams. The first suggestion Muhammad makes is to tell the dream to someone else: "A dream rests on the feathers of a bird and will not take effect unless it is related to someone." However, people should be careful not to reveal too much in public; "tell your dreams only to knowledgeable persons and loved ones," and beware those who will use your dreams against you (like Joseph's brothers did against him). Muhammad gives a colorful warning to those who abuse the practice of dream interpretation: "Whoever claims to have had a dream in which he says he saw something he did not shall be ordered [in Hell] to tie a knot between two barley grains and will not be able to do so."

To help people increase their chances of having a good dream, Muhammad offers suggestions about how to approach sleep in a state of ritual purity, with the specific instruction to try sleeping on the right side. Bad dreams come from Satan, and he says people should refrain from talking about these dreams and instead "offer a prayer" and "seek refuge with Allah from [the dream's] evil." The hadith that reads, "Whoever sees me [the Prophet] in dreams will see me in wakefulness [the Hereafter] for Satan cannot take my shape" has long been understood to mean that a dream in which Muhammad appears as a character is unquestionably a true dream. Every other kind of dream could be a malevolent deception sent by Satan, but a dream of Muhammad can be accepted with complete confidence as an authentic revelation because Satan does not have the power to assume the shape of God's Prophet.

Perhaps the most often quoted hadith on the subject of dreams reads, "The good dream is 1/46th of prophecy." While commentators have long debated the significance of this exact number, the general sense of the passage is clear: dreams are a legitimate source of divine knowledge. This basic attitude in the hadith-dreams are not the only source of religious revelation, but nevertheless a real and important one available to a wide spectrum of people-builds on the positive evaluation of dreams in the Qur'anic verses discussed above and gives a more definitive shaping to the beliefs and practices of later Muslims.

The hadith include two particular dreams of Muhammad that are worth mentioning. In the first, the Prophet explains how he interpreted one of his own dreams: "I saw in a dream that I waved a sword and it broke in the middle, and behold, that symbolized the casualties the believers suffered on the Day [of the battle] of Uhud. Then I waved the sword again, and it became better than it had ever been before; and behold, that symbolized the Conquest [of Mecca] which Allah brought about and the gathering of the leaders." The broken sword is a striking emblem of military defeat and social humiliation, a vivid imagistic reference that would be likely to resonate strongly with his battle-tested followers.

In that context, the suddenly restored and improved sword symbolizes the transcendent power of Muslim faith. What looks impossible can actually be done, what appears lost can be regained, what seems fractured can be made whole again-all of this is possible, if people are willing to give complete trust in the Almighty. Here again, a brief dream memorably expresses one of the preeminent themes of Islamic belief and practice. The second dream to note in the hadith is recounted by A'isha, the woman Muhammad married after the death of his first wife Khadija: "Allah's Apostle said to me [A'aisha], 'You were shown to me twice [in my dream] before I married you. I saw an angel carrying you in a silken piece of cloth, and I said to him, "Uncover

[her]," and behold, it was you. I said [to myself], "If this is from Allah, then it must happen."

Then you were shown to me, the angel carrying you in a silken piece of cloth, and I said [to him], "Uncover her," and behold, it was you. I said [to myself], "If this is from Allah, then it must happen." After the death of Khadija, we may imagine Muhammad felt some degree of uncertainty about whether he should take a new wife, and if yes, then whom he should choose. His decision would of course have profound implications for both his personal life and the political dynamics of the religious movement he was building. These twin dreams provide Muhammad with divine guidance in a potentially difficult situation, sanctioning his choice of A'aisha in a manner very much like his dreams legitimating the status of his successor 'Umar, mentioned above. The repetitive nature of the two dreams emphasizes the clarity of their message, which is that A'aisha has been presented to Muhammad as a gift from God. Not just in war but in love as well, dreams reveal the will of Allah.

Classical Topologies

Inspired by these teachings from the Qur'an and the hadith, Muslim philosophers and theologians in subsequent years continued the process of developing new techniques and conceptual frameworks for the practice of dream interpretation. The most famous of the early dream interpreters was Ibn Sirin, whose name was reverently attached to dream interpretation manuals for many centuries after his death in 728 C.E. One of the Ibn Sirin's key teachings was to pay close attention to the personal characteristics of the dreamer.

The following anecdote about his interpretive method appears in several texts: "Two dreamers came to Ibn Sirin within an hour of each other and each had dreamed of being the caller to prayer (muezzin). The first person was told that his dream foretold that he would perform the Muslim pilgrimage to Mecca. The second man, who seemed to be of a baser character, was told that he would be accused of a theft. [His] pupils then questioned how Ibn Sirin could come up with such radically different interpretations for the same dream. His response was that the character of each dreamer was evident from his appearance and demeanor.

Therefore, the first one's dream evoked the Qur'anic verse 'Proclaim to the people a solemn pilgrimage' (20:28) since he was clearly pious. The second man's dream evoked the verse 'Then a crier called after them, O company of travelers [Joseph's brothers], you are surely thieves' (12:70)." Ibn Sirin's reference to specific scriptural passages reflects the fact that Muslims are thoroughly steeped from an early age in the text of the Qur'an. Memorization of Qur'anic verses has long been a central feature of Muslim education, and Ibn Sirin's interpretive strategy relies heavily on people's intimate familiarity with the language, characters, and themes of the Qur'an. Perhaps of most interest to Western psychological researchers, Ibn Sirin explicitly teaches that a given dream's meaning cannot be determined without reference to the personality characteristics of the dreamer.

There is, in other words, no "one size fits all" interpretation for any particular dream symbol; the meaning depends on the personality and life circumstances of the dreamer. The same interpretive principle appears in the Oneirocritica of Artemidorus, a second C.E. writer from the Roman Empire. Artemidorus' work was translated into Arabic in 877, and it gave a major stimulus to the further development of Muslim dream theory and practice. Here is the point where Muslim traditions begin to expand beyond their Christian and Jewish counterparts. Indeed, I would argue (without having the space to defend my claim fully) that during its Medieval period Christianity effectively repudiated dreaming as a legitimate source of divine revelation by increasingly emphasizing the potential for demonic temptation in dreams.

Although religiously-oriented dream traditions continued and in some cases even flourished at the level of popular Christian practice, the attitude of theologians and church officials from Augustine through Aquinas, Luther, Calvin, and on into the present day has been generally hostile to dreams and dream interpretation. Judaism did not suffer this kind of decline in the religious authority of dreams. On the contrary, thinkers like Moses Maimonides (1135-1204) continued to develop creative new ways of conceptualizing the revelatory power of dreams. But Judaism never achieved anything like the geographic spread of Islam (from the Atlantic to the border of China in just its first 100 years), nor did Judaism ever produce the kind of spectacular efflorescence of scientific and philosophical discovery that occurred in the Classical Era of Islamic history (from approximately the ninth to thirteenth centuries C.E.).

Tabir, the Muslim science of dream interpretation, emerged in this period as dynamic body of knowledge integrating Islamic faith with the classical heritage of the Greeks and Romans. Nothing emerged in Judaism or Christianity to rival the breadth and sophistication of this tradition, and it is an open question whether any civilization from India, China, or anywhere else ever matched the richness of classical Islamic dream knowledge. Looking in more detail at the Muslim teachings, the first example to consider comes from the philosopher Ibn Arabi (1164-1240), who devised a grand metaphysical system merging Islamic theology with Greek philosophy. His typology of dreaming establishes the basic framework used throughout later Muslim history. According Ibn Arabi, there are three basic types of dream.

The first is an "ordinary" dream, produced by the imagination when it takes experiences from daily life and magnifies them as in a mirror, reflecting in a distorted symbolic fashion our wishes and desires. The second and much more significant type of dream draws its material not from daily life but from the "Universal Soul," a source of knowledge closely associated with the faculty of abstract reasoning. "Universal Soul" dreams reveal fundamental truths about reality, although like the first type of dream these ones are distorted by the imperfect mirror of the human imagination.

Interpretation is therefore required to discover what the symbolic images mean. The third and final type of dream involves a direct revelation of reality, with no distortion or symbolic mediation-a clear vision of divine truth. Ibn Arabi's typology portrays a wider range of dream experience than is usually acknowledged in Western psychological thinking, which focuses its attention almost exclusively on his first category, the "ordinary" dreams of daily life. A further elaboration of this three-part typology appears in the monumental Muqaddimah ("An Introduction to History") written by the philosopher Ibn Khaldun (1332-1402). He explains the different types of dreams in this way: "Real dream vision is an awareness on the part of the rational soul in its spiritual essence, of glimpses of the forms of events.... This happens to the soul [by means of] glimpses through the agency of sleep, whereby it gains the knowledge of future events that it desires and regains the perceptions that belong to it.

When this process is weak and indistinct, the soul applies to it allegory and imaginary pictures, in order to gain [the desired knowledge]. Such allegory, then, necessitates interpretation. When, on the other hand, this process is strong, it can dispense with allegory. Then, no interpretation is necessary, because the process is free from imaginary pictures.... One of the greatest hindrances [to this process] is the external senses. God, therefore, created man in such a way that the veil of the senses could be lifted through sleep, which is a natural function of man. When that veil is lifted, the soul is ready to learn the things it desires to know in the world of Truth. At times, it catches a glimpse of what it seeks.... Clear dream visions are from God.

Allegorical dream visions, which call for interpretation, are from the angels. And 'confused dreams' are from Satan, because they are altogether futile, as Satan is the source of futility." Ibn Khaldun refines the philosophical and theological foundations of Ibn Arabi's three-part typology. He emphasizes the idea that in sleep people are liberated from their senses, freeing their rational souls to gain glimpses of transcendent truth. This same theme runs throughout Platonic and Neoplatonic thinking about dreams, and it seems likely that Ibn Khaldun was familiar with those Graeco-Roman philosophical notions and used them to enrich his own understanding of dreams. The distinctive feature in Ibn Khaldun's theory is that God deliberately created sleep as an opportunity for humans to "lift the veil of the senses" and gain access to divine realities and higher forms of knowing. Dreaming appears in this light as one of God's gifts to humankind, a "natural" means of spiritual insight potentially available to all people. The foregoing is only the briefest of surveys of the vast wealth of Islamic dream teachings from the classical era.

A modestly sized scholarly literature exists in English that discusses this material, but much more work needs to be done by researchers from both Muslim and non-Muslim backgrounds. For example, it would be interesting to know more about how Islamic theologians understood the sexual dimensions of dreaming, a topic which has long troubled Christian thinking about dreams. It would also be useful to learn more about how dreams have served in Muslim caregiving practices as means of diagnosis and treatment for people suffering from physical and/or emotional distress. And, further information about the influence of dreams on political, legal, and military decision-making would offer excellent comparative material for the study of the problem-solving function of dreaming. My suspicion is that a vast amount of information on these and other questions does exist, but it has not yet received much attention from mainstream Western dream researchers.

Dreams in Contemporary Islam

Turning to the beliefs and practices of today's Muslims, who number over a billion people living in countries all over the globe, the main point to note is the strong historical continuity of the dream traditions discussed so far. The basic ideas about dreaming found in the Qur'an and the hadith are still a living influence in the contemporary Muslim world, and it appears that the people of several Muslim countries hold dreaming in a much higher regard than is generally true anywhere in North America or Western Europe. One detailed piece of research will have to suffice as evidence for this admittedly broad claim. Valerie J. Hoffman's work on the role of visions in contemporary Egypt indicates that for present-day Muslims religiously revelatory dreams are a surprisingly widespread phenomenon.

Hoffman argues that the experience of such dreams does not indicate a pre-modern or naively superstitious mentality; on the contrary, the people she describes are well-educated, technologically proficient, and psychologically healthy. Although many Westerners assume modern civilization and religious faith are mutually antithetical, the Egyptians Hoffman studies are living proof that this is not universally true. She says the Egyptian Muslims "believe that the ability to receive visions through dreams and in the waking state is a faculty that is latent in human beings, whose attachment to material things clouds their receptivity to impulses from the spiritual realm."

This is a remarkable indication that the fourteenth-century ideas of Ibn Khaldun are alive and well in the minds of twentieth-century Egyptian as they regard their dream experiences. Many of the people described by Hoffman have been deeply influenced by the Sufi mystical tradition of Islam, and this is most evident in their use of dreams as a means of seeking religious instruction: "In the course of my research I collected many stories in which dreams played a major role in guiding people to a particular spiritual guide. In two very similar cases, middle-class, college-educated women-whose families had no connections with Sufism and who claimed no previous knowledge of the major Sufi saints were afflicted by physical and psychological illnesses that medical doctors seemed unable to cure, when suddenly they were visited in their dreams by great Sufi saints, both deceased and living. They found themselves propelled by these dreams to seek the solace of the shrines of the great deceased saints and to seek blessing guidance and healing from specific living spiritual guides. Both of them found the guides they had seen in their visions, and one of them claimed that her dream had shown her the route and physical layout of the house of he woman who was to be her main spiritual guide."

The material gathered by Hoffman offers striking evidence that dreams continue to play an important part in the religious lives of present-day, "modernized" Muslims. Today as 1500 years ago, dreams provide Muslims with direct experiential confirmation their faith, connecting them with divine powers and realities and reassuring them of the living presence of God in their lives. Hoffman's concluding suggestion that "Egyptians may well be defining modernity in a manner that embraces experiences unrecognized by Western rationalism" is a thought-provoking challenge to Western researchers who may not fully appreciate the powerful influence of religious faith, devotional practice, and cultural history on people's dream experiences. What, then, are the most promising areas for Westerners and Muslims to develop further their mutual interest in dreams and dreaming? What are the best prospects for future investigation and dialogue? I have four suggestions, which certainly do not exhaust all possibilities but merely reflect some of my own research interests.

- Dream Patterns: C. G. Jung first was the first in the Western psychological tradition to investigate in real detail the question of whether certain dreams have fundamentally different psychological structures from other types of dreams. Jung's notion of "big dreams" has long been ignored by psychological researchers who focus exclusively on dream data produced in sleep laboratories. But in recent years, extraordinary dreams of unusual cognitive form, aesthetic vitality, and emotional intensity have been the subject of greater theoretical and empirical investigation. One common feature of these intense, highly memorable dreams is that when people describe them they often report a strong feeling that "it wasn't like a normal dream"; in many cases people say they're not even sure it was a dream, although they can't offer a better name for it.

This is reminiscent of our earlier discussion of Muhammad's "Night Journey" and the traditional Islamic debate about whether or not it was a dream or a physical transportation to heaven. I suggest the ambiguity of the Qur'anic text reflects the possibility that Muhammad experienced a type of "big dream" an experience that began in the physical state of sleep and ordinary dreaming but then soared away into the transcendent realm of revelation, inspiration, and divine presence. Seen in this light, the dream typologies of Ibn Arabi, Ibn Khaldun, and many other classical Muslim thinkers offer valuable observations about various types of extraordinary dream experience. Western researchers who aspire to a truly comprehensive understanding of the dreaming imagination could benefit greatly from a careful study of these texts.

Dreams and the Body

Although classical Muslim typologies recognize the transcendent dimensions of dreaming, they also provide detailed analyses of the bodily basis of dreaming experience, with a special focus on several different emotions (anger, fear, lust) that influence the formation of different kinds of dreams. Most Western researchers are on familiar ground here, and their findings about rapid eye moment (REM) sleep and the neuropsychology of dreaming should find a ready conceptual space in the Islamic tradition. For example, the common Muslim belief that dreams appearing just before waking are more truthful than dreams from earlier in the night could be correlated with the Western research finding that in most cases the longest REM period of the night (when the dreaming imagination seems to be especially active) comes during the last hour or two of the sleep cycle, right before waking.

Gender

The work of several Western scholars has focused on the significance of gender in dream beliefs, practices, and experiences. According to the content analysis work of Calvin Hall, Robert Van de Castle, and G. William Domhoff, men and women dream differently, and one of the major differences regards the rate in which the other gender appears in their dreams: women's dreams have an equal percentage of male and female characters, while men's dreams have twice as many male characters as females. This finding is based largely, though not exclusively, on Western populations, and it would be fascinating to know if the same pattern exists in various Muslim communities, where gender boundaries tend to be at least as sharply drawn and forcefully defended as in Western society.

A key question raised by the content analysis research is whether gender differences in dream content reflect genetically-determined psychophysiological differences between men and women, or the socializing influences of education, cultural expectation, and gender stereotyping, or some combination of the two. The best way to address this question is to investigate the dream lives of people from many different cultures, and here again the Islamic tradition offers an abundant source of comparative material.

What are contemporary Muslims dreaming right now? The Qur'an and hadith are clear about the special value of dreaming in times of military conflict, and I strongly suspect that many present-day Muslims are dreaming about the events of September 11 and talking with each other about what their dreams mean in relation to the current outbreak of warfare. I would be very, very interested in learning about those conversations. I know, based on my own research, that many people in the United States are experiencing profoundly troubling dreams related to September 11, dreams filled with planes crashing, bombs exploding, buildings crumbling, and terrorists attacking children and family members.

These dreams reflect the deep emotional impact of the events of September 11 on the American psyche, and in future work I hope to investigate these dreams as expressions of an extraordinary psychological effort to make meaning in a time of social trauma, anger, and confusion. As I contemplate that project, I wonder-do Muslim dream experiences contain any of these same themes, or do they express a totally different complex of perceptions, feelings, beliefs, and desires? Are Muslims dreaming of Westerners as much as Westerners are dreaming of Muslims?

9

Intellectual Life in the First Four Centuries of Islam

Arabic Poetry and Annalistic were developed independently of the learning of the schools. But as time went on, Literature and Historical Composition could not remain untouched by foreign influences. A few notices, confirmatory of this statement, must suffice us here. The introduction of Islam involved no break with the poetical tradition of the Arab race, such as had been occasioned by Christianity in the Teutonic world. The secular literature of the times even of the Omayyads handed down many wise sayings, partly taken from ancient Arabic poetry, which rivalled the preachings of the Qur'an . Abbasid Caliphs, like Mansur, Harun and Mamun, had more literary culture than Charlemagne.

The education of their sons was not confined to the reading of the Qur'an : it embraced acquaintance also with the ancient poets and with the history of the nation. Poets and literary men were drawn to the courts and rewarded in princely fashion. In these circumstances, Literature underwent the influence of scholarly culture and philosophical speculation, although, in most cases, in a very superficial manner. The result is specially exhibited in sceptical utterances, frivolous mockery of what is most sacred, and glorification of sensual pleasure. At the same time, however, wise sayings, serious reflections and mystic speculations made their way into the originally sober and realistic poetry of the Arabs. The place of the first natural freshness of representation was now taken by a wearisome play on thoughts and sentiments, and even on mere words, metres and rhymes.

The unpleasant Abu-l-Atahia (748-828), in his effeminate poetry, is nearly always talking about unhappy love and a longing for death. He gives expression to his wisdom in the following couplet:

"The mind guide thou with cautious hesitation:

'Gainst sin use the best shield, Renunciation".

Whoever possesses any faculty for appreciating life and the poetry of Nature will find little to enjoy in his world-renouncing songs; and just as little satisfaction will be afforded him in the verses of Mutanabbi (905-965), frightfully tedious in their contents, although epigrammatic in their form. And yet Mutanabbi has been praised as the greatest Arabic poet.

In like manner people have unduly extolled Abu-l-Ala al-Maarri (973—1058) as a philosophic poet. His occasionally quite respectable sentiments and sensible views are not philosophy, nor does the affected though often hackneyed expression of these amount to poetry. Under more favourable conditions,—for he was blind and not surpassingly rich,—this man might perhaps have rendered some service in the subordinate walks of criticism as a philologist or a historical writer. But, in place of an enthusiastic acceptance of life's duties, he is led to preach the joyless abandonment of them, and to grumble generally at political conditions, the opinions of the orthodox multitude, and the scientific assertions of the learned, without being able himself to advance anything positive. He is almost entirely wanting in the gift of combination. He can analyse, but he does not hit upon any synthesis, and his learning bears no fruit.

The, tree of his knowledge has its roots in the air, as he

himself confesses in one of his letters, though in a different sense. He leads a life of strict celibacy and vegetarianism, as becomes a pessimist. As he puts it in his poems "all is but an idle toy: Fate is blind; and Time spares neither the king who partakes of the joys of life, nor the devout man who spends his nights in watching and prayer. Nor does irrational belief solve for us the enigma of existence. Whatever is behind those moving heavens remains hidden from us for ever: Religions, which open up a prospect there, have been fabricated from motives of self-interest. Sects and factions of all kinds are utilized by the powerful to make their dominion secures though the truth about these matters can only be whispered. The wisest thing then is to keep aloof from the world, and to do good disinterestedly, and because it is virtuous and noble to do so, without any outlook for reward".

Other literary men had a more practical philosophy, and could make their weight more felt in the world. They subscribed to the wise doctrine of the Theatre-Manager in Goethe's Faust: "He who brings much, will something bring to many". The most perfect type of this species is Hariri (1054-1122), whose hero, the beggar and stroller, Abu Zaid of Serug, teaches as the highest wisdom:

"Hunt, instead of being hunted;
All the world's a wood for hunting.
If the falcon should escape you,
Take, content, the humble bunting:
If you finger not the dinars,
Coppers still are worth the counting"

The Annalistic of the ancient Arabs, like their Poetry, was distinguished by a clear perception of particulars, but was incapable of taking a general grasp of events. With the vast extension of the empire their view was necessarily widened. First a great mass of material was gathered together. Their historical and geographical knowledge was advanced by means of journeys undertaken to collect traditions, or for purposes of administration and trade, or simply to satisfy curiosity, more than it could have been by mere religious pilgrimages. Characteristic methods of research, brought to bear upon the value of tradition as a source of our knowledge, were elaborated.

With the same subtlety which they displayed in Grammar, they portioned out, in endless division and subdivision, the extended field of their observation, in a fashion more truly 'arabesque' than lucid; and in this way they formed a logic of history which must have appeared to an oriental eye much finer than the Aristotelian Organon with its austere structure. Their tradition,—in authenticating which they were, as a rule, less particular in practice than in theory,—was by many made equal in value to the evidence of the senses, and preferred to the judgment of the reason, which so easily admitted fallacious inferences.

There were always people, however, who impartially handed down contradictory reports, alongside of one another. Others, although exhibiting consideration for the feelings and requirements of the present, did not withhold their more or less well-founded judgment on the past, for it is often easier to be discerning in matters of history than in the affairs of the living world. New subjects of enquiry came up, together with new modes of treatment. Geography included somewhat of Natural Philosophy, for example in the geography of climate; while historical composition brought within the range of its description intellectual life, belief, morals, literature and science. Acquaintance also with other lands and nations invited comparison on many points; and thus an international, humanistic or cosmopolitan element was introduced.

A representative of the humanistic attitude of mind is met with in Masudi, who died about the year 956. He appreciates, and is interested in, everything that concerns humanity. Everywhere he is learning something from the men he meets with: and in consequence the reading of books, which occupies his privacy, is not without fruit. But it is neither the narrow, everyday practices of life and religion, nor the airy speculations of Philosophy, that specially appeal to him. He knows where his strength lies; and up to the last, when he is spending his old age in Egypt, far from his native home, he finds his consolation,—the medicine of his soul,—in the study of History. History for him is the all-embracing science: it is his philosophy; and its task is to set forth the truth of that which was and is.

Even the wisdom of the world, together with its development, becomes the subject of History; and without it all knowledge would long since have disappeared. For learned men come and go; but History records their intellectual achievements, and thereby restores the connection between the past and the present. It gives us unprejudiced information about events and about the views of men. Of course Masudi leaves it often to the intelligent reader to find out for himself the due synthesis of the facts and the individual opinion of the author.

A successor of his, the geographer Maqdasi, or Muqaddasi, who wrote in the year 985, deserves to be mentioned with high commendation. He journeyed through many countries, and exercised the most varied callings, in order to acquaint himself with the life of his time. He is a true Abu Zaid of Serug, but one with an object before him. He sets to work in critical fashion, and holds to the knowledge which is gained by research and enquiry, not by faith in tradition or by mere deductions of the reason. The geographical statements in the Qur'an be explains by the limited intellectual horizon of the ancient Arabs, to which Allah must have seen fit to adapt himself.

He describes then, *sine ira et studio,* the countries and races he has seen with own eyes. His plan is to set down, in the first place, results gathered from his own experience and observation; next, what he has heard from trustworthy people; and last of all what he has met with in books. The following sentences are extracted from his characterization of himself. "I have given instruction in the common subjects of education and morals: I have come forward as a preacher, and I have made the minaret of the mosque resound with the call to prayer. I have been present at the meetings of the learned and the devotions of the pious. I have partaken of broth with Sufis, gruel with monks, and ship's-fare with sailors.

Many Man a time I have been seclusion itself, and then again I have eaten forbidden fruit against my better judgment. I associated with the hermits of Lebanon, and in turn I lived at the court of the Prince. In wars I have participated: I have been detained as a captive and thrown into prison as a spy. Powerful princes and ministers have lent me their ear, and anon I have joined a band of robbers, or sat as a retail-dealer in the bazaar. I have enjoyed much honour and consideration, but I have likewise been fated to listen to many curses and to be reduced to the ordeal of the oath, when I was suspected of heresy or evil deeds". We are accustomed at the present day to picture to ourselves the Oriental as a being who, in contemplative repose, is completely bound to his ancestral faith and usages.

This representation is not quite correct, but still it agrees better with the situation which now exists than it does with the disposition of Islam in the first four centuries, for during that period it was inclined to take into its possession not only the outward advantages of the world, but also the intellectual acquisitions of Mankind. The rise, expansion, decline, and resurgence of Islamic civilization form one of the greatest epics in world history. In the course of the last fourteen centuries, Muslim philosophers and poets, artists and scientists, princes and laborers together created a unique culture that has directly and indirectly influenced societies on every continent.

What is Islam? The word means several things. Islam is the youngest of the world's three major monotheistic religions. Islam is a way of life governing all aspects of human behavior. Islam is an intellectual and emotional force that in our time binds together about one out of every five of the world's people, uniting its adherents through a common faith and a written language, despite diverse identities of race, nation, and political affiliation. Islamic culture has always demonstrated, within a unity of spiritual vision, a spectacularly broad diversity of style and expression. Heirs to earlier cultures of Asia, classical Greece and Rome, as well as Byzantium and Africa, Muslims took possession of their mixed heritage, preserving much of it and transforming much of it.

heir cultural and political experience had a profound influence on the late medieval world of Western Europe, where Muslim achievements played an essential part in the evolution of the Renaissance and thus on the formation of later societies, including our own. During the most recent three centuries the Western world has become familiar with many of the monuments and works of art and literature created in various Islamic periods and lands. The Taj Mahal, the great mosques of Cairo, Damascus, Istanbul, and Isfahan, the exquisite miniature paintings that enhance the historical and mythical sagas of Persian and Indian kings, the fabulous tales of the "Thousand Nights and One Night," Omar Khayyam's Rubayyat: these are but a few of the celebrated Islamic creations that we in the West now recognize as integral parts of our own cultural inheritance.

One part of the Islamic heritage has been until recent years less familiar to us, yet it has had a fundamental influence on all postmedieval lives: the historic achievement of Islamic philosopher-scientists, physicians, astronomers, mathematicians, technologists, and naturalists. Here was an elite community that included Christians and Jews as well as Muslims and comprised the first multiethnic and multinational group of its kind in the world's history. The accomplishments of this extraordinary scientific brotherhood are the subject of this illustrated introductory survey. From the ninth century on, scientists in Islamic lands acquired, through translations into Arabic, a treasury of Greek, Indian, Persian, and Babylonian philosophic and scientific thought.

They proceeded diligently to assimilate and systemize this intellectual legacy, all the while enriching it with innovation and invention, particularly in the areas of mathematics, optics, medicine, and astronomy. Their ultimate achievement was an unprecedented and harmoniously synthesized body of knowledge—the world's first truly international science. What inspired the early scientific effort of the Islamic world? What sustained it? What obstacles confronted its progress as the centuries passed? What factors, within and beyond Islamic lands, contributed to its eclipse? What, ultimately, was the extent of the Islamic scientific enterprise? How did it influence the development of our world of science today? A look at the dynamic birth of Islamic civilization can open the way toward finding answers to these questions.

The Gregorian and Islamic Calendars

For simplicity's sake, in the following text dates are given according to the Gregorian calendar now in use in most non-Islamic lands. However, any reader interested in deciphering dates found in historic Muslim manuscripts and on astronomical instruments may wish to relate the Muslim date to the corresponding Gregorian one. At the beginning of Islamic civilization, the Caliph 'Umar established a new calendar system, based on the first day of the year (AD 622 in which the Prophet Muhammad left Mecca. This day thus marked the start of Year One in the Islamic calendar. Since that time Muslims have preceded the date with Ax (anno hegirae, representing the year of Muhammad's emigration, the Hegira, as opposed to AD (anno Domini), which has either preceded or followed the Gregorian date since being introduced in Britain in the eighteenth century.

Inasmuch as the Islamic year is based on lunar months and amounts approximately to 354 days as opposed to the approximately 365 days of the Gregorian solar year, converting from one calendar to the other requires a bit of calculation. One basic equation does the job, approximately: AD = 622 + (32/33 x AH). Alternatively, AH = (33/32) x (AD - 622). The equation is derived from the fact that every 32 Gregorian years are about equal to 33 Muslim Hegira years. Thus, a Gregorian century amounts to about 103 Muslim Hegira years; ioo Muslim Hegira years equal about 97 Gregorian years. These discrepancies account for the fact that Muslim holidays and festivals may come around in any season. The Gregorian year AD 2000 will begin during the Islamic year AH 1421.

To avoid confusion for readers unfamiliar with the Arabic language, only two of Arabic's many symbols and diacritical marks have been included in the text: the 'ayn and the 'hamza. The 'ayn signifies a sort of rough breath, the 'hamza a glottal sound. Western spelling has been used for placenames most commonly known to Western readers.

Roots

The family tree of science traces a complicated ancestry. Egyptian and Babylonian processes of scientific inquiry that developed three thousand years before the birth of Christ were the precursors of Hellenic or Greek investigations, which in turn produced Hellenistic and Harranian (pre-Islamic northern Mesopotamian) and, in part, Persian science. All these influences nurtured the later scientific enterprise of Islamic civilization. This network of transmission was further extended before and during the Islamic era by direct connections, often commercial, between Egypt and other parts of the Hellenistic world, by links between Hellenic and Harranian science, and, last but not least, by important influences from India and China, the first passing through Persia, the second directly, if somewhat intermittently, carried by travelers to Islamic lands.

These varied legacies produced a far more international, intercultural, and abundant inheritance of intellectual riches than had ever before been received by any single civilization. It was a treasury long forgotten or unknown in much of the medieval world up to the Muslim conquests in the seventh century AD. Most important to it were the manuscript remnants that contained the greatest achievements of Greek science, those of the fourth and third centuries BC, in particular, as well as the achievements of Hellenistic scientists five centuries later. These works, long ignored, were found from the eighth century on by Muslim leaders and scholars when they explored Byzantine libraries and other collections of rarities.

The disintegration of Roman civilization during the early centuries of the Christian era was marked by the general deterioration of most of the basic endeavors that enable society to survive and flourish, from producing food in abundance to generating original ways of improving the conditions of daily life. These were not centuries of much significant or extensive cultural creativity. In Europe in the early Middle Ages intellectual and social progress was fitful when not atrophied. The times were more than usually propitious for superstition, belief in magic, and reliance on every kind of prophecy or divination—whatever might help to shore up faltering faith or provide a gratifying substitute for undeniable logic.

The Muslim conquerors at first gave little indication that they would revitalize cultural life in the communities they came to dominate politically and economically. The Arabs' pre-Islamic civilization had not been marked by notable scientific advance. Members of wandering Bedouin tribes or traders, Arabs and Berbers inevitably gained considerable practical knowledge of geology, plants, and animals in managing to survive in the inhospitable landscapes of the Arabian peninsula and North Africa. They knew well the limited pasture and the oases, caravan trails, and waterways in and adjacent to their lands; they had learned to use the stars in time-telling and travel. But the emergence of Islam, the vigor of the Muslim conquest, and the accompanying enthusiasm for exploring and exploiting the intellectual and commercial riches waiting in every major community that they conquered soon propelled Muslims beyond the development of practical technology.

The time was indeed at hand for the extraordinary intellectual, artistic, and scientific progress achieved throughout Islamic lands in the centuries between 800 and 1600. The development of the Muslims' imperial civilization turned cities such as Damascus, Baghdad, Cairo, and Córdoba into great cultural and commercial capitals, kept in regular contact through expanding networks of land and sea routes. Sponsored largely by caliphs and their royal courts, architecture and the decorative arts flourished, each in ways uniquely regional, yet each in ways recognizably Islamic. Great universities were founded, each one serving thousands of students. By the twelfth century the civilization of Islam was sophisticated far beyond that of Christian Europe.

Its society was increasingly urban in character, and its thriving commerce, dominating the entire Mediterranean basin, reflected shrewd, practical, and productive management of people, goods, and wealth. Scholars in the West have long given most of their studies of medieval history a Eurocentric orientation, despite the fact that for at least six centuries, Islam was a uniquely vital cultural and commercial force. In diverse national and ethnic ways Islam's culture displayed a unified religious spirit long after Islamic imperial power began to wane at the end of the tenth century. However, that spirit was increasingly challenged by a spreading worldliness, a growing focus on earthly as opposed to "celestial" or spiritual matters. This confrontation affected all areas of Muslim life, including the sciences.

We must remember that we are speaking generally of science written and carried on in the Arabic language, rather than simply of Muslim science: from the very beginning the Islamic scientific community included many Christians and Jews as well as Muslims, and it embraced Indians and

Persians as well as Arabs. This ethnic and religious mixture probably rendered early Muslim scientific endeavor more resistant to theological constraint than it would have been had only Muslim Arabs been involved. In any event, ancient Egyptian, Mesopotamian, Persian, and Hindu achievements greatly influenced virtually all scientific development during the first few centuries of the Islamic empire.

What seems remarkable is the fervor with which Muslim scientists as a whole embraced the diverse heritage they discovered in their new domains. As a crusading faith, Islam could have been expected to try to eradicate or denigrate most achievements of what were often ideologically perceived as profane, misguided, or inferior societies of the past. This did not happen, instead, the ancient legacy was treasured and utilized almost from the time of the conquerors' arrival. As a first step, an efficient and large-scale means of transmission from past to present was rapidly organized and put into service.

Period of Translation

The city of Gondeshapur in southwestern Persia was captured by the Arabs in AD 638; it became a center for the dissemination of Greek and other ancient philosophical and scientific knowledge throughout the new Islamic empire. Here flourished a large community of Nestorians, members of a Christian sect that had been charged with heresy and forced to flee from Christian territory late in the fifth century. The city had long supported a notable academy of scholars and physicians, many of whom spoke Greek and Sanskrit as well as Syriac, an Aramaic dialect then in wide use throughout the region. After the Arab conquest, these scholars quickly became familiar with Arabic.

An intensive program of translation into Arabic of philosophical, medical, and other scientific manuscripts was sponsored by the new Muslim caliphs, and soon this rapidly expanding enterprise spread to Baghdad and Damascus, the cultural centers of the Abbasid dynasty. Without historical precedent, the quantity of translations produced in Gondeshapur represented from the start an ecumenical as well as an international effort, involving many Christians and Jews as well as Muslims. It was most often an enterprise prompted by royal decree, reflecting interest on the part of caliphs and other high officials of court and government not only in practical sciences such as medicine and astronomy but also in the less exact precepts of astrology and alchemy. These two exotic disciplines, of course, had already enjoyed centuries of official and public support and would continue to do so for centuries more, in both East and West.

A parallel translation program, from Greek to Latin, was underway at the time in medieval Christian Europe. Sponsored by monasteries such as Monte Cassino and by rulers such as Charlemagne, its goal was the same as that of the effort being undertaken in the Islamic lands: to produce translations of classical Greek texts. This effort, however, did not match the Muslim output in scope or quantity until the twelfth century, when imperial Islam had begun to lose some of its political and cultural supremacy. Two centuries of Muslim translation succeeded in making the major works of Plato, Aristotle, Euclid, Archimedes, Hippocrates, Galen, Ptolemy, and many others available to Muslim scholars in settlements from Persia to Spain. Not all the translations were of the greatest fidelity or quality, but revisions became frequent as scholarship matured. Flexible and capable of accommodating new concepts, procedures, and the details of science as well as of philosophy, the Arabic language proved to be a resourceful vehicle.

At the outset of this enterprise emerged outstanding translators, such as Hunayn ibn Ishaq, a ninth-century Nestorian Christian who was expert in four languages and who produced a mass of work covering much of Greek philosophy and medicine. Another eminent scientist, Thabit ibn Qurra, was particularly noted for his translations and revisions of works on logic, mathematics, and astronomy. A member of a family of distinguished scientists and scholars, he never converted to Islam; he was a member of a pagan sect, the Sabians, who were mentioned in the Qur'an and thus had protected status. In the early selections of works to be translated, priority was given to subjects deemed most immediately useful, such as medicine, mathematics, and astronomy, the latter two needed in orientation for religious practice and for astrological prediction. However, within two centuries an encyclopedic classical treasury was available in Arabic, embracing Greek knowledge and Hellenistic contributions.

This store of cultural riches was capable of filling the intellectual needs of a new civilization even as that civilization was pursuing spiritual, political, and cultural aims radically different from those of ancient Greece and Rome. By the eleventh century Muslim rulers had established appropriate institutions designed to preserve and maintain this treasury and put it to Islamic use. Islam's first few centuries witnessed the establishment of great libraries and centers of learning in both East and West. The most celebrated of these were located in the seats of political or imperial power. A famous "house of wisdom" (*Bayt al-hikma*) flourished in ninth-century Abbasid Baghdad; it was a center not only for translation but also for specialized scholarly study and investigation. Notable libraries were established in several Persian cities. In tenth-century Cairo, under Fatimid dynasty rule, one of the libraries contained forty rooms holding many thousands of works devoted to the ancient sciences.

In Umayyad Spain, the great capital of Córdoba was, like Cairo and Baghdad, a center of higher learning that drew students and visiting scholars from all regions of Islam. Cairo's al-Azhar, founded late in the tenth century as a training school for preachers, later contained mosque schools (*madrasa*) and still flourishes today. After nearly a millennium of uninterrupted existence, it is the world's oldest university or college. A science academy was established during the tenth century at Córdoba, and another at Toledo. Generally, however, advanced education in science was carried out on a personal rather than an institutional scale, within the confines of royal courts and royally sponsored establishments such as observatories and hospitals. A young man seeking high-level education in the sciences had to wait until he had progressed beyond elementary school and the *madrasa,* where he could receive instruction in basic mathematics.

University curricula might include advanced mathematics, some astronomy, medicine, and natural sciences such as biology, but these subjects were treated largely within a framework of Qur'anic fundamentals and interpretation as well as principles of religious law. At the caliph's court, however, the young man might be fortunate enough to be admitted to a circle centered on one of the great teachers—often a person celebrated for achievement in more than one science, a philosopher-physician, perhaps, or a mathematician-astronomer. Such high-level scholarship represented the upper track of a two-track system. On the lower track, those of the general population who went through elementary education were offered mostly the curricula and concepts that were officially deemed appropriate or adequate for the many. In addition, the procedures of traditional Muslim elementary education did not promote original speculation.

Listening, reading, recitation, and preparation by rote formed a great part of the process of learning. As for prospects for young women who might be interested in learning more about the sciences or any other major academic subjects, they did not exist to any significant degree in any Islamic community until the second half of our own century. The character of Islam's specialized scientific education can be better understood if one considers the traditional Islamic concept of knowledge and the ways in which knowledge and the curriculum were organized and classified in early Islam. Not only was the pursuit of knowledge exhorted by many *hadith,* the statements traditionally attributed to Muhammad, the Qur'an emphasizes the value of knowledge in grasping the nature of the world around us.

As previously noted, Muslim religious doctrine defines the universe as a sign of God's activity; therefore, study of that activity is thought to provide knowledge of the right path toward the proper life on earth and salvation in the life beyond. Muslim religious leaders and educators devoted considerable time to classifying the sciences and clarifying their specific functions as they would help each person to acquire knowledge within an intellectual framework that would serve God's purpose. Definitive classifications were attempted by such intellectual giants as al-Farabi, Ibn Sina, and Ibn Khaldun, the greatest of the Muslim historianphilosophers.

Ibn Khaldun's system reveals basic distinctions that were widely adopted. First in his schema came the traditional religious sciences, dealing with examination and readings of the Qurán, the science of tradition, sciences of jurisprudence and dialectics (argument, speculative theology, mysticism, the interpretation of dreams, and philological science. A second major group, the philosophical sciences, included, first, Aristotelian logic; second, in a sort of umbrella category, physics, including medicine, agriculture, magic, alchemy, and other esoteric disciplines; third, metaphysics; and fourth, mathematics, covering numerical sciences such as arithmetic, calculation, algebra, commercial transactions, the apportioning of inheritances, geometrical sciences such as spherical and conical geometry, surveying, optics, and astronomy, including tabulation and astrology. Finally came music, which was considered a mathematical discipline.

Whatever the variations in degree, the different systems for the classification of learning all reflected a fundamental acceptance of the supremacy of the Islamic Revelation. Eventually there developed profound suspicion, even fear, of influences that might be exercised by intellectual disciplines inherited from the ancient world. There evolved a clear distinction between "revealed" subjects connected with religion and centered around the Qurán and those not connected with religion, considered "rational" subjects. What today we would call physics, biology, agronomy, and the earth sciences belonged to this latter group.

As a whole these sciences, termed "philosophical" because they were considered accessible through human reason rather than through faith, were regarded as foreign because of their origins in classical Greece and India. Among them, philosophy in particular, at first praised as a valuable tool inherited from the Greeks, was singled out by some orthodox scholars and leaders as alien and suspect. Ironically, the eleventh-century theologian al-Ghazali's belief in the value of logic in dealing with Islamic legal subjects helped to spread the acceptance of rational process as a valid tool in organizing knowledge. The mosque schools and the universities' legally oriented faculties took more or less exclusive charge of teaching the religious disciplines, leaving the philosophical, mathematical, and natural sciences to be taught mostly in the small, royal, elite groups described previously. There was little of a democratic character in medieval higher education, within or beyond Islamic lands.

A dynamic new faith, the vitality of a people freeing themselves from a struggle against the harsh elements of desert life, a pressing curiosity about the world that they encountered outside the Arabian heartland, a need for a share in that world's bounty, a language well-equipped for intellectual exploration: all these factors, binding together Muslims in greater unity than existed among any other civilization at the time, generated a powerful motive for Islam's scientific enterprise. The world, all its forms of life, and the heavens above were now subject to an unprecedented exploration and examination by Muslims and other scholars in Muslim lands. And even where spiritual motivation was less pressing than material enthusiasm and practical curiosity, there was power and material reward to be gained from learning more about what the world was made of and how such knowledge could be put to beneficial and profitable use.

In less than four centuries after the first Islamic conquest, philosophers, mathematicians, botanists, physicians, geographers, alchemists, and their peers in the other scientific disciplines, at work throughout the wide reaches of the Islamic empire, had accomplished the remarkable feat of unwrapping the vast intellectual legacy received from past civilizations, analyzing it in relentless detail, fussing with it, testing and retesting its hypotheses and answers, evolving new ones, and further revising, discarding, or reformulating many of those. From the broadest concepts of the physical universe to details of the smallest scale—including invisible processes within the human body—much was put in order and connected in ways some of which appear to reflect or to parallel the Muslim concept of cosmic unity spelled out in the Islamic Revelation. In sum, a new concept of the universe was put together, in many ways remarkably similar, or at least parallel, to the old ones, in other ways significantly simplified and clarified. More important, from macrocosmic to microcosmic element, this Islamic universe appeared, in general, orderly, functional, workable. It made sense. It represented a critical advance beyond contemporary non-Muslim concepts, most of which it would eventually affect profoundly. What, specifically, did Islam's medieval scientists accomplish? It seems appropriate to begin the inventory with Muslim ideas about the overall cosmos and all that was in it.

Basic Teachings of Islam

Islam is a system of religious beliefs and an allencompassing way of life. Muslims believe that God (Allah) revealed to the Prophet Muhammad the rules governing society and the proper conduct of society's members. Therefore, it is incumbent on the individual to live in a manner prescribed by the revealed law and incumbent on the community to build the perfect human society on earth according to holy injunctions. Islam recognizes no distinctions between church and state. The distinction between religious and secular law is a recent development that reflects the more pronounced role of the state in society and of Western economic and cultural penetration. Religion has a greater impact on daily life in Muslim countries than it has had in the largely Christian West since the Middle Ages.

Islam came to Ethiopia by way of the Arabian Peninsula, where in A.D. 610, Muhammad—a merchant of the Hashimite branch of the ruling Quraysh tribe in the Arabian town of Mecca—began to preach the first of a series of revelations he said had been granted him by God through the angel Gabriel. A fervent monotheist, Muhammad denounced the polytheism of his fellow Meccans. Because the town's economy was based in part on a thriving pilgrimage business to the shrine called the Kaaba and to numerous other pagan religious sites in the area, Muhammad's censure earned him the enmity of the town's leaders. In 622 he and a group of followers accepted an invitation to settle in the town of Yathrib, later known as Medina (the city), because it was the center of Muhammad's activities.

The move, or hijra, known in the West as the hegira, marks the beginning of the Islamic era and of Islam as a force in history; indeed, the Muslim calendar begins in 622. In Medina, Muhammad continued to preach, and he eventually defeated his detractors in battle. He consolidated the temporal and the spiritual leadership in his person before his death in 632. After Muhammad's death, his followers compiled those of his words regarded as coming directly from God into the Quran, the holy scriptures of Islam. Others of his sayings and teachings, recalled by those who had known him, became the hadith. The precedent of Muhammad's personal behavior is called the sunna. Together, these works form a comprehensive guide to the spiritual, ethical, and social life of the orthodox Sunni Muslim.

The duties of Muslims form the five pillars of Islam, which set forth the acts necessary to demonstrate and reinforce the faith. These are the recitation of the shahada ("There is no god but God [Allah], and Muhammad is his prophet."), salat (daily prayer), zakat (almsgiving), sawm (fasting), and hajj (pilgrimage). The believer is to pray in a prescribed manner after purification through ritual ablutions each day at dawn, midday, midafternoon, sunset, and nightfall. Prescribed genuflections and prostrations accompany the prayers, which the worshiper recites facing toward Mecca. Whenever possible, men pray in congregation at the mosque with an imam, or prayer leader, and on Fridays they make a special effort to do so. The Friday noon prayers provide the occasion for weekly sermons by religious leaders. Women may also attend public worship at the mosque, where they are segregated from the men, although women usually pray at home. A special functionary, the muezzin, intones a call to prayer to the entire community at the appropriate hour. Those out of earshot determine the time by the position of the sun.

The ninth month of the Muslim calendar is Ramadan, a period of obligatory fasting in commemoration of Muhammad's receipt of God's revelation. Throughout the month, all but the sick and weak, pregnant or lactating women, soldiers on duty, travelers on necessary journeys, and young children are enjoined from eating, drinking, smoking, or sexual intercourse during the daylight hours. Those adults who are excused are obliged to endure an equivalent fast at their earliest opportunity. A festive meal breaks the daily fast and inaugurates a night of feasting and celebration. The pious well-to-do usually perform little or no work during this period, and some businesses close for all or part of the day. Because the months of the lunar year revolve through the solar year, Ramadan falls at various seasons in different years.

A considerable test of discipline at any time of the year, a fast that falls in summertime imposes severe hardship on those who must do physical work. All Muslims, at least once in their lifetimes, are strongly encouraged to make the hajj to Mecca to participate in special rites held there during the twelfth month of the lunar calendar. Muhammad instituted this requirement, modifying pre-Islamic custom, to emphasize sites associated with God and Abraham (Ibrahim), considered the founder of monotheism and father of the Arabs through his son Ismail. Other tenets of the Muslim faith include the jihad (holy war), and the requirement to do good works and to avoid all evil thoughts, words, and deeds. In addition, Muslims agree on certain basic principles of faith based on the teachings of the Prophet Muhammad: there is one God, who is a unitary divine being, in contrast to the trinitarian belief of Christians; Muhammad, the last of a line of prophets beginning with Abraham and including Moses (Musa) and Jesus (Isa), was chosen by God to present His message to humanity; and there is to be a general resurrection on the last, or judgment, day.

During his lifetime, Muhammad was spiritual and temporal leader of the Muslim community. Religious and secular law merged, and all Muslims traditionally have been subject to sharia, or religious law. A comprehensive legal system, sharia developed gradually through the first four centuries of the Islamic era, primarily through the accretion of interpretations and precedents set by various judges and scholars. After Muhammad's death, Muslim community leaders chose Abu Bakr, the Prophet's father-in-law and one of his earliest followers, to succeed him. At that time, some persons favored Ali ibn Abu Talib, Muhammad's cousin and the husband of his daughter Fatima, but Ali and his supporters (the Shiat Ali, or Party of Ali) eventually recognized the community's choice. The next two caliphs (successors)—Umar, who succeeded in A.D. 634, and Uthman, who took power in 644—enjoyed the recognition of the entire community.

When Ali finally succeeded to the caliphate in 656, Muawiyah, governor of Syria, rebelled in the name of his murdered kinsman Uthman. After the ensuing civil war, Ali moved his capital to the area of present-day Iraq, where he was murdered shortly thereafter. Ali's death ended the last of the so-called four orthodox caliphates and the period in which the entire community of Islam recognized a single caliph. Muawiyah proclaimed himself caliph from Damascus. The Shiat Ali refused to recognize him or his line, the Umayyad caliphs, and withdrew in the great schism to establish the dissident sect, known as the Shia, who supported the claims of Ali's line to the caliphate based on descent from the Prophet.

The larger faction, the Sunnis, adhered to the position that the caliph must be elected, and over the centuries they have represented themselves as the orthodox branch. Early in Islam's history the Sufism movement emerged. It stressed the possibility of emotional closeness to God and mystical knowledge of God in contrast to the intellectual and legalistic emphasis of orthodox Sunni theology. By the twelfth century, this tendency had taken a number of forms. Orders, each emphasizing specific disciplines (ways) of achieving that closeness and knowledge, were organized. Disdained by orthodox Islamic theologians, Sufi orders nevertheless became an integral part of Islam, although their importance varied regionally.

10

Scientific and Philosophical Enquiry

Achievements and Reactions

Science in medieval Islam, also known as Islamic science, is a term used in the history of science to refer to the science developed in the Islamic world between 7th and 16th centuries, a period also known as the Islamic Golden Age. Most texts during this period were written in Arabic, a *lingua franca* of this period; although most scientists were Muslims but they were of diverse ethnicity (mostly Persian but also some of Arab, Berber, Moorish, and Turkic background), in addition to some from other religious backgrounds (Christian, Jewish, Sabian, Zoroastrian, and irreligious).

There are several different views on Islamic science among historians of science. The traditionalist view, as exemplified by Bertrand Russell, holds that Islamic science, while admirable in many technical ways, lacked the intellectual energy required for innovation and was chiefly important as a preserver of ancient knowledge and transmitter to medieval Europe. The revisionist view, as exemplified by Abdus Salam and George Saliba, holds that a Muslim scientific revolution occurred during the Middle Ages, an expression with which scholars such as Donald Routledge Hill and Ahmad Y Hassan express the view that Islam was the driving force behind the Muslim achievements, while Robert Briffault even sees Islamic science as the foundation of modern science.

The most prominent view in recent scholarship, however, as examplified by Toby E. Huff, Will Durant, Fielding H. Garrison, Muhammad Iqbal Hossein Nasr and Bernard Lewis, holds that Muslim scientists did help in laying the foundations for an experimental science with their contributions to the scientific method and their empirical, experimental and quantitative approach to scientific inquiry, but that their work cannot be considered a Scientific Revolution, like that which occurred in early modern Europe and led to the emergence of modern science, with the exception of Ibn al-Haytham's *Book of Optics* which is widely considered a revolution in the fields of optics and visual perception.

During the early Muslim conquests, the Muslim Arab forces, led primarily by Khalid ibn al-Walid, conquered the Sassanid Persian Empire and more than half of the Byzantine Roman Empire, establishing the caliphate across the Middle East, Central Asia, and North Africa, followed by further expansions across Pakistan, southern Italy and the Iberian Peninsula. As a result, the Islamic governments inherited the knowledge and skills of the ancient Middle East, of Greece, of Persia and of India.

The art of papermaking was obtained from two Chinese prisoners at the Battle of Talas (751), resulting in paper mills being built in Samarkand and Baghdad. The Arabs improved upon the Chinese techniques using linen rags instead of mulberry bark. Most notable Arab scientists and Iranian scientists lived and practiced during the Islamic Golden Age, though not all scientists in Islamic civilization were Arab or Muslim. Some argue that the term "Arab-Islamic" does not appreciate the rich diversity of eastern scholars who have contributed to science in that era.

During the Islamic Golden Age, Muslim scholars made significant advances in science, mathematics, medicine, astronomy, engineering, and many other fields. During this time, early Islamic philosophy developed and was often pivotal in scientific debates — key figures were usually scientists and philosophers. The number of important and original Arabic works written on the mathematical sciences is much larger than the combined total of Latin and Greek works on the mathematical sciences.

Scientific Institutions

A number of important institutions previously unknown in the ancient world have their origins in the medieval Islamic world, with the most notable examples being: the public hospital (which replaced healing temples and sleep temples) and psychiatric hospital, the public library and lending library, the academic degree-granting university, the astronomical observatory as a research institute (as opposed to a private observation post as was the case in ancient times), and the trust (Waqf).

The first universities which issued diplomas were the Bimaristan medical university-hospitals of the medieval Islamic world, where medical diplomas were issued to students of Islamic medicine who were qualified to be practicing doctors of medicine from the 9th century. Sir John Bagot Glubb wrote:

"By Mamun's time medical schools were extremely active in Baghdad. The first free public hospital was opened in Baghdad during the Caliphate of Haroon-ar-Rashid. As the system developed, physicians and surgeons were appointed who gave lectures to medical students and issued diplomas to those who were considered qualified to practice. The first hospital in Egypt was opened in 872 AD and thereafter public hospitals sprang up all over the empire from Spain and the Maghrib to Persia."

The Guinness Book of World Records recognizes the University of Al Karaouine in Fez, Morocco as the oldest university in the world with its founding in 859. Al-Azhar University, founded in Cairo, Egypt in the 10th century, offered a variety of academic degrees, including postgraduate degrees, and is often considered the first full-fledged university. A number of distinct features of the modern library were introduced in the Islamic world, where libraries not only served as a collection of manuscripts as was the case in ancient libraries, but also as a public library and lending library, a centre for the instruction and spread of sciences and ideas, a place for meetings and discussions, and sometimes as a lodging for scholars or boarding school for pupils. The concept of the library catalog was also introduced in medieval Islamic libraries, where books were organized into specific genres and categories.

Another common feature during the Islamic Golden Age was the large number of Muslim polymaths or "universal geniuses", scholars who contributed to many different fields of knowledge. Muslim polymaths were known as "Hakeems" and they had a wide breadth of knowledge in many different fields of religious and secular learning, comparable to the later "Renaissance Men", such as Leonardo da Vinci, of the European Renaissance period. Polymath scholars were so common during the Islamic Golden Age that it was rare to find a scholar who specialized in any single field at the time.

Notable Muslim polymaths included al-Biruni, al-Jahiz, al-Kindi, Abu Bakr Muhammad al-Razi, Ibn Sina, al-Idrisi, Ibn Bajja, Ibn Zuhr, Ibn Tufayl, Ibn Rushd, al-Suyuti Geber, al-Khwarizmi, the Banû Mûsâ, Abbas Ibn Firnas, al-Farabi, al-Masudi, al-Muqaddasi, Alhacen, Omar Khayyám, al-Ghazali, al-Khazini, Avempace, al-Jazari, Ibn al-Nafis, Nasîr al-Dîn al-Tûsî, Ibn al-Shatir, Ibn Khaldun, and Taqi al-Din, among many others.

Decline

Islamic science and the numbers of Islamic scientists were traditionally believed to have begun declining from the 12th or 13th centuries. It was believed that, though the Islamic civilization would still produce scientists, that they became the exception, rather than the rule. Recent scholarship, however, has come to question this traditional picture of decline, pointing to continued astronomical activity as a sign of a continuing and creative scientific tradition through to the 16th century, of which the work of Ibn al-Shatir (1304–1375) in Damascus is considered the most noteworthy example.

This was also the case for other areas of Islamic science, such as medicine, exemplified by the works of Ibn al-Nafis and Þerafeddin Sabuncuoolu, and the social sciences, exemplified by Ibn Khaldun's *Muqaddimah* (1370), which itself points out that science was declining in Iraq, Al-Andalus and Maghreb, but continuing to flourish in Persia, Syria and Egypt. One reason given for the scientific decline was when the orthodox Ash'ari school of theology challenged the more rational Mu'tazili school of theology, with al-Ghazali's *The Incoherence of the Philosophers* (*Tahafut al-falasifa*) being the most notable example. This interpretation was introduced by the Hungarian Orientalist Ignaz Goldziher, who believed that there was an intrinsic antagonism between Islamic orthodoxy and the Greek-influenced traditions of science.

Recent scholarship has questioned this traditional view, however, with a number of scholars pointing out that the Ash'ari school supported science but were only opposed to speculative philosophy and that some of the greatest Muslim scientists such as Alhazen, Biruni, Ibn al-Nafis and Ibn Khaldun were themselves followers of the Ash'ari school. Emilie Savage-Smith also pointed out that Al-Ghazali's positive views towards medicine, particularly anatomy, were a source of encouragement for the increased use of dissection by Muslim physicians (such as Avenzoar and Ibn al-Nafis) in the 12th and 13th centuries.

Other reasons for the decline of Islamic science include conflicts between the Sunni and Shia Muslims, and invasions by Crusaders and Mongols on Islamic lands between the 11th and 13th centuries, especially the Mongol invasions of the 13th century. The Mongols destroyed

Muslim libraries, observatories, hospitals, and universities, culminating in the destruction of Baghdad, the Abbasid capital and intellectual centre, in 1258, which is traditionally believed to have marked an end to the Islamic Golden Age. From the 13th century, some traditionalist Muslims believed that the Crusades and Mongol invasions may have been a divine punishment from God against Muslims deviating from the Sunnah, a view that was held even by the famous polymath Ibn al-Nafis.

Such traditionalist views as well as numerous wars and conflicts at the time are believed to have created a climate which made Islamic science less successful than before. However, Y. Ziedan has pointed out that the sack of Baghdad in 1258 was followed by intense scientific activity across Damascus and Cairo, as many Muslim scholars wrote huge encyclopedias (including an 80-volume medical encyclopedia by Ibn al-Nafis) in an attempt to preserve the scientific heritage of the Islamic world and cope with the loss of Baghdad.

Another reason given for the decline of Islamic science is the disruption to the cycle of equity based on Ibn Khaldun's famous model of Asabiyyah (the rise and fall of civilizations), which points to the decline being mainly due to political and economic factors rather than religious factors. With the fall of Islamic Spain in 1492, the scientific and technological initiative of the Islamic world was inherited by Europeans and laid the foundations for Europe's Renaissance and Scientific Revolution.

Influence on European Science

Contributing to the growth of European science was the major search by European scholars for new learning which they could only find among Muslims, especially in Islamic Spain and Sicily. These scholars translated new scientific and philosophical texts from Arabic into Latin. One of the most productive translators in Spain was Gerard of Cremona, who translated 87 books from Arabic to Latin, including

Muhammad ibn Mûsâ al-Khwârizmî's *On Algebra and Almucabala,* Jabir ibn Aflah's *Elementa astronomica,* al-Kindi's *On Optics,* Ahmad ibn Muhammad ibn Kathîr al-Farghânî's *On Elements of Astronomy on the Celestial Motions,* al-Farabi's *On the Classification of the Sciences,* the chemical and medical works of Razi, the works of Thabit ibn Qurra and Hunayn ibn Ishaq, and the works of Arzachel, Jabir ibn Aflah, the Banû Mûsâ, Abû Kâmil Shujâ ibn Aslam, Abu al-Qasim, and Ibn al-Haytham (including the *Book of Optics*).

Other Arabic works translated into Latin during the 12th century include the works of Muhammad ibn Jâbir al-Harrânî al-Battânî and Muhammad ibn Mûsâ al-Khwârizmî (including *The Compendious Book on Calculation by Completion and Balancing*), the works of Abu al-Qasim (including the *al-Tasrif*), Muhammad al-Fazari's *Great Sindhind* (based on the *Surya Siddhanta* and the works of Brahmagupta), the works of Razi and Avicenna (including *The Book of Healing* and *The Canon of Medicine*), the works of Averroes, the works of Thabit ibn Qurra, al-Farabi, Ahmad ibn Muhammad ibn Kathîr al-Farghânî, Hunayn ibn Ishaq, and his nephew Hubaysh ibn al-Hasan, the works of al-Kindi, Abraham bar Hiyya's *Liber embadorum,* Ibn Sarabi's (Serapion Junior) *De Simplicibus,* the works of Qusta ibn Luqa, the works of Maslamah Ibn Ahmad al-Majriti, Ja'far ibn Muhammad Abu Ma'shar al-Balkhi, and al-Ghazali, the works of Nur Ed-Din Al Betrugi, including *On the Motions of the Heavens,* Ali ibn Abbas al-Majusi's medical encyclopedia, *The Complete Book of the Medical Art,* Abu Mashar's *Introduction to Astrology,* the works of Maimonides, Ibn Zezla (Byngezla), Masawaiyh, Serapion, al-Qifti, and Albe'thar. Abû Kâmil Shujâ ibn Aslam's *Algebra,* the chemical works of Geber, and the *De Proprietatibus Elementorum,* an Arabic work on geology written by a pseudo-Aristotle. By the beginning of the 13th century, Mark of Toledo translated the Qur'an and various medical works.

Fibonacci presented the first complete European account of the Hindu-Arabic numeral system from Arabic sources in his *Liber Abaci* (1202). Al-Khazini's *Zij as-Sanjari* was translated into Greek by Gregory Choniades in the 13th century and was studied in the Byzantine Empire. The astronomical corrections to the Ptolemaic model made by al-Battani and Averroes and the non-Ptolemaic models produced by Mo'ayyeduddin Urdi (Urdi lemma), Nasîr al-Dîn al-Tûsî (Tusi-couple) and Ibn al-Shatir were later adapted into the Copernican heliocentric model. Al-Kindi's (Alkindus) law of terrestrial gravity influenced Robert Hooke's law of celestial gravity, which in turn inspired Newton's law of universal gravitation. Abû al-Rayhân al-Bîrûnî's *Ta'rikh al-Hind* and *Kitab al-qanun al-Mas'udi* were translated into Latin as *Indica* and *Canon Mas'udicus* respectively.

Ibn al-Nafis' *Commentary on Compound Drugs* was translated into Latin by Andrea Alpago (died 1522), who may have also translated Ibn al-Nafis' *Commentary on Anatomy in the Canon of Avicenna*, which first described pulmonary circulation and coronary circulation, and which may have had an influence on Michael Servetus, Realdo Colombo and William Harvey. Translations of the algebraic and geometrical works of Ibn al-Haytham, Omar Khayyám and Nasîr al-Dîn al-Tûsî were later influential in the development of non-Euclidean geometry in Europe from the 17th century. Ibn Tufail's *Hayy ibn Yaqdhan* was translated into Latin by Edward Pococke in 1671 and into English by Simon Ockley in 1708 and became "one of the most important books that heralded the Scientific Revolution." Ibn al-Baitar's *Kitab al-Jami fi al-Adwiya al-Mufrada* also had an influence on European botany after it was translated into Latin in 1758.

Muslim scientists placed a greater emphasis on experimentation than previous ancient civilizations (for example, Greek philosophy placed a greater emphasis on rationality rather than empiricism), which was due to the emphasis on empirical observation found in the Qur'an and Sunnah, and the rigorous historical methods established in the science of hadith. Muslim scientists thus combined precise observation, controlled experiment and careful records with a new approach to scientific inquiry which led to the development of the scientific method. In particular, the empirical observations and experiments of Ibn al-Haytham (Alhacen) in his *Book of Optics* (1021) is seen as the beginning of the modern scientific method, which he first introduced to optics and psychology. Rosanna Gorini writes:

"According to the majority of the historians al-Haytham was the pioneer of the modern scientific method. With his book he changed the meaning of the term optics and established experiments as the norm of proof in the field. His investigations are based not on abstract theories, but on experimental evidences and his experiments were systematic and repeatable."

Other early experimental methods were developed by Geber (for chemistry), Muhammad al-Bukhari (for history and the science of hadith), al-Kindi (for the Earth sciences), Avicenna (for medicine), Abû Rayhân al-Bîrûnî (for astronomy and mechanics), Ibn Zuhr (for surgery) and Ibn Khaldun (for the social sciences). The most important development of the scientific method, the use of experimentation and quantification to distinguish between competing scientific theories set within a generally empirical orientation, was introduced by Muslim scientists. Ibn al-Haytham, a pioneer of modern optics, used the scientific method to obtain the results in his *Book of Optics*.

In particular, he combined observations, experiments and rational arguments to show that his modern intromission theory of vision, where rays of light are emitted from objects rather than from the eyes, is scientifically correct, and that the ancient emission theory of vision supported by Ptolemy and Euclid (where the eyes emit rays of light), and the ancient intromission theory supported by Aristotle (where objects emit physical particles to the eyes), were both wrong. It is known that Roger Bacon was familiar with Ibn al-Haytham's work. Ibn al-Haytham is featured on the 10,000 Iraqi dinar note.

Ibn al-Haytham developed rigorous experimental methods of controlled scientific testing in order to verify theoretical hypotheses and substantiate inductive conjectures. Ibn al-Haytham's scientific method was similar to the modern scientific method in that it consisted of the following procedures:

1. Observation
2. Statement of problem
3. Formulation of hypothesis
4. Testing of hypothesis using experimentation
5. Analysis of experimental results
6. Interpretation of data and formulation of conclusion
7. Publication of findings

The development of the scientific method is considered to be fundamental to modern science and some – especially philosophers of science and practicing scientists – consider earlier inquiries into nature to be prescientific. Some consider Ibn al-Haytham to be the "first scientist" for this reason. In *The Model of the Motions*, Ibn al-Haytham also describes an early version of Occam's razor, where he employs only minimal hypotheses regarding the properties that characterize astronomical motions, as he attempts to eliminate from his planetary model the cosmological hypotheses that cannot be observed from Earth.

Robert Briffault wrote in *The Making of Humanity*:

"The debt of our science to that of the Arabs does not consist in startling discoveries or revolutionary theories; science owes a great deal more to Arab culture, it owes its existence. The ancient world was, as we saw, pre- scientific. The astronomy and mathematics of the Greeks were a foreign importation never thoroughly acclimatized in Greek culture. The Greeks systematized, generalized and theorized, but the patient ways of investigation, the accumulation of positive knowledge, the minute methods of science, detailed and prolonged observation, experimental inquiry, were altogether alien to the Greek temperament. [...] What we call science arose in Europe as a result of a new spirit of inquiry, of new methods of investigation, of the method of experiment, observation, measurement, of the development of mathematics in a form unknown to the Greeks. That spirit and those methods were introduced into the European world by the Arabs."

Science is the most momentous contribution of Arab civilization to the modern world, but its fruits were slow in ripening. Not until long after Moorish culture had sunk back into darkness did the giant to which it had given birth, rise in his might. It was not science only which brought Europe back to life. Other and manifold influences from the civilization of Islam communicated its first glow to European life."

George Sarton wrote in the *Introduction to the History of Science*:

"The main, as well as the least obvious, achievement of the Middle Ages was the creation of the experimental spirit and this was primarily due to the Muslims down to the 12th century."

Oliver Joseph Lodge wrote in the *Pioneers of Science*:

"The only effective link between the old and the new science is afforded by the Arabs. The dark ages come as an utter gap in the scientific history of Europe, and for more than a thousand years there was not a scientific man of note except in Arabia."

Muhammad Iqbal wrote in *The Reconstruction of Religious Thought in Islam*:

"Thus the experimental method, reason and observation introduced by the Arabs were responsible for the rapid advancement of science during the medieval times."

The first documented description of a peer review process is found in the *Ethics of the Physician* written by Ishaq bin Ali al-Rahwi (854–931) of al-Raha, Syria, who describes the first medical peer review process. His work, as well as later Arabic medical manuals, state that a visiting physician must always make duplicate notes of a patient's condition on every visit. When the patient was cured or had died, the notes of the physician were examined by a local medical council of other physicians, who would review the practising physician's notes to decide whether his/her performance have met the required standards of medical care. If their reviews were negative, the practicing physician could face a lawsuit from a maltreated patient.

Applied Sciences

Fielding H. Garrison wrote in the *History of Medicine*:

"The Saracens themselves were the originators not only of algebra, chemistry, and geology, but of many of the so-called improvements or refinements of civilization, such as street lamps, window-panes, firework, stringed instruments, cultivated fruits, perfumes, spices, etc..."

In the applied sciences, a significant number of inventions and technologies were produced by medieval Muslim scientists and engineers such as Abbas Ibn Firnas, Taqi al-Din, and particularly al-Jazari, who is considered a pioneer in modern engineering. Some of the inventions believed to have come from the medieval Islamic world include the programmable automaton, coffee, the soap bar, shampoo, pure distillation, liquefaction, crystallisation, purification, oxidisation, evaporation, filtration, distilled alcohol, uric acid, nitric acid, alembic, the crankshaft, the valve,the combination lock, quilting, the pointed arch, the scalpel, the bone saw, forceps, surgical catgut, the windmill, inoculation, the fountain pen, cryptanalysis, frequency analysis, the three-course meal, stained glass and quartz glass, Persian carpet, the celestial globe, explosive rockets and incendiary devices, and artificial pleasure gardens.

Agricultural Sciences

During the Muslim Agricultural Revolution, Muslim

scientists made significant advances in botany and laid the foundations of agricultural science. Muslim botanists and agriculturists demonstrated advanced agronomical, agrotechnical and economic knowledge in areas such as meteorology, climatology, hydrology, soil occupation, and the economy and management of agricultural enterprises. They also demosntrated agricultural knowledge in areas such as pedology, agricultural ecology, irrigation, preparation of soil, planting, spreading of manure, killing herbs, sowing, cutting trees, grafting, pruning vine, prophylaxis, phytotherapy, the care and improvement of cultures and plants, and the harvest and storage of crops.

Al-Dinawari (828-896) is considered the founder of Arabic botany for his *Book of Plants*, in which he described at least 637 plants and discussed plant evolution from its birth to its death, describing the phases of plant growth and the production of flowers and fruit. In the 13th century, the Andalusian-Arabian biologist Abu al-Abbas al-Nabati developed an early scientific method for botany, introducing empirical and experimental techniques in the testing, description and identification of numerous materia medica, and separating unverified reports from those supported by actual tests and observations.

His student Ibn al-Baitar published the *Kitab al-Jami fi al-Adwiya al-Mufrada*, which is considered one of the greatest botanical compilations in history, and was a botanical authority for centuries. It contains details on at least 1,400 different plants, foods, and drugs, 300 of which were his own original discoveries. His work was also influential in Europe after it was translated into Latin in 1758.

Medicine

Muslim physicians made many significant advances and contributions to medicine, including anatomy, ophthalmology, pathology, the pharmaceutical sciences (including pharmacy and pharmacology), physiology, and surgery. Muslim physicians set up some of the earliest dedicated hospitals, which later spread to Europe during the Crusades, inspired by the hospitals in the Middle East. Al-Kindi wrote *De Gradibus*, in which he first demonstrated the application of quantification and mathematics to medicine, particularly in the field of pharmacology. This includes the development of a mathematical scale to quantify the strength of drugs, and a system that would allow a doctor to determine in advance the most critical days of a patient's illness.

Razi (Rhazes) (865-925), a pioneer of pediatrics, recorded clinical cases of his own experience and provided very useful recordings of various diseases. His *Comprehensive Book of Medicine*, which introduced measles and smallpox, was very influential in Europe. In his *Doubts about Galen*, al-Razi was also the first to prove both Galen's theory of humorism and Aristotle's theory of classical elements false using experimentation. He also introduced urinalysis and stool tests. Abu al-Qasim (Abulcasis), considered a pioneer of modern surgery, wrote the *Al-Tasrif* (1000), a 30-volume medical encyclopedia which was taught at Muslim and European medical schools until the 17th century. He invented numerous surgical instruments, including the first instruments unique to women, as well as the surgical uses of catgut and forceps, the ligature, surgical needle, scalpel, curette, retractor, surgical spoon, sound, surgical hook, surgical rod, and specula, bone saw, and plaster.

In 1021, Ibn al-Haytham (Alhacen) made important advances in eye surgery, as he studied and correctly explained the process of sight and visual perception for the first time in his *Book of Optics* (1021). Avicenna, who was a pioneer of experimental medicine and was also an influential thinker and medical scholar, wrote *The Canon of Medicine* (1025) and *The Book of Healing* (1027), which remained standard textbooks in both Muslim and European universities until at least the 17th century.

Avicenna's contributions include the introduction of systematic experimentation and quantification into the study of physiology, the discovery of the contagious nature of infectious diseases, the introduction of quarantine to limit the spread of contagious diseases, the introduction of experimental medicine, evidence-based medicine, clinical trials, randomized controlled trials, efficacy tests, and clinical pharmacology, the importance of dietetics and the influence of climate and environment on health, the distinction of mediastinitis from pleurisy, the contagious nature of phthisis and tuberculosis, the distribution of diseases by water and soil, and the first careful descriptions of skin troubles, sexually transmitted diseases, perversions, and nervous ailments, as well the use of ice to treat fevers, and the separation of medicine from pharmacology, which was important to the development of the pharmaceutical sciences.

Ibn Zuhr (Avenzoar) is considered a pioneer of experimental surgery, for introducing the experimental method into surgery in the 12th century, as he was the first to employ animal testing in order to experiment with surgical procedures before applying them to human patients. He also performed the first dissections and postmortem autopsies on both humans as well as animals. In 1242, Ibn al-Nafis, considered a pioneer of circulatory physiology, was the first to describe pulmonary circulation and coronary circulation, which form the basis of the circulatory system, for which he is considered one of the greatest physiologists in history.

He also described the earliest concept of metabolism, and developed new systems of physiology and psychology to replace the Avicennian and Galenic systems, while discrediting many of their erroneous theories on the four humours, pulsation, bones, muscles, intestines, sensory organs, bilious canals, esophagus, stomach, etc. Ibn al-Lubudi (1210-1267) rejected the theory of four humours supported by Galen and Hippocrates, discovered that the body and its preservation depend exclusively upon blood, rejected Galen's idea that women can produce sperm, and discovered that the movement of arteries are not dependent upon the movement of the heart, that the heart is the first organ to form in a fetus' body (rather than the brain as claimed by Hippocrates), and that the bones forming the skull can grow into tumors.

The *Tashrih al-badan* (*Anatomy of the body*) of Mansur ibn Ilyas (c. 1390) contained comprehensive diagrams of the body's structural, nervous and circulatory systems. During the Black Death bubonic plague in 14th century al-Andalus, Ibn Khatima and Ibn al-Khatib hypothesized that infectious diseases are caused by "contagious entities" which enter the human body. Other medical innovations first introduced by Muslim physicians include the discovery of the immune system, the use of animal testing, and the combination of medicine with other sciences (including agriculture, botany, chemistry, and pharmacology), as well as the invention of the injection syringe by Ammar ibn Ali al-Mawsili in 9th century Iraq, the first drugstores in Baghdad (754), the distinction between medicine and pharmacy by the 12th century, and the discovery of at least 2,000 medicinal and chemical substances.

Formal Sciences

Logic

Early Islamic law placed importance on formulating standards of argument, which gave rise to a novel approach to logic in Kalam, but this approach was later influenced by ideas from Greek philosophy and Hellenistic philosophy with the rise of the Mu'tazili theologians, who highly valued Aristotle's *Organon*. The works of Hellenistic-influenced Islamic philosophers were crucial in the reception of Aristotelian logic in medieval Europe, along with the commentaries on the *Organon* by Averroes. The works of al-Farabi, Avicenna, al-Ghazali and other Muslim logicians who often criticized and corrected Aristotelian logic and introduced their own forms of logic, also played a central role in the subsequent development of medieval European logic.

Islamic logic not only included the study of formal patterns of inference and their validity but also elements of the philosophy of language and elements of epistemology and metaphysics. Due to disputes with Arabic grammarians, Islamic philosophers were very interested in working out the relationship between logic and language, and they devoted much discussion to the question of the subject matter and aims of logic in relation to reasoning and speech. In the area of formal logical analysis, they elaborated upon the theory of terms, propositions and syllogisms. They considered the syllogism to be the form to which all rational argumentation could be reduced, and they regarded syllogistic theory as the focal point of logic. Even poetics was considered as a syllogistic art in some fashion by many major Islamic logicians.

Important developments made by Muslim logicians included the development of "Avicennian logic" as a replacement of Aristotelian logic. Avicenna's system of logic was responsible for the introduction of hypothetical syllogism, temporal modal logic, and inductive logic. Other important developments in Islamic philosophy include the development of a strict science of citation, the isnad or "backing", and the development of a scientific method of open inquiry to disprove claims, the ijtihad, which could be generally applied to many types of questions. From the 12th century, despite the logical sophistication of al-Ghazali, the rise of the Asharite school in the late Middle Ages slowly limited original work on logic in the Islamic world, though it did continue into the 15th century.

Mathematics

John J. O'Connor and Edmund F. Robertson wrote in the *MacTutor History of Mathematics archive*:

"Recent research paints a new picture of the debt that we owe to Islamic mathematics. Certainly many of the ideas which were previously thought to have been brilliant new conceptions due to European mathematicians of the sixteenth, seventeenth and eighteenth centuries are now known to have been developed by Persian/Islamic mathematicians around four centuries earlier."

Al-Khwarizmi (780-850) (born in Iran) , from whose name the word algorithm derives, contributed significantly to algebra, which is named after his book, *Kitab al-Jabr*, the first book on elementary algebra. He also introduced what is now known as Arabic numerals, which originally came from India, though Muslim mathematicians did make several refinements to the number system, such as the introduction of decimal point notation. Al-Kindi (801-873) was a pioneer in cryptanalysis and cryptology. He gave the first known recorded explanations of cryptanalysis and frequency analysis in *A Manuscript on Deciphering Cryptographic Messages*.

The first known proof by mathematical induction appears in a book written by Al-Karaji around 1000 AD, who used it to prove the binomial theorem, Pascal's triangle, and the sum of integral cubes. The historian of mathematics, F. Woepcke, praised Al-Karaji for being "the first who introduced the theory of algebraic calculus." Ibn al-Haytham was the first mathematician to derive the formula for the sum of the fourth powers, and using the method of induction, he developed a method for determining the general formula for the sum of any integral powers, which was fundamental to the development of integral calculus. The 11th century poet-mathematician Omar Khayyám was the first to find general geometric solutions of cubic equations and laid the foundations for the development of analytic geometry, algebraic geometry and non-Euclidean geometry.

Sharaf al-Din al-Tusi (1135-1213) found algebraic and numerical solutions to cubic equations and was the first to discover the derivative of cubic polynomials, an important result in differential calculus. Other achievements of Muslim mathematicians include the invention of spherical trigonometry, the discovery of all the trigonometric functions besides sine and cosine, early inquiry which aided the development of analytic geometry by Ibn al-Haytham, the first refutations of Euclidean geometry and the parallel postulate by Nasîr al-Dîn al-Tûsî, the first attempt at a non-Euclidean geometry by Sadr al-Din, the development of symbolic algebra by Abû al-Hasan ibn Alî al-Qalasâdî, and numerous other advances in algebra, arithmetic, calculus, cryptography, geometry, number theory and trigonometry.

Natural Sciences

Astrology

Islamic astrology, in Arabic *ilm al-nujum* is the study of the heavens by early Muslims. In early Arabic sources, *ilm al-nujum* was used to refer to both astronomy and astrology. In medieval sources, however, a clear distinction was made between *ilm al-nujum* (science of the stars) or *ilm al-falak* (science of the celestial orbs), referring to astrology, and *ilm al-haya* (science of the figure of the heavens), referring to astronomy. Both fields were rooted in Greek, Persian, and Indian traditions. Despite consistent critiques of astrology by scientists and religious scholars, astrological prognostications required a fair amount of exact scientific knowledge and thus gave partial incentive for the study and development of astronomy.

The first semantic distinction between astronomy and astrology was given by al-Biruni in the 11th century, though he himself refuted the study of astrology. The study of astrology was also refuted by other Muslim astronomers at the time, including al-Farabi, Ibn al-Haytham, Avicenna and Averroes. Their reasons for refuting astrology were both due to the methods used by astrologers being conjectural rather than empirical and also due to the views of astrologers conflicting with orthodox Islam.

Astronomy

In astronomy, the works of Egyptian/Greek astronomer Ptolemy, particularly the *Almagest,* and the Indian work of Brahmagupta, were significantly refined over the years by Muslim astronomers. The astronomical tables of Al-

Khwarizmi and of Maslamah Ibn Ahmad al-Majriti served as important sources of information for Latinized European thinkers rediscovering the works of astronomy, where extensive interest in astrology was discouraged. In the 11th century, Muslim astronomers began questioning the Ptolemaic system, beginning with Ibn al-Haytham, and they were the first to conduct elaborate experiments related to astronomical phenomena, beginning with Abû al-Rayhân al-Bîrûnî's introduction of the experimental method into astronomy. Many of them made changes and corrections to the Ptolemaic model and proposed alternative non-Ptolemaic models within a geocentric framework.

In particular, the corrections and critiques of al-Battani, Ibn al-Haytham, and Averroes, and the non-Ptolemaic models of the Maragha astronomers, Nasir al-Din al-Tusi (Tusi-couple), Mo'ayyeduddin Urdi (Urdi lemma), and Ibn al-Shatir, were later adapted into the heliocentric Copernican model, and that Copernicus' arguments for the Earth's rotation were similar to those of al-Tusi and Ali al-Qushji. Some have referred to the achievements of the Maragha school as a "Maragha Revolution", "Maragha School Revolution", or "Scientific Revolution before the Renaissance".

Other contributions from Muslim astronomers include Biruni speculating that the Milky Way galaxy is a collection of numerous nebulous stars, the development of a planetary model without any epicycles by Ibn Bajjah (Avempace), the development of universal astrolabes, the invention of numerous other astronomical instruments, continuation of inquiry into the motion of the planets, Ja'far Muhammad ibn Mûsâ ibn Shâkir's discovery that the heavenly bodies and celestial spheres are subject to the same physical laws as Earth, the first elaborate experiments related to astronomical phenomena and the first semantic distinction between astronomy and astrology by Abû al-Rayhân al-Bîrûnî, the use of exacting empirical observations and experimental techniques, the discovery that the celestial spheres are not solid and that the heavens are less dense than the air by Ibn al-Haytham, the separation of natural philosophy from astronomy by Ibn al-Haytham and al-Qushji, the rejection of the Ptolemaic model on empirical rather than philosophical grounds by Ibn al-Shatir, and the first empirical observational evidence of the Earth's rotation by al-Tusi and al-Qushji. Several Muslim astronomers also discussed the possibility of a heliocentric model with elliptical orbits, such as Ja'far ibn Muhammad Abu Ma'shar al-Balkhi, Ibn al-Haytham, Abû al-Rayhân al-Bîrûnî, al-Sijzi, 'Umar al-Katibi al-Qazwini, and Qutb al-Din al-Shirazi.

Chemistry

The 9th century chemist, Geber (Jabir ibn Hayyan), is considered a pioneer of chemistry, for introducing an early experimental method for chemistry, as well as the alembic, still, retort, pure distillation, liquefaction, crystallisation, purification, oxidisation, evaporation, and filtration. Al-Kindi was the first to refute the study of traditional alchemy and the theory of the transmutation of metals, followed by Abû Rayhân al-Bîrûnî, Avicenna, and Ibn Khaldun. Avicenna also invented steam distillation and produced the first essential oils, which led to the development of aromatherapy. Razi first distilled petroleum, invented kerosene and kerosene lamps, soap bars and modern recipes for soap, and antiseptics. In his *Doubts about Galen*, al-Razi was also the first to prove both Aristotle's theory of classical elements and Galen's theory of humorism wrong using an experimental method. In the 13th century, Nasîr al-Dîn al-Tûsî stated an early version of the law of conservation of mass, noting that a body of matter is able to change, but is not able to disappear.

Will Durant wrote in *The Story of Civilization IV: The Age of Faith*:

"Chemistry as a science was almost created by the Moslems; for in this field, where the Greeks (so far as we know) were confined to industrial experience and vague hypothesis, the Saracens introduced precise observation, controlled experiment, and careful records. They invented and named the alembic (al-anbiq), chemically analyzed innumerable substances, composed lapidaries, distinguished alkalis and acids, investigated their affinities, studied and manufactured hundreds of drugs. Alchemy, which the Moslems inherited from Egypt, contributed to chemistry by a thousand incidental discoveries, and by its method, which was the most scientific of all medieval operations."

George Sarton wrote in the *Introduction to the History of Science*:

"We find in his (Jabir, Geber) writings remarkably sound views on methods of chemical research, a theory on the geologic formation of metals (the six metals differ essentially because of different proportions of sulphur and mercury in them); preparation of various substances (e.g., basic lead carbonatic, arsenic and antimony from their sulphides)."

Earth Sciences

Muslim scientists made a number of contributions to the Earth sciences. Alkindus was the first to introduce experimentation into the Earth sciences. Biruni is considered a pioneer of geodesy for his important contributions to the field, along with his significant contributions to geography and geology.

Among his writings on geology, Biruni wrote the following on the geology of India:

"But if you see the soil of India with your own eyes and meditate on its nature, if you consider the rounded stones found in earth however deeply you dig, stones that are huge near the mountains and where the rivers have a violent current: stones that are of smaller size at a greater distance from the mountains and where the streams flow more slowly: stones that appear pulverised in the shape of sand where the streams begin to stagnate near their mouths and near the sea - if you consider all this you can scarcely help thinking that India was once a sea, which by degrees has been filled up by the alluvium of the streams."

John J. O'Connor and Edmund F. Robertson write in the *MacTutor History of Mathematics archive*:

"Important contributions to geodesy and geography were also made by al-Biruni. He introduced techniques to measure the earth and distances on it using triangulation. He found the radius of the earth to be 6339.6 km, a value not obtained in the West until the 16th century. His *Masudic canon* contains a table giving the coordinates of six hundred places, almost all of which he had direct knowledge."

Fielding H. Garrison wrote in the *History of Medicine*:

"The Saracens themselves were the originators not only of algebra, chemistry, and geology, but of many of the so-called improvements or refinements of civilization..."

George Sarton wrote in the *Introduction to the History of Science*:

"We find in his (Jabir, Geber) writings remarkably sound views on methods of chemical research, a theory on the geologic formation of metals (the six metals differ essentially because of different proportions of sulphur and mercury in them)..."

In geology, Avicenna hypothesized on two causes of mountains in *The Book of Healing* (1027) and developed the law of superposition and concept of uniformitarianism. In cartography, the Piri Reis map drawn by the Ottoman cartographer Piri Reis in 1513, was one of the earliest world maps to include the Americas, and perhaps the first to include Antarctica. His map of the world was considered the most accurate in the 16th century.

The earliest known treatises dealing with environmentalism and environmental science, especially pollution, were Arabic treatises written by al-Kindi, al-Razi, Ibn Al-Jazzar, al-Tamimi, al-Masihi, Avicenna, Ali ibn Ridwan, Abd-el-latif, and Ibn al-Nafis. Their works covered a number of subjects related to pollution such as air pollution, water pollution, soil contamination, municipal solid waste mishandling, and environmental impact assessments of certain localities. Cordoba, al-Andalus also had the first waste containers and waste disposal facilities for litter collection.

Physics

In the optics field of physics, Ibn Sahl (c. 940-1000), a mathematician and physicist connected with the court of Baghdad, wrote a treatise *On Burning Mirrors and Lenses* in 984 in which he set out his understanding of how curved mirrors and lenses bend and focus light. Ibn Sahl is now credited with first discovering the law of refraction, usually called Snell's law. He used this law to work out the shapes of lenses that focus light with no geometric aberrations, known as anaclastic lenses. Ibn al-Haytham (Alhazen) (965-1039), who is considered a pioneer of optics and the scientific method, developed a broad theory of light and optics in his *Book of Optics* which explained vision, using geometry and anatomy, and stated that each point on an illuminated area or object radiates light rays in every direction, but that only one ray from each point, which strikes the eye perpendicularly, can be seen.

The other rays strike at different angles and are not seen. He used the example of the camera obscura and pinhole camera, which produces an inverted image, to support his argument. This contradicted Ptolemy's theory of vision that objects are seen by rays of light emanating from the eyes. Alhacen held light rays to be streams of minute particles that travelled at a finite speed. He improved accurately described the refraction of light, and discovered the laws of refraction. He dealt at length with the theory of various physical phenomena like shadows, eclipses, and the rainbow. He also attempted to explain binocular vision and the moon illusion. Through these extensive researches on optics, he is considered a pioneer of modern optics. His *Book of Optics* was later translated into Latin, and has been ranked alongside

Isaac Newton's *Philosophiae Naturalis Principia Mathematica* as one of the most influential books in the history of physics, for initiating a revolution in optics and visual perception.

Avicenna (980-1037) agreed that the speed of light is finite, as he "observed that if the perception of light is due to the emission of some sort of particles by a luminous source, the speed of light must be finite." Abû Rayhân al-Bîrûnî (973-1048) also agreed that light has a finite speed, and he was the first to discover that the speed of light is much faster than the speed of sound. Qutb al-Din al-Shirazi (1236-1311) and Kamâl al-Dîn al-Fârisî (1260-1320) gave the first correct explanations for the rainbow phenomenon. In mechanics, Ja'far Muhammad ibn Mûsâ ibn Shâkir (800-873) of the Banû Mûsâ hypothesized that heavenly bodies and celestial spheres were subject to the same laws of physics as Earth, and in his *Astral Motion* and *The Force of Attraction*, he also hypothesized that there was a force of attraction between heavenly bodies. Abû Rayhân al-Bîrûnî (973-1048), and later al-Khazini, developed experimental scientific methods for mechanics, especially the fields of statics and dynamics, particularly for determining specific weights, such as those based on the theory of balances and weighing.

Muslim physicists unified statics and dynamics into the science of mechanics, and they combined the fields of hydrostatics with dynamics to give birth to hydrodynamics. They applied the mathematical theories of ratios and infinitesimal techniques, and introduced algebraic and fine calculation techniques into the field of statics. They were also generalized the theory of the centre of gravity and applied it to three-dimensional bodies. They also founded the theory of the ponderable lever and created the "science of gravity" which was later further developed in medieval Europe. Al-Biruni also theorized that acceleration is connected with non-uniform motion. In mechanics, Ibn al-Haytham discussed the theory of attraction between masses, and it seems that he was aware of the magnitude of acceleration due to gravity, and he stated that the heavenly bodies "were accountable to the laws of physics".

Ibn al-Haytham also enunciated the law of inertia when he stated that a body moves perpetually unless an external force stops it or changes its direction of motion. He also developed the concept of momentum, though he did not quantify this concept mathematically. Avicenna (980-1037) developed the concept of momentum, referring to impetus as being proportional to weight times velocity. His theory of motion was also consistent with the concept of inertia in classical mechanics. In 1121, al-Khazini, in *The Book of the Balance of Wisdom*, proposed that the gravity and gravitational potential energy of a body varies depending on its distance from the centre of the Earth, and in statics, he clearly differentiated between force, mass and weight. Avempace (d. 1138) argued that there is always a reaction force for every force exerted, though he did not refer to the reaction force as being equal to the exerted force.

His theory of motion had an important influence on later physicists like Galileo Galilei. Hibat Allah Abu'l-Barakat al-Baghdaadi (1080-1165) wrote a critique of Aristotelian physics entitled *al-Mu'tabar*, where he negated Aristotle's idea that a constant force produces uniform motion, as he theorized that a force applied continuously produces acceleration. He also described acceleration as the rate of change of velocity. Averroes (1126–1198) defined and measured force as "the rate at which work is done in changing the kinetic condition of a material body" and correctly argued "that the effect and measure of force is change in the kinetic condition of a materially resistant mass." In the early 16th century, al-Birjandi developed a hypothesis similar to "circular inertia." The Muslim developments in mechanics laid the foundations for the later development of classical mechanics in early modern Europe.

Zoology

In the zoology field of biology, Muslim biologists developed theories on evolution which were widely taught in medieval Islamic schools. John William Draper, a contemporary of Charles Darwin, considered the

"Mohammedan theory of evolution" to be developed "much farther than we are disposed to do, extending them even to inorganic or mineral things." According to al-Khazini, ideas on evolution were widespread among "common people" in the Islamic world by the 12th century. The first Muslim biologist to develop a theory on evolution was al-Jahiz (781-869). He wrote on the effects of the environment on the likelihood of an animal to survive, and he first described the struggle for existence. Al-Jahiz was also the first to discuss food chains, and was also an early adherent of environmental determinism, arguing that the environment can determine the physical characteristics of the inhabitants of a certain community and that the origins of different human skin colors is the result of the environment.

Ibn al-Haytham wrote a book in which he argued for evolutionism (although not natural selection), and numerous other Islamic scholars and scientists, such as Ibn Miskawayh, the Brethren of Purity, al-Khazini, Abû Rayhân al-Bîrûnî, Nasir al-Din Tusi, and Ibn Khaldun, discussed and developed these ideas. Translated into Latin, these works began to appear in the West after the Renaissance and appear to have had an impact on Western science. Ibn Miskawayh's *al-Fawz al-Asghar* and the Brethren of Purity's *Encyclopedia of the Brethren of Purity* (*The Epistles of Ikhwan al-Safa*) expressed evolutionary ideas on how species evolved from matter, into vapor, and then water, then minerals, then plants, then animals, then apes, and then humans. These works were known in Europe and likely had an influence on Darwinism.

Social Sciences

Sociology and Anthropology

Significant contributions were made to the social sciences in the Islamic civilization. Abû al-Rayhân al-Bîrûnî (973-1048) has been described as "the first anthropologist". He wrote detailed comparative studies on the anthropology of peoples, religions and cultures in the Middle East,

Mediterranean and South Asia. Biruni's anthropology of religion was only possible for a scholar deeply immersed in the lore of other nations. Biruni has also been praised by several scholars for his Islamic anthropology. Biruni is also considered a pioneer of Indology. Al-Saghani (died 990) wrote some of the earliest comments on the history of science, which included a comparison between the more theoretical approach of the "ancients" (including the ancient Egyptians, Babylonians, Greeks and Indians) to that of the more experimental approach of the "modern scholars" (the Muslim scientists of his time). Al-Muqaddasi (b. 945) also made contributions to the social sciences.

Ibn Khaldun (1332-1406) is considered a forerunner of several social sciences such as demography, cultural history, historiography, the philosophy of history, sociology, and economics. He is best known for his *Muqaddimah* (Latinized as *Prolegomenon*). Some of the ideas he introduced in the *Muqaddimah* include social philosophy, social conflict theories, social cohesion, social capital, social networks, dialectics, the Laffer curve, the historical method, systemic bias, the rise and fall of civilizations, feedback loops, systems theory, and corporate social responsibility. He also introduced the scientific method into the social sciences.

Franz Rosenthal wrote in the *History of Muslim Historiography*:

"Muslim historiography has at all times been united by the closest ties with the general development of scholarship in Islam, and the position of historical knowledge in Muslim education has exercised a decisive influence upon the intellectual level of historicai writing....The Muslims achieved a definite advance beyond previous historical writing in the sociological understanding of history and the systematisation of historiography. The development of modern historical writing seems to have gained considerably in speed and substance through the utilization of a Muslim Literature which enabled western historians, from the seventeenth century on, to see a large section of the world through foreign eyes. The Muslim historiography helped indirectly and modestly to shape present day historical thinking."

Psychology

"Islamic psychology" or *Ilm-al Nafsiat* refers to the study of the *Nafs* ("self" or "psyche") in the Islamic world and encompassed a "broad range of topics including the *qalb* (heart), the *ruh* (spirit), the *aql* (intellect) and *irada* (will)." Al-Kindi (Alkindus) was the first to experiment with music therapy, and Ali ibn Sahl Rabban al-Tabari was the first to practice '*al-'ilaj al-nafs* ("psychotherapy"). The concepts of *al-tibb al-ruhani* ("spiritual health") and "mental hygiene" were introduced by Ahmed ibn Sahl al-Balkhi, who was "probably the first cognitive and medical psychologist to clearly differentiate between neuroses and psychoses, to classify neurotic disorders, and to show in detail how rational and spiritual cognitive therapies can be used to treat each one of his classified disorders." Al-Razi (Rhazes) made significant advances in psychiatry in his landmark texts *El-Mansuri* and *Al-Hawi*, which presented definitions, symptoms and treatments for mental illnesses and problems related to mental health. He also ran the psychiatric ward of a Baghdad hospital. Such institutions could not exist in Europe at the time because of fear of demonic possessions.

Al-Farabi wrote the first treatises on social psychology and dealt with consciousness studies. In al-Andalus, Abulcasis pioneered neurosurgery, while Ibn Zuhr (Avenzoar) gave the first accurate descriptions on neurological disorders and contributed to modern neuropharmacology, and Averroes suggested the existence of Parkinson's disease. Ali ibn Abbas al-Majusi discussed "the relationship between certain psychological events to the physiological changes in the body", while Avicenna anticipated the word association test, discussed neuropsychiatry in *The Canon of Medicine*, and described the first thought experiments on self-awareness and self-consciousness.

Ibn al-Haytham (Alhazen) is considered by some a forerunner of experimental psychology, for his experimental work on the psychology of visual perception in the *Book of Optics*, where he was the first scientist to argue that vision occurs in the brain, rather than the eyes. He pointed out that personal experience has an effect on what people see and how they see, and that vision and perception are subjective. He was also the first to combine physics and psychology to form psychophysics, and his investigations and experiments on psychology and visual perception included sensation, variations in sensitivity, sensation of touch, perception of colours, perception of darkness, the psychological explanation of the moon illusion, and binocular vision. Biruni was also a pioneer of experimental psychology, as he was the first to empirically describe the concept of reaction time.

The history of science in the Islamic world, like all history, is filled with questions of interpretation. Historians of science generally consider that the study of Islamic science, like all history, must be seen within the particular circumstances of time and place. A. I. Sabra opened a recent overview of Arabic science by noting, "I trust no one would wish to contest the proposition that all of history is local history ... and the history of science is no exception." Some scholars avoid such local historical approaches and seek to identify essential relations between Islam and science that apply at all times and places. The Pakistani physicist, Pervez Hoodbhoy, portrayed "religious fanaticism to be the dominant relation of religion and science in Islam". Sociologist Toby Huff claimed that Islam lacked the "rationalist view of man and nature" that became dominant in Europe.

The Persian philosopher and historian of science, Seyyed Hossein Nasr saw a more positive connection in "an Islamic science that was spiritual and antisecular" which "point[ed] the way to a new 'Islamic science' that would avoid the dehumanizing and despiritualizing mistakes of Western science."

Nasr identified a distinctly Muslim approach to science, flowing from Islamic monotheism and the related theological prohibition against portraying graven images. In science, this is reflected in a philosophical disinterest in describing individual material objects, their properties and characteristics and instead a concern with the ideal, the Platonic form, which exists in matter as an expression of the will of the Creator. Thus one can "see why mathematics was to make such a strong appeal to the Muslim: its abstract nature furnished the bridge that Muslims were seeking between multiplicity and unity."

Some historians of science, however, question the value of drawing boundaries that label the sciences, and the scientists who practice them, in specific cultural, civilizational, or linguistic terms. Consider the case of Nasir al-Din Tusi (1201–1274), who invented his mathematical theorem, the Tusi Couple, while he was director of Maragheh observatory. Tusi's patron and founder of the observatory was the non-Muslim Mongol conqueror of Baghdad, Hulagu Khan. The Tusi-couple "was first encountered in an Arabic text, written by a man who spoke Persian at home, and used that theorem, like many other astronomers who followed him and were all working in the "Arabic/Islamic" world, in order to reform classical Greek astronomy, and then have his theorem in turn be translated into Byzantine Greek towards the beginning of the fourteenth century, only to be used later by Copernicus and others in Latin texts of Renaissance Europe."

The relationship between science and Islam is a matter of controversy. In the Muslim world, many believe that modern science was first developed in the Muslim world rather than in Europe and Western countries, that "all the wealth of knowledge in the world has actually emanated from Muslim civilization," and what people call "the scientific method", is actually "the Islamic method." Muslims often cite verse 239 from Surah Al-Baqara —- *He has taught you what you did not know* in support of their view that the Qur'an promotes the acquisition of new knowledge.

In stark contrast, others worry that the contemporary Muslim world suffers from a "profound lack of scientific understanding," and lament that, for example, in countries like Pakistan even postgraduate physics students have been known to blame earthquakes on "sinfulness, moral laxity, deviation from the Islamic true path," while "only a couple of muffled voices supported the scientific view that earthquakes are a natural phenomenon unaffected by human activity."

The development of scientific thought and knowledge has caused differing reactions among Muslims. In the Muslim world today, most of the focus on the relation between Islam and science involves scientific interpretations of the Quran (and sometimes the Sunna) that claim to show these sources make prescient statements about the nature of the universe, biological development and other phenomena later confirmed by scientific research, and proof of the divine origin of the Qur'an. This effort has been criticized by some scientists and philosophers as containing logical fallacies, being unscientific, likely to be disproven by evolving scientific theories.

The religion Islam has its own worldview system including beliefs about "ultimate reality, epistemology, ontology, ethics, purpose, etc." Muslims believe that the Qur'an is the literal word and the final revelation of God for the guidance of humankind. Science in the broadest sense refers to any falsifiable system of knowledge attained by verifiable means, and in a narrower sense to a system of acquiring knowledge based on empiricism, experimentation, and methodological naturalism, as well as to the organized body of knowledge humans have gained by such research. Scientists maintain that scientific investigation must adhere to the scientific method, a process for evaluating empirical knowledge that explains observable events in nature as results of natural causes, rejecting supernatural notions.

One of the most important features of Science, notably Physics is the precise quantitative prediction based on its current level understanding of a phenomenon. In this aspect it differs from many religious texts where physical phenomena are depicted in a very qualitative way, often by the use of words carrying several meanings.

Classical Islamic Science

In the history of science, Islamic science refers to the science developed under Islamic civilization between the 8th and 16th centuries, during what is known as the Islamic Golden Age. It is also known as Arabic science since the majority of texts during this period were written in Arabic, the *lingua franca* of Islamic civilization. Despite these terms, not all scientists during this period were Muslim or Arab, as there were a number of notable non-Arab scientists (most notably Persians), as well as some non-Muslim scientists, who contributed to scientific studies in the Islamic world. A number of modern scholars such as Fielding H. Garrison, Bertrand Russell, Abdus Salam and Hossein Nasr consider modern science and the scientific method to have been greatly influenced by Muslim scientists who introduced a modern empirical, experimental and quantitative approach to scientific inquiry.

Some scholars, notably Donald Routledge Hill, Ahmad Y Hassan, Abdus Salam, and George Saliba, have referred to their achievements as a Muslim scientific revolution, though this does not contradict the traditional view of the Scientific Revolution which is still supported by most scholars. According to many historians, science in Islamic civilization flourished during the Middle Ages, but began declining at some time around the 14th to 16th centuries. At least some scholars blame this on the "rise of a clerical faction which froze this same science and withered its progress." Examples of conflicts with prevailing interpretations of Islam and science - or at least the fruits of science - thereafter include the demolition of Taqi al-Din's great Istanbul observatory of al-Din in Galata, "comparable in its technical equipment and its specialist personnel with that of his celebrated contemporary, the Danish astronomer Tycho Brahe." But while Brahe's observatory "opened the way to a vast new development of astronomical science," Taqi al-Din's was demolished by a squad of Janissaries, "by order of the sultan, on the recommendation of the Chief Mufti," sometime after 1577 AD.

It is believed that it was the empirical attitude of the Qur'an and Sunnah which inspired medieval Muslim scientists, in particular Alhazen (965-1037), to develop the scientific method. It is also known that certain advances made by medieval Muslim astronomers, geographers and mathematicians was motivated by problems presented in Islamic scripture, such as Al-Khwarizmi's (c. 780-850) development of algebra in order to solve the Islamic inheritance laws, and developments in astronomy, geography, spherical geometry and spherical trigonometry in order to determine the direction of the Qibla, the times of Salah prayers, and the dates of the Islamic calendar.

Other such examples include Ibn al-Nafis (1213-1288), who discovered the pulmonary circulation in 1242 and used his discovery as evidence for the orthodox Islamic doctrine of bodily resurrection. Ibn al-Nafis also used Islamic scripture as justification for his rejection of wine as self-medication. Ali Kuºçu's (1403-1474) support for the Earth's rotation and his rejection of Aristotelian cosmology (which advocates a stationary Earth) was also motivated by religious opposition to Aristotle by orthodox Islamic theologians such as Al-Ghazali. Criticisms against alchemy and astrology were also motivated by religion, such as the views of astrologers conflicting with orthodox Islam.

Arrival of Modern Science in Islamic World

At the beginning of the nineteenth century, modern science arrived in the Muslim world but it wasn't the science itself that affected Muslim scholars. Rather, it "was the transfer of various philosophical currents entangled with science that had a profound effect on the minds of Muslim scientists and intellectuals. Schools like Positivism and Darwinism penetrated the Muslim world and dominated its academic circles and had a noticeable impact on some Islamic theological doctrines." There were different responses to this among the Muslim scholars: These reactions, in words of Professor Mehdi Golshani, were the following:

- Some rejected modern science as corrupt foreign thought, considering it incompatible with Islamic teachings, and in their view, the only remedy for the stagnancy of Islamic societies would be the strict following of Islamic teachings.
- Other thinkers in the Muslim world saw science as the only source of real enlightenment and advocated the complete adoption of modern science. In their view, the only remedy for the stagnation of Muslim societies would be the mastery of modern science and the replacement of the religious worldview by the scientific worldview.
- The majority of faithful Muslim scientists tried to adapt Islam to the findings of modern science; they can be categorized in the following subgroups: (a) Some Muslim thinkers attempted to justify modern science on religious grounds. Their motivation was to encourage Muslim societies to acquire modern knowledge and to safeguard their societies from the criticism of Orientalists and Muslim intellectuals. (b) Others tried to show that all important scientific discoveries had been predicted in the Qur'an and Islamic tradition and appealed to modern science to explain various aspects of faith. (c) Yet other scholars advocated a reinterpretation of Islam. In their view, one must try to construct a new theology that can establish a viable relation between Islam and modern science. The Indian scholar, Sayyid Ahmad

Khan, sought a theology of nature through which one could reinterpret the basic principles of Islam in the light of modern science. (d) Then there were some Muslim scholars who believed that empirical science had reached the same conclusions that prophets had been advocating several thousand years ago. The revelation had only the privilege of prophecy.

- Finally, some Muslim philosophers separated the findings of modern science from its philosophical attachments. Thus, while they praised the attempts of Western scientists for the discovery of the secrets of nature, they warned against various empiricist and materialistic interpretations of scientific findings. Scientific knowledge can reveal certain aspects of the physical world, but it should not be identified with the alpha and omega of knowledge. Rather, it has to be integrated into a metaphysical framework—consistent with the Muslim worldview—in which higher levels of knowledge are recognized and the role of science in bringing us closer to God is fulfilled.

Compatibility of Islam and the Development of Science

Whether Islamic culture has promoted or hindered scientific advancement is disputed. Islamists such as Sayyid Qutb argue that since "Islam appointed" Muslims "as representatives of God and made them responsible for learning all the sciences," science cannot but prosper in a society of true Muslims. Many "classical and modern [sources] agree that the Qur'an condones, even encourages the acquisition of science and scientific knowledge, and urges humans to reflect on the natural phenomena as signs of God's creation." Some scientific instruments produced in classical times in the Islamic world were inscribed with Qur'anic citations. Many Muslims agree that doing science is an act of religious merit, even a collective duty of the Muslim community.

Others say traditional interpretations of Islam are not compatible with the development of science. Author Rodney Stark, explains Islam's lag behind the West in scientific advancement after (roughly) 1500 AD to opposition by traditional ulema to efforts to formulate systematic explanation of natural phenomenon with "natural laws." They believed such laws were blasphemous because they limit "Allah's freedom to act" as He wishes. This principle was enshired in aya 14:4: "Allah sendeth whom He will astray, and guideth whom He will," which (they believed) applied to all of creation not just humanity.

In the early twentieth century ulema forbade the learning of foreign languages and dissection of human bodies in the medical school in Iran. The ulama at the Islamic university of Al-Azhar in Cairo taught the Ptolemaic astronomical system (in which the sun circles the earth) until compelled to adopt the Copernican system by the Egyptian government in 1961. In recent years, the lagging of the Muslim world in science is manifest in the disproportionately small amount of scientific output as measured by citations of articles published in internationally circulating science journals, annual expenditures on research and development, and numbers of research scientists and engineers. Skepticism of science among some Muslims is reflected in issues such as resistance in Muslim northern Nigeria to polio inoculation, which some believe is "an imaginary thing created in the West or it is a ploy to get us to submit to this evil agenda."

Qur'an and Science

The belief that Qur'an had prophesied scientific theories and discoveries has become a strong and widespread belief in the contemporary Islamic world; these prophecies are often provided as a proof of the divine origin of the Qur'an. The scientific facts claimed to be in the Qur'an exist in different subjects, including creation, astronomy, the animal and vegetables kingdom, and human reproduction "a time is fixed for every prophecy; you will come to know in time". Islamic scholar Zaghloul El-Naggar thinks that this verse refers to the scientific facts in the Qur'an that would be discovered by the world in modern time, centuries after the revelation.

This belief is, however, arguable in the Muslim world, while some support it, other Muslim scholars oppose the believe, claiming that the Qur'an is not a book of science; al-Biruni, one of the most celebrated Muslim scientists of the classical period, assigned to the Qur'an a separate and autonomous realm of its own and held that the Qur'an "does not interfere in the business of science nor does it infringe on the realm of science." These scholars argued for the possibility of multiple scientific explanation of the natural phenomena, and refused to subordinate the Qur'an to an ever-changing science.

Fossils of Ancient Humans

Here are three basic verses in Qur'an which are related to human creation: According to the first two verses, Adam and Eve were directly created by God from clay that give sound. They did not descend from any other species as proposed by Charles Darwin. The rest of mankind is the progeny of Adam and Eve. The third verse implies that there were three stages in their creation, and can be interpreted as follows:

- Adam and Eve were created from clay that gives sound
- They subsequently developed the ability to reproduce at a later age
- Finally, after some more time elapsed, they entered the third phase in which they were perfected both physically and spiritually, and received the divine spirit from God

Conception and Inherited Characteristics

The most prominent of the ancient Greek thinkers who wrote on medicine were Hippocrates, Aristotle, and Galen.

Hippocrates and Galen, in contrast with Aristotle, wrote that the contribution of females to children is equal to that of males, and the vehicle for it is a substance similar to the semen of males. Basim Musallam writes that the ideas of these men were widespread through the pre-modern Middle East: "Hippocrates, Aristotle, and Galen were as much a part of Middle Eastern Arabic culture as anything else in it." The sayings in the Quran and those attributed to Muhammad in the Hadith influenced generations of Muslim scientists by siding with Galen and Hippocrates. Basim Musallam writes: "... the statements about parental contribution to generation in the *hadith* paralleled the Hippocratic writings, and the view of fetal development in the Quran agreed in detail with Galen's scientific writings." He reports that the highly influential medieval Hanbali scholar Ibn Qayyim, in his book *Kitab al-tibyan fi aqsam al-qur'an*, cites the following statement of the prophet from the Sahih Muslim:

"The male semen is white and the female semen is yellowish. When the two meet and the male semen overpowers the female semen, it will be male; when the female semen overpowers the male semen, it will be female."

Ibn Qayyim also quotes a different hadith from the same collection, which is quoted by other Muslim authors as well. Having been asked the question "from what is man created," the Prophet replies:

"He is created of both, the semen of the man and the semen of the woman. The man's semen is thick and forms the bones and the tendons. The woman's semen is fine and forms the flesh and blood."

The relation between Qur'an and science is strongly affirmed in Islamic thought. Almost all sources, classical and modern, agree that the Qur'an encourages the acquisition of science and scientific knowledge.

The contemporary Islamic discourse on the Qur'an and science abounds with assertions of the relationship between the two. This presumed relationship is construed in a variety of ways, the most common of which are the efforts to prove the divine nature of the Qur'an through modern science.

The belief that Qur'an had prophesied scientific theories and discoveries - known as Ijaz al-Qur'an - has become a strong and widespread belief in the contemporary Islamic world. Alleged prophecies are often provided to show a connection between the Qur'an and miracles, and to support the belief of divine origin for the Qur'an.

Science-related Prophecies

According to Qur'an; natural phenomena comprises a large portion of the divine signs; nature itself praises God, and God proclaims that he will show humankind his signs on the furthest horizons we well as deep within themselves. Islamic scholar Zaghloul El-Naggar thinks that this verse refers to the scientific signs in the Qur'an that would be discovered by the world in modern time, centuries after the revelation. The scientific signs claimed to be in the Qur'an exist in different subjects, including creation, astronomy, the animal and vegetables kingdom, and human reproduction. Some of those claimed prophecies are:

- The Qur'an contains a number of verses pertaining to some biological specificities regarding human reproduction and development. According to Keith L. Moore (professor emeritus of anatomy at the University of Toronto, and son of a Protestant clergyman) the scientific meaning of certain surahs in the Qur'an has become clear only recently. Moore has concluded that God revealed the Qur'an to Muhammad, and has disseminated this view in many lectures, panel discussions and articles.
- The Qur'an referenced the heavens and earth as originally being an integrated mass before God split them *"Have not those who disbelieve known that the heavens and the earth were of one piece, then We parted them"*, which has been interpreted by some as being "nothing short of a condensed version of the Big bang theory".

- The Qur'an talked about cosmic orbital motion: "*It is not for the sun to overtake the moon, nor doth the night outstrip the day. They float each in an orbit*" at a period of time when the common belief was that earth was stationary.

The most famous proponent of this argument is perhaps Maurice Bucaille, a French physician and author of the popular book *The Bible, The Quran and Science*. Maurice Bucaille asserts in his book that "he could not find a single error in the Qur'an", and that the Qur'an does "not contain a single statement which is assailable from a modern scientific point of view", which led him to believe that no human author in the seventh century could have written "facts" which "today are shown to be keeping with modern scientific knowledge". Bucaille's opinion did not gain scientific consensus on the matter; critics believe that "Bucaille bends the meaning of the Arabic words to suit his own ideas." and "Bucaille proposes new meanings for Qur'anic words to bring them into accord with modern scientific knowledge, without requiring any standard philological justification."

The translator of "The Bible, The Quran and Science" into Indonesian, Dr. Muhammad Rasjidi, former Professor for Islamic Studies at McGill University and former Indonesian Minister for Religious Affairs characterizes as "a half-baked mish-mash of pseudo-science and pseudo-exegesis". The search for Qur'anic references to and prophecies of modern scientific discoveries has become a "popular trend" in some Muslim societies as a manifestation of the popularity of the scientific miracles belief, the Muslim World League at Mecca formed a committee named Committee on the Scientific Miracles of the Qur'ân and the Sunna to investigate the relation between Qur'an and science, headed by Zaghloul El-Naggar.

According to some recent studies of the relationship between science education and religion, one of the ways in which science education in strongly Islamic societies is impacted by religiosity is when "acceptable" scientific discoveries can be found to have been anticipated or "identified" by the Qur'an, with consequent implications for what is taught and not taught.

Scientific Exegesis of the Qur'an

Scientific exegesis of the Qur'an is the assumption that all sorts of findings of the modern natural sciences have been anticipated in the Qur'an and that many unambiguous references to them can be discovered in its verses. Many Islamic authors, classical and modern, believe that all the sciences were contained in the Qur'an. The practise of *tafsir 'ilmi*, or scientific exegesis, which was "almost forgotten, has been revived in modern times; the classical attempt to incorporate all streams of human knowledge into the Qur'an has been updated with a special focus on the natural sciences.

This method of scientific interpretation did not find general approval among Muslim authors. Many classical Muslim commentators and scientists, notably al-Biruni, assigned to the Qur'an a separate and autonomous realm of its own and held that the Qur'an "does not interfere in the business of science nor does it infringe on the realm of science." These medieval scholars argued for the possibility of multiple scientific explanation of the natural phenomena, and refused to subordinate the Qur'an to an ever-changing science.

Author Rotraud Wielandt summarizes the arguments of the modern Muslim commentators such as Mahmud Shaltut and Sayyid Qutb who reject a scientific method of interpretation of the Qur'an as follows:

1. It is lexicographically untenable, since it falsely attributes modern meanings to the quranic vocabulary.
2. It neglects the contexts of words or phrases within the quranic text, and also the occasions of revelation where these are transmitted.
3. It ignores the fact that, for the Quran to be comprehensible for its first audience, the words of the Qur'ân had to

conform to the language and the intellectual horizon of the ancient Arabs at the Prophet's time—an argument already used by the Andalusian Mâlikite scholar al-Shâmibî against the scientific exegesis of his time.

4. It does not take notice of the fact that scientific knowledge and scientific theories are always incomplete and provisory by their very nature; therefore, the derivation of scientific knowledge and scientific theories in qur¾ânic verses is actually tantamount to limiting the validity of these verses to the time for which the results of the science in question are accepted.
5. Most importantly, it fails to comprehend that the Qur'an is not a scientific book, but a religious one designed to guide human beings by imparting to them a creed and a set of moral values.

   In defense of their efforts the exegetes use two verses in the Qur'an: one that states *"and We have sent down to thee the Book explaining all things"* and another which says *"We have neglected nothing in the Book"*. The classical objection to these verses being used as a basis for intensive *tafsir 'ilmi* is that the "Book" mentioned in these verses is not the Qur'an itself, but a "well-preserved tablet" in heaven, of which the earthly Qur'an is a reflection.

Creationism

The Qur'an is insistent that Allah is the sole creator of all things; the universe and humans. Qur'an does not assert that God created the universe at some definable point in the past. As opposed to deism or to certain readings of Newtonian physics, God continues to sustain the creation during every moment of its existence. And in fact the Qur'an is deeply impressed with the ongoing order of nature and summons all humankind to share in its admiration and to learn from it:

Your Guardian-Lord is Allah, Who created the heavens and the earth in six days, and is firmly established on the throne (of authority): He draweth the night as a veil o'er the day, each seeking the other in rapid succession: He created the sun, the moon, and the stars, (all) governed by laws under His command. Is it not His to create and to govern? Blessed be Allah, the Cherisher and Sustainer of the worlds!

God's purpose in the creation of the universe was focused on humanity. This is manifest, for example, in the fact that the universe is admirably designed to provide for human needs and wants. The Qur'an offers its own version of cosmic anthropic principle.

Universal Creation

Qur'an contains many verses describing the universe creation; God created heavens and earth in six days, the heavens and earth were completed in two days, and in four days God furnished the creation of the earth with mountains, rivers and fruit-gardens. Heavens and earth formed from an integrated disk-shaped mass which had to be split, the seven heavens were created from smoke, forming layers, one above the other. God and angels inhabit the seventh heaven . The lowest heaven is adorned with lights, the sun and the moon (which follow a regular path), the stars and the constellations of the zodiac.

Human Creation

According to Qur'an, Adam is the first human being and the father of humankind. First Adam was created from clay, God himself formed the material of which Adam is made and breathed his spirit into him, and then Eve was created from Adam, the Qur'an does not report when she was created . Subsequently all humankind was created from clay. Today, some modern Muslim commentators have decided that, since the Qur'an makes no mention of the evolution of one species to another kind of species, the Darwinian theory of evolution is contrary to the teachings of the Qur'an. An apt verse that summarizes the process of human creation is:

"From the (earth) did We create you, and into it shall We return you, and from it shall We bring you out once again"

However, on multiple occasions, the Quran states that life and living creatures originated from water. (21:30, and 24:45) Furthermore, it also states on multiple occasions that mankind was "created", *then* "fashioned." This has been interpreted as a hint toward evolution, in that after creation of life, modifications can occur through natural selection. Verse 95:4 states: "We created Man in the finest state." An alternative translation has been "We created man according to the best organizational plan." Verses that have previously been interpreted as pertaining to human embryological development have also been open to interpretation in regards to evolution. Verse 71:14 states: (God)"has created you stage by stage." The Quran also mentions the wrath of God being at work when one community of people is punished for its sins through annihilation, and replaced with another community. The text is thus open to interpretation.

Embryology

In Qur'an reference is made to fetal development and growth, explanations of these verses express the view that "sperm" and "safe lodging" refer to sperm within the female uterus. Prior to fertilization, sperm bind to the zona pellucida or outer covering of the ovum. Following such lines of interpretation, *clot* could be a reference to this, i.e. to sperm clinging to the ovum. However, *clot* is also interpreted by some exegetes as *blood clot* and taken to refer to "something that clings" to the uterus. For those modern commentators who then extrapolate this interpretation scientifically, the *blood clot* could be taken to represent the fertilized ovum or early embryo implanting itself in the endometrium or uterine lining. Some modern interpreters combine these verses with, seeing in the reference to the "three veils of darkness" a reflection of the three anatomical layers that protect the fetus

— the abdominal wall, the uterus wall and amniotic sac.

It is widely recognized that the Qur'an and hadith contain a number of verses pertaining to human reproduction and development. In his book *A History of Embryology*, Professor Joseph Needham describes some of the embryological passages in the Qur'an, verses. For the past 100 years this verse has been translated to describe the second stage of the embryo being a "clot of blood", but it has been argued that the word "alaqa", prior to one hundred years ago, and during the prophet Muhammad's lifetime, the definition of this word "alaqa" and the context in which it was used was "that which clings".

Dr. Keith L. Moore, who is most known for his textbooks on the subjects of anatomy and human embryology, had to say of the Qur'an and Muhammad, "It is clear to me that these statements (of the Qur'an about human development) must have come to Muhammad from God, because almost all of this knowledge was not discovered until many centuries later. This proves to me that Muhammad must have been a messenger of God", then he was asked does this mean you believe that the Qur'an is the word of God? He replied "I found no difficulty in accepting this as a seventh century echo of Aristotle and Ayurveda." According to Dr. Moore, professor emeritus of Anatomy at the University of Toronto, the scientific meaning of certain surahs in the Quran has become clear only recently. An example cited by him is verse.

However when asked in a 2002 if he would be willing to be interviewed about Qur'anic scientific miracles, Moore declined saying, "it's been 10 or 11 years since I was involved in the Quran."

France's professoriate was roiled early this year by a capaciously sourced polemic masquerading as a major work of revisionist intellectual history. According to the startling thesis propounded in Lyon University Professor Sylvain Gouguenheim's *Aristote au Mont Saint–Michel: les raciness grecques de l'Europe*, the revival of learning in Europe had little to do with Islam's transmission of Hellenic philosophy and science. Indeed, Professor Gouguenheim believes that, given Islam's inculcation of revealed authority, Muslim scholars could not have really assimilated the intrinsic rationalism animating Greek thought. Rather, he attributes the preservation and translation of that learning into Aramaean and Syriac by Christian holy men living under the protection of Muslim caliphs. He follows the documentary underground of Syriac translations to a handful of receiving stations in Dark Ages Europe, of which the great Norman bastion of Mont St–Michel was one of the most important.

The Renaissance for Sylvain Gouguenheim, then, mainly amounts to the splendid work of a few assiduous Catholic monks restoring the lost corpus of classical antiquity to the West long before those Arab scholars to whom most contemporary historians give credit had achieved real mastery of Aristotle, Plato, Ptolemy, and Euclid. In France, where willful historical distortion can be punished by law, informed academic reaction to *Aristote au Mont Saint Michel* was quite censorious. The book will likely have a more favorable reception in the United States, where innocence of the fruitful cohabitation of Islamdom and Christendom in the millennium after the collapse of the Roman Empire is widespread and deep. As Michael Hamilton Morgan reminds us in *Lost History*, his interpretively venturesome and felicitously written panorama of Islamic thought and science, "most Westerners have been taught that the greatness of the West has its intellectual roots in Greece and Rome, and that after the thousand–year sleep of the Dark Ages, Europe miraculously reawakened to its Greco–Roman roots."

The more general problem of agnosticism about the historic interaction of Islam and the Occident has been compounded in America by the Huntingtonian thesis of civilizational clash and the ascendancy of a neo–conservative scholarship and policy agendas clamorously asserting an oil–and–water incompatibility of the culture of the West and that of the Muslim world. In this conception of the Muslim "problem" (of "what went wrong?" in Bernard Lewis's famous interrogation), Muslim retrogression into radical religious fundamentalism and political terrorism is stipulated as having been inevitable, notwithstanding the acknowledgement of various important Muslim contributions to the post–Roman West. Islam's long ago remarkable attainments merely serve as ammunition to indict a civilization deemed to have forfeited the post–industrial world's confidence.

Lost History is an anti–text to the literature of inevitable decline and titanic clash, a robustly researched work of popular history, the author of which announces from the outset a game choice "to emphasize the bright side of a very complex [Muslim] civilization." Mr. Morgan proceeds from the Meccan origins of the world's third Abrahamic monotheism to its irrepressible advance across the Fertile Crescent at a pace that mimics the *jihad* launched in 636 C.E. by the "rightly guided" Umar, Islam's second caliph. One world empire (Sassanian Iran) crashes upon contact; the other (Greco–Roman) survives territorially much reduced and on life support for another eight centuries. *Jihad*, as the author makes clear, obeyed the Prophet's Qur'anic interdiction of forced religious conversion.

The poll tax *(jizya)* exacted from nonbelievers also powerfully incentivized a policy of religious laissez faire. That many of the conquered peoples looked upon Muslim rule as preferable to the religious oppression or labor exploitation they knew previously explains both their readiness to surrender and to convert. Think of the analogy of the Roman Empire ruling a heterogeneous mass of humanity and demanding respect for its laws and remission of taxes, but otherwise indulgent of cultural variety and accepting a high degree of local autonomy. A mere 79 years after Muhammad's death, the Muslim Empire leapfrogged in 711 from North Africa to a Mediterranean beachhead and on to the swift occupation of Iberia after defeating its brutal and fiercely anti–Semitic Visigoth oligarchy.

Germanic–Latin Iberia became Muslim *al–Andalus* in a flash, after which the jihad swept over and around the Pyrenees on its seemingly unstoppable course of conquest and incorporation. In 732, a large Muslim expeditionary army encountered a much smaller Frankish force on the old Roman road to Poitiers. "For some reason," observes Morgan of books written by countless generations of European historians, "this particular struggle will be painted in apocalyptic terms." Although he mistakenly believes that the actual site (viz., the tiny village of Moussais–la–Bataille) "cannot be located on a map," the author reconstructs the Battle of Poitiers with a cinematic detail of considerable plausibility. As for what it all meant – Dark–Ages Christianity saved by a wily German tribal chieftain; Muslim occupation of Gaul temporarily interrupted; a quest for booty gone awry? – *Lost History* decides that "this debate will never be settled."

It seems clear, however, that, whether or not the Umayyad caliphate planned to add the lands beyond the Pyrenees to the *dar al–Islam* (Morgan thinks not), Europe has drawn vastly more significance than Muslims did from Charles the Hammer's victory. Indeed, the neologism "europenses" first applied by an Andalusian scribe to the Poitiers winners comported with a civilizationist mindset of perpetual clash that would become dogma for Westerners by the 11th century. More to the point, the Carolingian regime founded by Charles and his descendants on the mythos of Poitiers and in alliance with the Catholic papacy shaped a future of militant Christianity in which no other faiths were tolerated and a master–class of cavalrymen ruled by intimidation and slaughter (though not with the newfangled Arab stirrups Mr. Morgan erroneously believes the Hammer's men stripped from fallen Andalusian cavalry.) A major skirmish devoid of religious animus between Arab and German warriors at the foot of the Pyrenees became the signature of a civilization. Poitiers was traumatic, writes Morgan, "leaving a wound that has never fully healed."

But if the Pyrenees traced a scarlet cicatrice on the European continent, a Muslim civilization of cultural sophistication and fabulous prosperity evolved west of the mountain range. Although roiled for more than a decade by sanguinary violence that obliterated the 100–year–old Umayyad dynasty, Umayyad rule eventually returned to the Iberian peninsula in the remarkable persons of Abd al–Rahman I and III, whose policies fostered the legendary *convivencia* that could have served as model for an alternative Europe of interfaith tolerance and philosophical rationalism. *Lost History* engagingly recycles the familiar story of Cordoba, "the ornament of the world," with its lighted streets, bath houses, and large libraries, its chess–playing cosmopolites, Sephardic notables, and Arabized Christians.

A vignette unexpected by this reader was Mr. Morgan's account of the late ninth–century aerial feat of one Abbas ibn Firnas, a septuagenarian polymath whose winged flight over Cordoba from the Sierra Morena Leonardo da Vinci would have envied. Cordoba cradled the high philosophizing of Ibn Rushd (Averroes) and Musa bin Maimun (Maimonides) – both of whom made reason revelation's handmaiden – as well as the medical ingenuity of al–Zahrawi, whose forceps transformed pediatrics and experimental mastectomies into advanced surgery. The translation from Greek into Arabic of Diascorides's *De Materia Medica* by a Byzantine Greek, a Muslim scholar, and a Catholic priest under the direction of Hasdai ibn Shaprut, a Cordoban Jew, was an inconceivable undertaking in Christian Europe.

Mr. Morgan's "lost history" of Abbasid Baghdad undermines Professor Gouguenheim's claim of indispensable Syriac scribes and merely imitative Muslim thinkers. Rising on the banks of the Tigris under the command of the second Abbasid caliph, al–Mansur (712–775), Baghdad surpassed Constantinople in scale and wealth. By comparison,

Umayyad Cordoba was only a simulacrum. With Gundeshapur, the destroyed Iranian Empire's city of science and medicine, as prototype, Caliph Harun al–Rashid is said to have inaugurated Baghdad's House of Wisdom (Bayt al–Hikma), the Muslim world's great research center from which almost four centuries of caliphal patronage nurtured breakthrough achievements in astronomy, mathematics, and medicine.

Royal patronage of learning being a standard feature of empires, it was not incumbent upon Mr. Morgan to do more than to describe examples of it. Hence, in contrast to George Saliba's recent *Islamic Science and the Making of the European Renaissance* (2007), we encounter few real–world facts of life in Morgan's book that necessitated and incentivized the Umayyad and Abbasid regimes' investment in the sciences: the role of the zero, decimals, and simple Hindu numerals in order to pay soldiers' salaries and circulate standardized specie, for example, or the mathematics and rudimentary astronomy involved in aligning lunar and solar calendars or in plying Indian Ocean trade routes.

Mr. Morgan's strength is the captivating descriptive flair with which he recounts histories of patronized achievements. Summoned from remote Khurasan by the scholarly Caliph al–Mamun (813–833), Muhammad al–Khwarizmi, eponymous father of the algorithm and re–discoverer of the Hindu zero and the Babylonian sixty–second minute, distills his lifetime epiphanies into the House of Wisdom algebraic masterwork *Al–Jabr wa al–Muqabala (The Compendious Book on Calculation by Completion and Balancing.)* Soon after the House of Wisdom opened its doors, a peripatetic Uzbekistan stargazer named al–Farghani rendered the first Arabic summary of Ptolemy's foundational *Almagest*. Another wandering genius recruited to al–Mamun's House of Wisdom, Jabir ibn Haiyan of Yemeni descent, mixed alchemy and chemistry so liberally that the author tells us Jabir is the source of the word "jibberish."

Although he fails to transmute gold from lead, Jabir creates *aqua regia* that dissolves gold and platinum, discovers hydrochloric acid, originates the concept of alkali, and, as Christian Europe's "Geber," achieves renown as a father of alchemy and chemistry. By no means does Baghdad capture all the best scientific talent, especially not after the Abbasid caliphs become pawns of their Buyid and Mamluk ancillaries and then ciphers under the conquering Seljuk Turks in the 11th century. From the House of Knowledge of the upstart Fatimid caliphate of Egypt came Ibn al–Haytham's rejection of Ptolemy's theory that light rays emanate from the eye. Christian Europe knew him as Alhacen, author of the arbitral *Book of Optics*. From sophisticated Isfahan, another 11th–century center of power and learning, came Omar Khayyam's demonstration of the rotating axis of the earth and calculation of the year almost as precise as the length established eleven hundred years later by the Hubble telescope.

Another Isfahan scholar, Ibn Sina, identified tuberculosis as a virus and assembled the known medical knowledge in his *Canon of Medicine*, an ecumenical commentary that would hold sway in the medical schools of Europe for centuries. Taken to India by warring Sultan Mahmud of Ghazna, the captive scholar, Raihan al–Biruni, learned of the Hindu theory of lunar tides. *Lost History* reproduces al–Biruni's diagram of a lunar eclipse. Southeast of Anatolia, another genius in service to a warrior Seljuk sultan designed revolutionary machines and instruments (the crankshaft, giant water pumps). The author tells us that, although parts of it became known, al–Jazari's remarkable *Book of Ingenious Mechanical Devices* was only translated into English in the 20th century. Otherwise, al–Jazari "would be as well known to the world as Leonardo da Vinci."

It has become a commonplace observation among Western scholars that the cause of much of the disjunction between the Western democracies and the Muslim world lies in the latter's failure to experience a religious upheaval analogous to the European Reformation of the 16th and 17th centuries. However, as Mr. Morgan's second chapter reminds us, the umma experienced a comparable philosophical and theological upheaval some six centuries before Europe did. A dozen or more competing schools of traditionalist and radical philosophy, theology, and law – Hanafites, Hanbalites, *Mutakallimun, fuqaha* – contended for primacy in Abbasid Baghdad. Citing the translated writings of Aristotle and Plato in support of their causes, learned men such as al–Kindi and al–Farabi not only argued that no conflict existed between reason and revelation ("the work of God and the word of God,") those like Ibn Sina, belonging to the Mu'tazalite school, claimed that the Qur'an was created in time and that Aristotelian reason was the path to revealed truth.

Before the rationalist wave broke against traditionalist outrage in the early 11th century, some Mu'tazalites even proposed to interpret parts of the Qur'an metaphorically. But while the work of astronomers, mathematicians, chemists, and physicians progressed apace, independent rational inquiry (*ijtihad*) formally ended in caliphal proscription in the reign of al–Qadir (991–1031). *Ijtihad* survived somewhat longer in al Andalus and was even tolerated by some of the Almohad caliphs. In a book that is avowedly celebratory, it may not surprise us that the fateful "closing of the gates of *ijtihad*" passes as a dutiful observation rather than as an opportunity to explore its immense cultural ramifications. Writing of the deaths within eight years of each other of three of Islam's greatest rationalists — Andalusis al–Bitruji, Ibn Rushd, and Maimonides – Morgan might have made more of their adversity than the understatement that "their deaths mark a passing and the beginning of even more turbulent times to come."

The Mongol tsunami that rolled across Mesopotamia in 1258 killed the last Abbasid caliph, obliterated Baghdad, decimated its population, and wiped the empire from the face of the earth. Two years later, the Mongol steamroller commanded by Hulegu, Genghis Khan's grandson, was stopped against all odds by the Mamluk rulers of Egypt at the battle of Ain Jalut in Palestine. Ain Jalut was "the Battle of Poitiers cubed" in terms of civilizational meaning. The Mongol rupture and the aftermath of relatively short–lived Mongol–Turkic sultanates eventually divided the dar al–Islam into three principal civilizations: Sefavid Persia; Mughal India; and Ottoman Asia Minor and North Africa. Each of these empires was larger, richer, more powerful, architecturally superior, and, arguably, more civilized than the warring, religiously divided nation–states of Europe. *Lost History* resumes its endlessly engaging story of scientific, intellectual, and artistic achievements in the grand capitals of Isfahan, Samarkand, Delhi, Maragheh, and Istanbul. From his observatory in Mongolian Azerbaijan, one of the few survivors of Baghdad scans the heavens and calculates precisely the two equinoxes.

Muhammad al–Tusi dedicates his catalog of stars to his master, Hulegu the Ilkhan, tries to square Ptolemy's geocentric universe with observed discrepancies, and leaves to Copernicus' time his influential *Memoir on the Science of Astronomy*. In later times, Portuguese mariners will tack down the African coast in caravels modeled on the Muslim *qarib* with its lateen sails. Ottoman armies will besiege Vienna with Chinese rockets less than a century after capturing Constantinople. To call the 16th century "the century of Suleiman the Magnificent" would not be an overstatement. In the end, Morgan offers no explanation for the asymmetrical development of Europe and the Muslim world, resulting in the West's primacy, although he seems tempted to stress the importance of the terrible 13th–century Mongol body blow.

Yet, from the abundance of his own examples of imperial magnificence and sustained technological achievements well into the 17th century, it seems that substantial recovery after Ain Jalut – such as Muzaffar Iqbal's in his fine theoretical work, *Islam and Science* (1998) – is more likely than not.

Michael Hamilton Morgan's *Lost History* leaves us better informed and intellectually stimulated, but still at an explanatory loss. It is clear, though, that he believes that deterministic thinking is the bane of historiography. "History might have taken another course," he hypothesizes:

At that moment of rare equipoise between China, India, the Muslim world, and Europe in the late 15th and 16th centuries, any one of Europe's rivals could have made the same fateful decisions that Spain, Portugal, and England undertook to support voyages of exploration and conquest. .. Christianity could have become ever more locked in anti–materialism and zealotry; a few blips in royal succession could have brought the Inquisition to England; and Oliver Cromwell could have become the key patron of English political philosophy and not John Locke. In this parallel universe, the Muslim world could have led and enjoyed the benefits of the Renaissance and the Enlightenment it seeded. .. This author does not believe there was any inevitability to the rise of the West.

This is a fine antidote to the hubris of our post–9/11 era. Yet, if we cannot predict the past, does that leave us facing a future in which little can ever be said to be certain?

Spirit of Muslim Culture

Muhammad of Arabia ascended the highest Heaven and returned. I swear by God that if I had reached that point, I should never have returned.' These are the words of a great Muslim saint, 'AbdulQuddës of Gangoh. In the whole range of Sufi literature it will be probably difficult to find words which, in a single sentence, disclose such an acute perception of the psychological difference between the prophetic and the mystic types of consciousness. The mystic does not wish to return from the repose of 'unitary experience'; and even when he does return, as he must, his return does not mean much for mankind at large. The prophet's return is creative. He returns to insert himself into the sweep of time with a view to control the forces of history, and thereby to create a fresh world of ideals. For the mystic the repose of 'unitary experience' is something final; for the prophet it is the awakening, within him, of world-shaking psychological forces, calculated to completely transform the human world. The desire to see his religious experience transformed into a living world-force is supreme in the prophet. Thus his return amounts to a kind of pragmatic test of the value of his religious experience.

In its creative act the prophet's will judges both itself and the world of concrete fact in which it endeavours to objectify itself. In penetrating the impervious material before him the prophet discovers himself for himself, and unveils himself to the eye of history. Another way of judging the value of a prophet's religious experience, therefore, would be to examine the type of manhood that he has created, and the cultural world that has sprung out of the spirit of his message. In this lecture I want to confine myself to the latter alone. The idea is not to give you a description of the achievements of Islam in the domain of knowledge. I want rather to fix your gaze on some of the ruling concepts of the culture of Islam in order to gain an insight into the process of ideation that underlies them, and thus to catch a glimpse of the soul that found expression through them. Before, however, I proceed to do so it is necessary to understand the cultural value of a great idea in Islam - I mean the finality of the institution of prophethood.

A prophet may be defined as a type of mystic consciousness in which 'unitary experience' tends to overflow its boundaries, and seeks opportunities of redirecting or refashioning the forces of collective life. In his personality the finite centre of life sinks into his own infinite depths only to spring up again, with fresh vigour, to destroy the old, and to disclose the new directions of life. This contact with the root of his own being is by no means peculiar to man. Indeed the way in which the word WaÁâ (inspiration) is used in the

Qur'an shows that the Qur'an regards it as a universal property of life; though its nature and character are different at different stages of the evolution of life. The plant growing freely in space, the animal developing a new organ to suit a new environment, and a human being receiving light from the inner depths of life, are all cases of inspiration varying in character according to the needs of the recipient, or the needs of the species to which the recipient belongs.

Now during the minority of mankind psychic energy develops what I call prophetic consciousness - a mode of economizing individual thought and choice by providing readymade judgements, choices, and ways of action. With the birth of reason and critical faculty, however, life, in its own interest, inhibits the formation and growth of non-rational modes of consciousness through which psychic energy flowed at an earlier stage of human evolution. Man is primarily governed by passion and instinct. Inductive reason, which alone makes man master of his environment, is an achievement; and when once born it must be reinforced by inhibiting the growth of other modes of knowledge. There is no doubt that the ancient world produced some great systems of philosophy at a time when man was comparatively primitive and governed more or less by suggestion. But we must not forget that this system-building in the ancient world was the work of abstract thought which cannot go beyond the systematization of vague religious beliefs and traditions, and gives us no hold on the concrete situations of life.

Looking at the matter from this point of view, then, the Prophet of Islam seems to stand between the ancient and the modern world. In so far as the source of his revelation is concerned he belongs to the ancient world; in so far as the spirit of his revelation is concerned he belongs to the modern world. In him life discovers other sources of knowledge suitable to its new direction. The birth of Islam, as I hope to be able presently to prove to your satisfaction, is the birth of inductive intellect. In Islam prophecy reaches its perfection in discovering the need of its own abolition. This involves the keen perception that life cannot for ever be kept in leading strings; that, in order to achieve full self-consciousness, man must finally be thrown back on his own resources. The abolition of priesthood and hereditary kingship in Islam, the constant appeal to reason and experience in the Qur'an, and the emphasis that it lays on Nature and History as sources of human knowledge, are all different aspects of the same idea of finality. The idea, however, does not mean that mystic experience, which qualitatively does not differ from the experience of the prophet, has now ceased to exist as a vital fact. Indeed the Qur'an regards both *Anfus* (self) and *ïjf«q* (world) as sources of knowledge.

God reveals His signs in inner as well as outer experience, and it is the duty of man to judge the knowledge-yielding capacity of all aspects of experience. The idea of finality, therefore, should not be taken to suggest that the ultimate fate of life is complete displacement of emotion by reason. Such a thing is neither possible nor desirable. The intellectual value of the idea is that it tends to create an independent critical attitude towards mystic experience by generating the belief that all personal authority, claiming a supernatural origin, has come to an end in the history of man. This kind of belief is a psychological force which inhibits the growth of such authority. The function of the idea is to open up fresh vistas of knowledge in the domain of man's inner experience. Just as the first half of the formula of Islam has created and fostered the spirit of a critical observation of man's outer experience by divesting the forces of nature of that Divine character with which earlier cultures had clothed them. Mystic experience, then, however unusual and abnormal, must now be regarded by a Muslim as a perfectly natural experience, open to critical scrutiny like other aspects of human experience.

This is clear from the Prophet's own attitude towards Ibn Âayy«d's psychic experiences. The function of Sufism in Islam has been to systematize mystic experience; though it must be admitted that Ibn Khaldën was the only Muslim who approached it in a thoroughly scientific spirit. But inner experience is only one source of human knowledge. According to the Qur'an , there are two other sources of knowledge - Nature and History; and it is in tapping these sources of knowledge that the spirit of Islam is seen at its best. The Qur'an sees signs of the Ultimate Reality in the 'sun', the 'moon', 'the lengthening out of shadows', 'the alternation of day and night', 'the variety of human colours and tongues',10 'the alternation of the days of success and reverse among peoples' - in fact in the whole of Nature as revealed to the sense-perception of man. And the Muslim's duty is to reflect on these signs and not to pass by them 'as if he is dead and blind', for he 'who does not see these signs in this life will remain blind to the realities of the life to come'. This appeal to the concrete combined with the slow realization that, according to the teachings of the Qur'an , the universe is dynamic in its origin, finite and capable of increase, eventually brought Muslim thinkers into conflict with Greek thought which, in the beginning of their intellectual career, they had studied with so much enthusiasm.

Not realizing that the spirit of the Qur'an was essentially anti-classical, and putting full confidence in Greek thinkers, their first impulse was to understand the Qur'an in the light of Greek philosophy. In view of the concrete spirit of the Qur'an , and the speculative nature of Greek philosophy which enjoyed theory and was neglectful of fact, this attempt was foredoomed to failure. And it is what follows their failure that brings out the real spirit of the culture of Islam, and lays the foundation of modern culture in some of its most important aspects. This intellectual revolt against Greek philosophy manifests itself in all departments of thought. I am afraid I am not competent enough to deal with it as it discloses itself in Mathematics, Astronomy, and Medicine. It is clearly visible in the metaphysical thought of the Ash'arite, but appears as a most well-defined phenomenon in the Muslim criticism of Greek Logic. This was only natural; for dissatisfaction with purely speculative philosophy means the search for a surer method of knowledge. It was, I think, Naïï«m who first formulated the principle of 'doubt' as the beginning of all knowledge. Ghazz«lâ further amplified it in his 'Revivification of the Sciences of Religion', and prepared the way for 'Descartes' Method'. But Ghazz«lâ remained on the whole a follower of Aristotle in Logic.

In his *Qists* he puts some of the Quranic arguments in the form of Aristotelian figures, but forgets the Quranic *Sërah* known as *Shu'ar'* where the proposition that retribution follows the gainsaying of prophets is established by the method of simple enumeration of historical instances. It was Ishr«qâand Ibn Taimâyyah who undertook a systematic refutation of Greek Logic. Abë Bakr R«zâ was perhaps the first to criticize Aristotle's first figure, and in our own times his objection, conceived in a thoroughly inductive spirit, has been reformulated by John Stuart Mill. Ibn Àazm, in his 'Scope of Logic', emphasizes sense-perception as a source of knowledge; and Ibn Taimâyyah in his 'Refutation of Logic', shows that induction is the only form of reliable argument. Thus arose the method of observation and experiment. It was not a merely theoretical affair. Al-Bârënâ's discovery of what we call reaction-time and al-Kindâ's discovery that sensation is proportionate to the stimulus, are instances of its application in psychology. It is a mistake to suppose that the experimental method is a European discovery. Dü hring tells us that Roger Bacon's conceptions of science are more just and clear than those of his celebrated namesake.

And where did Roger Bacon receive his scientific training? - In the Muslim universities of Spain. Indeed Part V of his *Opus Majus* which is devoted to 'Perspective' is practically a copy of Ibn Haitham's *Optics*. Nor is the book, as a whole, lacking in evidences of Ibn Hazm's influence on its author. Europe has been rather slow to recognize the Islamic origin of her scientific method. But full recognition of the fact has at last come. Let me quote one or two passages from Briffault's *Making of Humanity*,'. . . it was under their successors at that Oxford school that Roger Bacon learned Arabic and Arabic science. Neither Roger Bacon nor his later namesake has any title to be credited with having introduced the experimental method. Roger Bacon was no more than one of the apostles of Muslim science and method to Christian Europe; and he never wearied of declaring that a knowledge of Arabic and Arabian science was for his contemporaries the only way to true knowledge. Discussions as to who was the originator of the experimental method . . . are part of the colossal misrepresentation of the origins of European civilization. The experimental method of the Arabs was by Bacon's time widespread and eagerly cultivated throughout Europe'. . . .

'Science is the most momentous contribution of Arab civilization to the modern world, but its fruits were slow in ripening. Not until long after Moorish culture had sunk back into darkness did the giant to which it had given birth rise in his might. It was not science which brought Europe back to life. Other and manifold influences from the civilization of Islam communicated its first glow to European life'.

'For although there is not a single aspect of European growth in which the decisive influence of Islamic culture is not traceable, nowhere is it so clear and momentous as in the genesis of that power which constitutes the paramount distinctive force of the modern world, and the supreme source of its victory - natural science and the scientific spirit'.

'The debt of our science to that of the Arabs does not consist in startling discoveries or revolutionary theories; science owes a great deal more to Arab culture, it owes its existence. The ancient world was, as we saw, pre-scientific. The astronomy and mathematics of the Greek were a foreign importation never thoroughly acclimatized in Greek culture. The Greeks systematized, generalized, and theorized, but the patient ways of investigation, the accumulation of positive knowledge, the minute methods of science, detailed and prolonged observation, experimental inquiry, were altogether alien to the Greek temperament. Only in Hellenistic Alexandria was any approach to scientific work conducted in the ancient classical world. What we call science arose in Europe as a result of a new spirit of inquiry, of new methods of investigation, of the method of experiment, observation, measurement, of the development of mathematics in a form unknown to the Greeks. That spirit and those methods were introduced into the European world by the Arabs'.

The first important point to note about the spirit of Muslim culture then is that, for purposes of knowledge, it fixes its gaze on the concrete, the finite. It is further clear that the birth of the method of observation and experiment in Islam was due not to a compromise with Greek thought but to a prolonged intellectual warfare with it. In fact, the influence of the Greeks who, as Briffault says, were interested chiefly in theory, not in fact, tended rather to obscure the Muslims' vision of the Qur'an , and for at least two centuries kept the practical Arab temperament from asserting itself and coming to its own. I want, therefore, definitely to eradicate the misunderstanding that Greek thought, in any way, determined the character of Muslim culture. Part of my argument you have seen; part you will see presently.

Knowledge must begin with the concrete. It is the intellectual capture of and power over the concrete that makes it possible for the intellect of man to pass beyond the concrete. As the Qur'an says:

'O company of djinn and men, if you can overpass the bounds of the heaven and the earth, then overpass them. But by power alone shall ye overpass them'.

But the universe, as a collection of finite things, presents itself as a kind of island situated in a pure vacuity to which time, regarded as a series of mutually exclusive moments, is nothing and does nothing. Such a vision of the universe leads the reflecting mind nowhere. The thought of a limit to perceptual space and time staggers the mind. The finite, as such, is an idol obstructing the movement of the mind; or, in order to overpass its bounds, the mind must overcome serial time and the pure vacuity of perceptual space. 'And verily towards thy God is the limit', says the Qur'an . This verse embodies one of the deepest thoughts in the Qur'an ; for it definitely suggests that the ultimate limit is to be sought not in the direction of stars, but in an infinite cosmic life and spirituality. Now the intellectual journey towards this ultimate limit is long and arduous; and in this effort, too, the thought of Islam appears to have moved in a direction entirely different to the Greeks. The ideal of the Greeks, as Spengler tells us, was proportion, not infinity. The physical presentness of the finite with its well-defined limits alone absorbed the mind of the Greeks.

In the history of Muslim culture, on the other hand, we find that both in the realms of pure intellect and religious psychology, by which term I mean higher Sufism, the ideal revealed is the possession and enjoyment of the Infinite. In a culture, with such an attitude, the problem of space and time becomes a question of life and death. In one of these lectures I have already given you some idea of the way in which the problem of time and space presented itself to Muslim thinkers, especially the Ash'arite.

One reason why the atomism of Democritus never became popular in the world of Islam is that it involves the assumption of an absolute space. The Ash'arite were, therefore, driven to develop a different kind of atomism, and tried to overcome the difficulties of perceptual space in a manner similar to modern atomism. On the side of Mathematics it must be remembered that since the days of Ptolemy (A.D. 87-165) till the time of NaÄâr ñësâ (A.D. 120-74)nobody gave serious thought to the difficulties of demonstrating the certitude of Euclid's parallel postulate on the basis of perceptual space. It was ñësâ who first disturbed the calm which had prevailed in the world of Mathematics for a thousand years; and in his effort to improve the postulate realized the necessity of abandoning perceptual space. He thus furnished a basis, however slight, for the hyperspace movement of our time.

It was, however, al-Bârënâ who, in his approach to the modern mathematical idea of function saw, from a purely scientific point of view, the insufficiency of a static view of the universe. This again is a clear departure from the Greek view. The function-idea introduces the element of time in our world-picture. It turns the fixed into the variable, and sees the universe not as being but as becoming. Spengler thinks that the mathematical idea of function is the symbol of the West of which 'no other culture gives even a hint'. In view of al-Bârënâ, generalizing Newton's formula of interpolation from trignometrical function to any function whatever. Spengler's claim has no foundation in fact. The transformation of the Greek concept of number from pure magnitude to pure relation really began with Khw«rizmâs movement from Arithmetic to Algebra. al-Bârënâ took a definite step forward towards what Spengler describes as chronological number which signifies the mind's passage from being to becoming. Indeed, more recent developments in European mathematics tend rather to deprive time of its living historical character, and to reduce it to a mere representation of space. That is why Whitehead's view of Relativity is likely to appeal to Muslim students more than that of Einstein in whose theory time loses its character of passage and mysteriously translates itself into utter space.

Side by side with the progress of mathematical thought in Islam we find the idea of evolution gradually shaping itself. It was Ja'hiz who was the first to note the changes in bird-life caused by migrations. Later Ibn Maskawaih who was a contemporary of al-Bârënâ gave it the shape of a more definite theory, and adopted it in his theological work - *al-Fauz al-Asghar*. I reproduce here the substance of his evolutionary hypothesis, not because of its scientific value, but because of the light which it throws on the direction in which Muslim thought was moving.

According to Ibn Maskawaih plant-life at the lowest stage of evolution does not need any seed for its birth and growth. Nor does it perpetuate its species by means of the seed. This kind of plant-life differs from minerals only in some little power of movement which grows in higher forms, and reveals itself further in that the plant spreads out its branches, and perpetuates its species by means of the seed. The power of movement gradually grows farther until we reach trees which possess a trunk, leaves, and fruit. At a higher stage of evolution stand forms of plant-life which need better soil and climate for their growth. The last stage of development is reached in vine and date-palm which stand, as it were, on the threshold of animal life.

In the date-palm a clear sex-distinction appears. Besides roots and fibres it develops something which functions like the animal brain, on the integrity of which depends the life of the date-palm. This is the highest stage in the development of plant-life, and a prelude to animal life. The first forward step towards animal life is freedom from earth-rootedness which is the germ of conscious movement. This is the initial state of animality in which the sense of touch is the first, and the sense of sight is the last to appear. With the development of the senses of animal acquires freedom of movement, as in the case of worms, reptiles, ants, and bees.

Animality reaches its perfection in the horse among quadrupeds and the falcon among birds, and finally arrives at the frontier of humanity in the ape which is just a degree below man in the scale of evolution. Further evolution brings physiological changes with a growing power of discrimination and spirituality until humanity passes from barbarism to civilization. But it is really religious psychology, as in 'Iraq and Khw«jah Muhammad P«rs«, which brings us much nearer to our modern ways of looking at the problem of space and time. 'Iraq's view of time-stratifications I have given you before. I will now give you the substance of his view of space.

According to 'Iraq the existence of some kind of space in relation to God is clear from the following verses of the Qur'an:

'Dost thou not see that God knoweth all that is in the heavens and all that is in the earth? Three persons speak not privately together, but He is their fourth; nor five, but He is their sixth; nor fewer nor more, but wherever they be He is with them' (58:7).

'Ye shall not be employed in affairs, nor shall ye read a text out of the Qur'an , nor shall ye do any work, but We will be witness over you when you are engaged therein; and the weight of an atom on earth or in heaven escapeth not thy Lord; nor is there aught that is less than this or greater, but it is in the Perspicuous Book' (10:61).

'We created man, and We know what his soul whispereth to him, and We are closer to him than his neck-vein' (50:16).

But we must not forget that the words proximity, contact, and mutual separation which apply to material bodies do not apply to God. Divine life is in touch with the whole universe on the analogy of the soul's contact with the body. The soul is neither inside nor outside the body; neither proximate to nor separate from it. Yet its contact with every atom of the body is real, and it is impossible to conceive this contact except by positing some kind of space which befits the subtleness of the soul. The existence of space in relation to the life of God, therefore, cannot be denied; only we should carefully define the kind of space which may be predicated of the Absoluteness of God. Now, there are three kinds of space - the space of material bodies, the space of immaterial beings, and the space of God.

The space of material bodies is further divided into three kinds. First, the space of gross bodies of which we predicate roominess. In this space movement takes time, bodies occupy their respective places and resist displacement. Secondly, the space of subtle bodies, e.g. air and sound. In this space too bodies resist each other, and their movement is measurable in terms of time which, however, appears to be different to the time of gross bodies. The air in a tube must be displaced before other air can enter into it; and the time of sound-waves is practically nothing compared to the time of gross bodies. Thirdly, we have the space of light. The light of the sun instantly reaches the remotest limits of the earth. Thus in the velocity of light and sound time is reduced almost to zero. It is, therefore, clear that the space of light is different to the space of air and sound. There is, however, a more effective argument than this. The light of a candle spreads in all directions in a room without displacing the air in the room; and this shows that the space of light is more subtle than the space of air which has no entry into the space of light. In view of the close proximity of these spaces, however, it is not possible to distinguish the one from the other except by purely intellectual analysis and spiritual experience.

Again, in the hot water the two opposites - fire and water - which appear to interpenetrate each other cannot, in view of their respective natures, exist in the same space. The fact cannot be explained except on the supposition that the spaces of the two substances, though closely proximate to each other, are nevertheless distinct. But while the element of distance is not entirely absent, there is no possibility of mutual resistance in the space of light. The light of a candle reaches up to a certain point only, and the lights of a hundred candles intermingle in the same room without displacing one another.

Having thus described the spaces of physical bodies possessing various degrees of subtleness 'Iraq proceeds briefly to describe the main varieties of space operated upon by the various classes of immaterial beings, e.g. angels. The element of distance is not entirely absent from these spaces; for immaterial beings, while they can easily pass through stone walls, cannot altogether dispense with motion which, according to 'Ir«qâ, is evidence of imperfection in spirituality.

The highest point in the scale of spatial freedom is reached by the human soul which, in its unique essence, is neither at rest nor in motion. Thus passing through the infinite varieties of space we reach the Divine space which is absolutely free from all dimensions and constitutes the meeting point of all infinities.

From this summary of 'Iraq's view you will see how a cultured Muslim Sufi intellectually interpreted his spiritual experience of time and space in an age which had no idea of the theories and concepts of modern Mathematics and Physics. 'Iraq is really trying to reach the concept of space as a dynamic appearance. His mind seems to be vaguely struggling with the concept of space as an infinite continuum; yet he was unable to see the full implications of his thought partly because he was not a mathematician and partly because of his natural prejudice in favour of the traditional Aristotelian idea of a fixed universe. Again, the interpenetration of the super-spatial 'here' and super-eternal 'now' in the Ultimate Reality suggests the modern notion of space-time which Professor Alexander, in his lectures on 'Space, Time, and Deity', regards as the matrix of all things.

A keener insight into the nature of time would have led 'Iraq to see that time is more fundamental of the two; and that it is not a mere metaphor to say, as Professor Alexander does say, that time is the mind of space. 'Iraq conceives God's relation to the universe on the analogy of the relation of the human soul to the body; but, instead of philosophically reaching this position through a criticism of the spatial and temporal aspects of experience, he simply postulates it on the basis of his spiritual experience. It is not sufficient merely to reduce space and time to a vanishing point-instant. The philosophical path that leads to God as the omnipsyche of the universe lies through the discovery of living thought as the ultimate principle of space-time. 'Iraq's mind, no doubt, moved in the right direction, but his Aristotelian prejudices, coupled with a lack of psychological analysis, blocked his progress. With his view that Divine Time is utterly devoid of change - a view obviously based on an inadequate analysis of conscious experience - it was not possible for him to discover the relation between Divine Time and serial time, and to reach, through this discovery, the essentially Islamic idea of continuous creation which means a growing universe.

Thus all lines of Muslim thought converge on a dynamic conception of the universe. This view is further reinforced by Ibn Maskawaih's theory of life as an evolutionary movement, and Ibn Khaldën's view of history. History or, in the language of the Qur'an , 'the days of God', is the third source of human knowledge according to the Qur'an . It is one of the most essential teachings of the Qur'an that nations are collectively judged, and suffer for their misdeeds here and now. In order to establish this proposition, the Qur'an constantly cites historical instances, and urges upon the reader to reflect on the past and present experience of mankind.

"Of old did We send Moses with Our signs, and said to him: 'Bring forth thy people from the darkness into the light, and remind them of the days of God." Verily, in this are signs for every patient, grateful person' (14:5).

'And among those whom We had created are a people who guide others with truth, and in accordance therewith act justly. But as for those who treat Our signs as lies, We gradually ring them down by means of which they know not; and though I lengthen their days, verily, My stratagem is effectual' (7:181-83).

'Already, before your time, have precedents been made. Traverse the Earth then, and see what hath been the end of those who falsify the signs of God!' (3:137).

'If a wound hath befallen you, a wound like it hath already befallen others; We alternate the days of successes and reverses among peoples' (3:140).

'Every nation hath its fixed period' (7:34).

The last verse is rather an instance of a more specific

historical generalization which, in its epigrammatic formulation, suggests the possibility of a scientific treatment of the life of human societies regarded as organisms. It is, therefore, a gross error to think that the Qur'an has no germs of a historical doctrine. The truth is that the whole spirit of the 'Prolegomena' of Ibn Khaldën appears to have been mainly due to the inspiration which the author must have received from the Qur'an. Even in his judgements of character he is, in no small degree, indebted to the Qur'an. An instance in point is his long paragraph devoted to an estimate of the character of the Arabs as a people. The whole paragraph is a mere amplification of the following verses of the Qur'an :

'The Arabs of the desert are most stout in unbelief and dissimulation; and likelier it is that they should be unaware of the laws which God hath sent down to His Apostle; and God is Knowing, Wise.

'Of the Arabs of the desert there are some who reckon what they expend in the cause of God as tribute, and wait for some change of fortune to befall you: a change for evil shall befall them! God is the Hearer, the Knower' (9:97-98).

However, the interest of the Qur'an in history, regarded as a source of human knowledge, extends farther than mere indications of historical generalizations. It has given us one of the most fundamental principles of historical criticism: Since accuracy in recording facts which constitute the material of history is an indispensable condition of history as a science, and an accurate knowledge of facts ultimately depends on those who report them, the very first principle of historical criticism is that the reporter's personal character is an important factor in judging his testimony. The Qur'an says:

'O believers! if any bad man comes to you with a report, clear it up at once' (49:6).

It is the application of the principle embodied in this verse to the reporters of the Prophet's traditions out of which were gradually evolved the canons of historical criticism. The growth of historical sense in Islam is a fascinating subject. The Quranic appeal to experience, the necessity to ascertain the exact sayings of the Prophet, and the desire to furnish permanent sources of inspiration to posterity - all these forces contributed to produce such men as Ibn Ish«q, ñabarâ, and Mas'ëdâ. But history, as an art of firing the reader's imagination, is only a stage in the development of history as a genuine science. The possibility of a scientific treatment of history means a wider experience, a greater maturity of practical reason, and finally a fuller realization of certain basic ideas regarding the nature of life and time. These ideas are in the main two; and both form the foundation of the Quranic teaching.

1. *The Unity of Human Origin.* 'And We have created you all from one breath of life', says the Qur'an . But the perception of life as an organic unity is a slow achievement, and depends for its growth on a people's entry into the main current of world-events. This opportunity was brought to Islam by the rapid development of a vast empire. No doubt, Christianity, long before Islam, brought the message of equality to mankind; but Christian Rome did not rise to the full apprehension of the idea of humanity as a single organism. As Flint rightly says, 'No Christian writer and still less, of course, any other in the Roman Empire, can be credited with having had more than a general and abstract conception of human unity.' And since the days of Rome the idea does not seem to have gained much in depth and rootage in Europe. On the other hand, the growth of territorial nationalism, with its emphasis on what is called national characteristics, has tended rather to kill the broad human element in the art and literature of Europe. It was quite otherwise with Islam. Here the idea was neither a concept of philosophy nor a dream of poetry. As a social movement the aim of Islam was to make the idea a living factor in the Muslim's daily life, and thus silently and imperceptibly to carry it towards fuller fruition.
2. *A Keen Sense of the Reality of Time, and the Concept of Life*

as a Continuous Movement in Time. It is this conception of life and time which is the main point of interest in Ibn Khaldën's view of history, and which justifies Flint's eulogy that 'Plato, Aristotle, and Augustine were not his peers, and all others were unworthy of being even mentioned along with him'. From the remarks that I have made above I do not mean to throw doubt on the originality of Ibn Khaldën. All that I mean to say is that, considering the direction in which the culture of Islam had unfolded itself, only a Muslim could have viewed history as a continuous, collective movement, a real inevitable development in time. The point of interest in this view of history is the way in which Ibn Khaldën conceives the process of change. His conception is of infinite importance because of the implication that history, as a continuous movement in time, is a genuinely creative movement and not a movement whose path is already determined. Ibn Khaldën was not a metaphysician. Indeed he was hostile to Metaphysics.

But in view of the nature of his conception of time he may fairly be regarded as a forerunner of Bergson. I have already discussed the intellectual antecedents of this conception in the cultural history of Islam. The Quranic view of the 'alternation of day and night' as a symbol of the Ultimate Reality which 'appears in a fresh glory every moment', the tendency in Muslim Metaphysics to regard time as objective, Ibn Maskawaih's view of life as an evolutionary movement, and lastly al-Bârënâ's definite approach to the conception of Nature as a process of becoming - all this constituted the intellectual inheritance of Ibn Khaldën. His chief merit lies in his acute perception of, and systematic expression to, the spirit of the cultural movement of which he was a most brilliant product. In the work of this genius the anti-classical spirit of the Qur'an scores its final victory over Greek thought; for with the Greeks time was either unreal, as in Plato and Zeno, or moved in a circle, as in Heraclitus and the Stoics. Whatever may be the criterion by which to judge the forward steps of a creative movement, the movement itself, if conceived as cyclic, ceases to be creative. Eternal recurrence is not eternal creation; it is eternal repetition.

We are now in a position to see the true significance of the intellectual revolt of Islam against Greek philosophy. The fact that this revolt originated in a purely theological interest shows that the anti-classical spirit of the Qur'an asserted itself in spite of those who began with a desire to interpret Islam in the light of Greek thought.

It now remains to eradicate a grave misunderstanding created by Spengler's widely read book, *The Decline of the West*. His two chapters devoted to the problem of Arabian culture constitute a most important contribution to the cultural history of Asia. They are, however, based on a complete misconception of the nature of Islam as a religious movement, and of the cultural activity which it initiated. Spengler's main thesis is that each culture is a specific organism, having no point of contact with cultures that historically precede or follow it. Indeed, according to him, each culture has its own peculiar way of looking at things which is entirely inaccessible to men belonging to a different culture. In his anxiety to prove this thesis he marshals an overwhelming array of facts and interpretations to show that the spirit of European culture is through and through anti-classical.

And this anti-classical spirit of European culture is entirely due to the specific genius of Europe, and not to any inspiration she may have received from the culture of Islam which, according to Spengler, is thoroughly 'Magian' in spirit and character. Spengler's view of the spirit of modern culture is, in my opinion, perfectly correct. I have, however, tried to show in these lectures that the anti-classical spirit of the modern world has really arisen out of the revolt of Islam against Greek thought. It is obvious that such a view cannot be acceptable to Spengler; for, if it is possible to show that the anti-classical spirit of modern culture is due to the inspiration which it received from the culture immediately preceding it, the whole argument of Spengler regarding the complete mutual independence of cultural growths would collapse. I am afraid Spengler's anxiety to establish this thesis has completely perverted his vision of Islam as a cultural movement.

By the expression 'Magian culture' Spengler means the common culture associated with what he calls 'Magian group of religions', i.e. Judaism, ancient Chaldean religion, early Christianity, Zoroastrianism, and Islam. That a Magian crust has grown over Islam, I do not deny. Indeed my main purpose in these lectures has been to secure a vision of the spirit of Islam as emancipated from its Magian overlayings which, in my opinion, have misled Spengler. His ignorance of Muslim thought on the problem of time, as well as of the way in which the 'I', as a free centre of experience, has found expression in the religious experience of Islam, is simply appalling. Instead of seeking light from the history of Muslim thought and experience, he prefers to base his judgement on vulgar beliefs as to the beginning and end of time. Just imagine a man of overwhelming learning finding support for the supposed fatalism of Islam in such Eastern expressions and proverbs as the 'vault of time', and 'everything has a time!' However, on the origin and growth of the concept of time in Islam, and on the human ego as a free power, I have said enough in these lectures. It is obvious that a full examination of Spengler's view of Islam, and of the culture that grew out of it, will require a whole volume. In addition to what I have said before, I shall offer here one more observation of a general nature.

'The kernel of the prophetic teaching,' says Spengler, 'is already Magian. There is one God - be He called *Yahweh, Ahuramazda,* or *Marduk-Baal* - who is the principle of good, and all other deities are either impotent or evil. To this doctrine there attached itself the hope of a Messiah, very clear in Isaiah, but also bursting out everywhere during the next centuries, under pressure of an inner necessity. It is the basic idea of Magian religion, for it contains implicitly the conception of the world-historical struggle between Good and Evil, with the power of Evil prevailing in the middle period, and the Good finally triumphant on the Day of Judgement.'

If this view of the prophetic teaching is meant to apply to Islam it is obviously a misrepresentation. The point to note is that the Magian admitted the existence of false gods; only they did not turn to worship them. Islam denies the very existence of false gods. In this connexion Spengler fails to appreciate the cultural value of the idea of the finality of prophethood in Islam. No doubt, one important feature of Magian culture is a perpetual attitude of expectation, a constant looking forward to the coming of Zoroaster's unborn sons, the Messiah, or the Paraclete of the fourth gospel. I have already indicated the direction in which the student of Islam should seek the cultural meaning of the doctrine of finality in Islam. It may further be regarded as a psychological cure for the Magian attitude of constant expectation which tends to give a false view of history. Ibn Khaldën, seeing the spirit of his own view of history, has fully criticized and, I believe, finally demolished the alleged revelational basis in Islam of an idea similar, at least in its psychological effects, to the original Magian idea which had reappeared in Islam under the pressure of Magian thought.

Bibliography

Armstrong, Karen. *Islam: A Short History*. New York: Modern Library, revised ed., 2002.

Ali, Syed Ameer. *The Spirit of Islam: A History of the Evolution and Ideals of Islam,* with *a Life of the Prophet.* London: Chatto & Windus, 1978.

Bloom, Jonathan and Sheila Blair. *Islam: A Thousand Years of Faith and Power.* New Haven, CT: Yale University Press, 2002.

Booth, E. *Aristotelian Aporetic Ontology in Islamic and Christian Thinkers.* Cambridge, 1983.

Bowker, John. *What Muslims Believe.* Oxford, UK: Onewworld, 1999.

Burrell, D. *Freedom and Creation in Three Traditions.* Notre Dame, 1993.

Burrell, D. *Knowing the Unknowable God: Ibn Sina, Maimonides, Aquinas* (Notre Dame: 1986).

Cook, Michael. *The Koran: A Very Short Introduction.* Oxford, UK: Oxford University Press, 2000.

Corbin, H. *History of Islamic Philosophy,* trans. L. Sherrard. London, 1993.

Craig, E. (ed.), *Routledge Encyclopedia of Philosophy.* London, 1998.

Davidson, H.A. *Proofs for Eternity, Creation and the Existence of God in Medieval Islamic and Jewish Philosophy.* Oxford, 1987.

Elias, Jamal J. *Islam.* Upper Saddle River, NJ: Prentice Hall, 1999.

Fakhry, M. *A History of Islamic Philosophy* , 2nd ed. New York, 1983.

Gibb, Hamilton A.R. and J.H. Kramers, eds. *Shorter Encyclopedia of Islam.* Leiden: E.J. Brill, 1997 (reprint ed.).

Hodgson, Marshall G.S. *The Venture of Islam,* 3 Vols. Chicago, IL: University of Chicago Press, 1974.

Keller, Nuh Ha Mim, trans. *Al-Nawawi's Manual of Islam.* Cambridge, UK: The Islamic Texts Society, 1996.

Leaman, O. *An Introduction to Classical Islamic Philosophy.* Cambridge, 2002.

Marmura , M.E. (ed.), *Islamic Theology and Philosophy.* Albany, 1984.

Nasr, Seyyed Hossein. *The Heart of Islam: Enduring Values for Humanity.* San Francisco, CA, Harper San Francisco, 2002.

Newby, Gordon D. *A Concise Encyclopedia of Islam.* Oxford, UK, Oneworld, 2002.

Peters, F.E. *A Reader on Classical Islam.* Princeton, NJ: Princeton University Press, 1994.

Qadir , C.A. *Philosophy and Science in the Islamic World.* London, 1990.

Renard, John, ed. *Windows on the House of Islam: Muslim Sources on Spirituality.* Berkeley, CA: University of California Press, 1998.

Renard, John. *Seven Doors to Islam: Spirituality and the Religious Life of Muslims.* Berkeley, CA: University of California Press, 1996.

Ruthven, Malise. *Islam in the World.* New York: Oxford University Press, 2nd ed., 2000.

Schimmel, Annemarie. *Islam: An Introduction.* Albany, NY: State University of New York Press, 1992.

Schuon, Frithjof. *Islam and the Perennial Philosophy.* London: World of Islam Festival Publ. Co., 1976.

Sharif, M.M. *A History of Muslim Philosophy,* 2 vols. (Wiesbaden: 1963-6).

Stern, S.M. *Medieval Arabic and Hebrew Thought* , ed. F. Zimmermann, London, 1983.

Stern, S.M., Hourani, H. and Brown, V. (eds.), *Islamic Philosophy and the Classical Tradition.* Oxford, 1972.

Waines, David. *An Introduction to Islam.* Cambridge, UK: Cambridge University Press, 1995.

Watt, M.W. Islamic Philosophy and Theology. Edinburgh, 1962, revised ed. 1985.

Watt, William Montgomery. *The Formative Period of Islamic Thought.* Oxford, UK: Oneworld,1998.

Watt, William Montgomery. *What is Islam?* London: Longman, 1970.

Williams, John Alden, ed. *The Word of Islam.* Austin, TX: University of Texas Press, 1994.

Wolfson, H.A. *Studies in the History of Philosophy and Religion* , ed. I. Twersky, G.H. Williams, in 2 vols. Cambridge, MA, 1973, 1977.

Wolfson, H.A. *The Philosophy of the Kalam.* Cambridge, MA, 1976.

Ziai, H. "Islamic Philosophy," in *The Oxford Companion to Philosophy,* ed. T. Honderich. Oxford , 1955.

Index

I

J

L

M

N

O

P

R

S

T

U

W